THE DIGITAL BANAL

LITERATURE NOW

LITERATURE NOW

Matthew Hart, David James, and Rebecca L. Walkowitz, Series Editors

Literature Now offers a distinct vision of late-twentieth- and early-twenty-first-century literary culture. Addressing contemporary literature and the ways we understand its meaning, the series includes books that are comparative and transnational in scope as well as those that focus on national and regional literary cultures.

Caren Irr, *Toward the Geopolitical Novel: U.S. Fiction in the Twenty-First Century*

Heather Houser, *Ecosickness in Contemporary U.S. Fiction: Environment and Affect*

Mrinalini Chakravorty, *In Stereotype: South Asia in the Global Literary Imaginary*

Héctor Hoyos, *Beyond Bolaño: The Global Latin American Novel*

Rebecca L. Walkowitz, *Born Translated: The Contemporary Novel in an Age of World Literature*

Carol Jacobs, *Sebald's Vision*

Sarah Phillips Casteel, *Calypso Jews: Jewishness in the Caribbean Literary Imagination*

Jeremy Rosen, *Minor Characters Have Their Day: Genre and the Contemporary Literary Marketplace*

Jesse Matz, *Lasting Impressions: The Legacies of Impressionism in Contemporary Culture*

Ashley T. Shelden, *Unmaking Love: The Contemporary Novel and the Impossibility of Union*

Theodore Martin, *Contemporary Drift: Genre, Historicism, and the Problem of the Present*

THE DIGITAL BANAL

NEW MEDIA
AND AMERICAN LITERATURE
AND CULTURE

ZARA DINNEN

Columbia University Press
New York

Columbia University Press
Publishers Since 1893
New York   Chichester, West Sussex
cup.columbia.edu
Copyright © 2018 Columbia University Press
Paperback edition, 2022
All rights reserved

Cataloging-in-Publication Data available from the Library of Congress.

ISBN 978-0-231-18428-1 (cloth)
ISBN 978-0-231-18429-8 (pbk.)
ISBN 978-0-231-54540-2 (e-book)

Cover design: Jordan Wannemacher

CONTENTS

Acknowledgments vii

INTRODUCTION: THINKING WITH THE DIGITAL BANAL 1

1. DAVID FINCHER'S GRAMMAR OF CODE 19

2. JONATHAN LETHEM'S AND MARK AMERIKA'S COMMON WRITING 47

3. BEING SOCIAL IN A POSTDIGITAL WORLD IN *CATFISH* AND *HOW SHOULD A PERSON BE?* 73

4. TWENTY YEARS OF CALIFORNIAN IDEOLOGY IN *THE BUG* AND *THE CIRCLE* 97

5. REFRESH, UPDATE, WAIT, OR, LIVING WITH THE DIGITAL BANAL IN *CHRONIC CITY* AND *REFRESH REFRESH* 119

6. SPECULATING ON THE REAL ESTATE OF THE DIGITAL BANAL 141

CONCLUSION: AFTER THE DIGITAL BANAL 163

Notes 169
Bibliography 199
Index 217

ACKNOWLEDGMENTS

I have never been very attached to the process of thinking just by myself, and so I am truly grateful to all those who have given their care and time by way of conversing, organizing, reading, advising, advocating, and hanging out. This book exists in the way it does because of the following people: Sam McBean (I talked the whole thing out with you), Holly Pester, Bianca Leggett, Rob Gallagher, Daniel Rourke, Tony Venezia, Anna Hartnell, Caroline Bassett, Gill Partington, Danielle Fuller, Sarah Palmer, Sandie Dinnen, Lucy Dinnen, and Matt Parker.

The research for this book began at Birkbeck, University of London. I was fortunate to be supervised by Joe Brooker, mentored by Anna Hartnell, and part of a PhD cohort that made study a lively thing. Before Birkbeck, there was Jay Prosser, who got me started with academic life. Since Birkbeck, there has been Caroline Bassett, who has consistently championed this project and who gave me the title of this book. I was supported throughout my MA and PhD by Arts and Humanities Research Council grants. As a lecturer at the University of Birmingham, I have been fortunate enough to work alongside brilliant colleagues. I especially want to thank Danielle Fuller for her generosity as a mentor, friend, and advocate. I have had much support from colleagues in the Centre for Contemporary Literature and Culture as well as across my department and school; I'd especially like to thank Michele Aaron and Dan Moore for comments on this as a work-in-progress. At Birmingham I have also had the privilege of working out the ideas for this book while teaching the material on the "Imagining the Digital" module—thank you to all the students who made it a such formative experience for me. While working on this book I have presented at, participated in, and organized many conferences and events. Special thanks go to those present at C21 (2017, University of Brighton), What Happens Now (2016, University of Lincoln), MLA (2012, Seattle), the Art of English (2013, Queen Mary, University of London), the International Conference on Narrative (2013, Manchester), and all the Contemporary Fiction Research Seminars and their related symposia and events (2009–15, London).

David James suggested I submit this manuscript to the Literature Now series at Columbia University Press. I did, and now this book is in the world—thank you. The support from the series editors, Matthew Hart, David James, and Rebecca Walkowitz, and from Abby Graves, Miriam Grossman, Kathryn Jorge, and Philip Leventhal at Columbia University Press, has been immense; I appreciate the way you have all shaped and championed this project. I would like to thank the anonymous readers for Columbia University Press as well for their astute and constructive comments.

One of the best aspects of publishing this book is that it gives me the opportunity to thank my friends and family. Thank you, friends, for all the stuff that isn't work and for caring so much about the work. Lucy, you are the person I want to keep growing up with. Sandie, I can do this because you showed us how to have independent and loving lives, and because you sat and did your homework while we did ours. Matt, I have done this all with you; thank you for being in it all with me.

Earlier versions of material in this book have appeared as "Things That Matter: Representing Everyday Technological Things in Comics," *Studies in Comics* 3, no. 2 (Winter 2013); "Breaking Out That Perl Script: The Imaging and Imagining of Code in *The Social Network* and *Catfish*," *European Journal of American Culture* 32, no. 2 (Summer 2013); and "In the Mix: The Potential Convergence of Literature and New Media in Jonathan Lethem's 'Ecstasy of Influence,'" *Journal of Narrative Theory* 42, no. 2 (Summer 2012). This material is reproduced here with permission from the *European Journal of American Culture*, the *Journal of Narrative Theory*, and *Studies in Comics*.

THE DIGITAL BANAL

INTRODUCTION

Thinking with the Digital Banal

The digital banal is the condition by which we don't notice the affective novelty of becoming-with digital media. In other words, the way we use media makes us unaware of the ways we are co-constituted as subjects with media. In a culture where Facebook can claim to be a platform that simply "helps us to connect and share," it is vital to consider how we end up at a place where we think such a particular technological instantiation of sociality is instead a general situation that we have always had coming. Technology companies make banal rhetoric out of revolutionary energy and progress; the iPhone 4 was released to the fanfare of "This Changes Everything. Again."[1] Just as the "platformativity" of Facebook is both a means for knowledge and connection and at the same time a radical rewriting of what those terms mean, so are digital media, in general, complex mediational entanglements that are too often presented as inevitably progressive.[2] A platform such as Facebook is part of a media ecology wherein the massive material impact of servers is effaced by metaphors of "the Cloud" and stories of Silicon Valley liberalism efface the bodies and voices of smartphone factory workers in China and rare-earth-mineral miners in the Democratic Republic of the Congo. Digital media works by reifying the political and social arrangements it instantiates as novelty objects (devices) and narratives of "newness" (the sharing economy, and before that, cyber-utopianism), while effacing (by blocking access to) the affective stakes of life determined by algorithms and life at the edge of the earth's resources. Narrative culture records these stakes in ways that we can critically apprehend. In *The Digital Banal* I examine a variety of fictional works that set out to recover novelty from the banal, to recover the novelty of living with digital media from scenes of the digital banal. What may elsewhere be written off as just another detail of contemporary life—a fleeting expression of technology within a narrative about something else—is here sought out as a potentially generative encounter with the affective novelty of new media.

REALITY EFFECTS

In A. M. Homes's 2012 novel *May We Be Forgiven*, the narrator and protagonist, Harry Silver, uses the Internet. He also uses a laptop, a computer (which is presumably shorthand for a PC desktop, as laptops and computers are separate devices in the novel), and a mobile phone. As is typical of Homes's work, *May We Be Forgiven* "considers unsparingly the fate of both the individual and the novel in a postmodern, posthuman/ism, postrealism world."[3] The novel charts Harry's midlife crisis by way of a dramatic catalyst: his brother, George, drives into oncoming traffic and kills a couple; the couple's son survives. After the crash George is hospitalized, and Harry stays with George's wife, Jane, to comfort her. George, having escaped from the hospital, comes home to find Harry in bed with Jane—Harry and Jane have been having an affair since George's hospitalization. On seeing the pair in bed, George bludgeons Jane to death with a lamp. George is sent away. Harry takes over George's life in the wake of this disaster, while his own domestic world crumbles: Harry's wife leaves him, his credit card debts are mounting, and he is fired from his job as a lecturer in history because he has failed to publish new research.[4] *May We Be Forgiven* is a realist novel in the sense that it, like Homes's work more generally, "frets and answers ... problems according to a realist faith in methodical fretting and answering via a narrative that will lead to resolution."[5] An aspect of real life that *May We Be Forgiven* rarely addresses as such, but is often found fretting over, is digital technology. The novel is about digital media to the extent that it continually references digital networks and devices, but it also does so no more frequently than the networks and devices are used in everyday life and, ostensibly, with no more interest or knowledge than most everyday users might possess.

Harry is an "Internet idiot" who has "Internet escapades" courtesy of an online dating site. He asks a man he is e-mailing in a small village near Durban, South Africa, if he has the Internet, to which the man replies, "'Of course, that is how we are talking. . . . [We] have our own satellite.'"[6] In less conspicuously digital encounters Harry "log[s] onto the computer to cancel [his] lunch date"; he reserves accommodation to visit his niece and nephew's school online, and the "school's Web site has a list of local accommodations"; he locates "Ryan" (a rabbi in training, now AWOL) "by methodically searching the web and little postings, like rabbit droppings . . . his thumbs-up 'like' of a site called 'Embracing the Gap (Can Jews and Gentiles Really Be Friends?)' is what leads [Harry] to him."[7] There are some anachronisms here and elsewhere ("Web site," not "website," or "site" even), but it is in moments like these that this novel is a contemporary fiction that lives with contemporary technology. Toward the end of the novel Harry's nephew, Nate, brings a friend home from school: "Nate's friend Josh is dyslexic. He calls Nate 'Ante.'" Nate explains that whenever Josh texts, he types "Ante" instead of "Nate," and "the nickname stuck."[8] The detail of typing rather than writing appears significant—it appears to distinguish a particular kind of communication—but throughout, the novel's characters frequently switch between writing and typing in ways that express these actions as interchangeable.[9] For Roland Barthes, literature's "reality effect" resides in such asides; details that are "neither incongruous nor significant."[10] Technology is in the background of the everyday life of the novel; the characters have "absorbed . . . , invisibly and unremarkably, the forces of mediation."[11] While there are moments in *May We Be Forgiven* where digital media is foregrounded as a concern, especially for Harry, life is de facto mediational, and so digital media is also, more ambivalently, the implied context for everyday life. For example, when Harry is writing his book, the reader likely assumes he is working on a digital device: "I work for an hour or two. I move paragraphs here and there and then back again."[12]

In *May We Be Forgiven* technology is a banal sort of figure because it is neither a properly delineated subject nor entirely absent. Instead, the technological is effaced in deference to the narrative: information is googled, e-mails are sent; in other moments, facts are learned and communication takes place. Mediational encounters are integrated with other narrative concerns, which is precisely the default mode of media in general. To better understand contemporary culture and the stories we tell about it, we need to be able to recognize processes of mediation as forms of effacement. When a medium is working, it disappears from view. Books work best when we forget they are there: if a book is too heavy, our arms get tired and we disengage; if we drop a book in the bath, its paperiness becomes an obstacle to our reading. As new media theorists have long argued, "the digital" is a reification of the effacing condition of all media.[13] When we watch YouTube, we watch "videos"; social media is social *life*; when code runs properly, we don't see it. In the words of Jay David Bolter and Richard Grusin, digital media specifically "remediates" older media; we multiply and expand our media universe while wanting to "erase all traces" of mediation.[14] The model of remediation is helpful for thinking about digital media in discrete instances, but is strained when digital media are considered in their full complexity. Is Uber a remediation of public transport for the neoliberal age? Is the Internet of Things a remediation of domestic labor? Is "following" a remediation of friendship? We can more helpfully think about digital media in terms of mediation. In a recent work by Sarah Kember and Joanna Zylinska, mediation "stands for the differentiation of, as well as connection between, media and, more broadly, for the acts and processes of producing and temporarily stabilizing the world into media, agents, relations, and networks."[15] The open-endedness of "meditation" is necessary in order to apprehend the operations of media that do not arrest us, that do not appear as discrete objects or procedures, but that form and reform as temporary instantiations of media, agents, relations, and networks.

We are, in Kember and Zylinska's terms, living lives "*after* new media." We are "becoming-with" technology, that is, we exist through the "mutual co-constitution of 'media' and 'us,'" in ways that are ordinary and perpetual rather than novel or notable.[16] It is difficult to think about "becoming-with" when digital media is sold as an endless procession of shiny new things, a journey through a technologically determined future. Often the novelty of the commodity is given in place of engagement with the novelty of mediation. The reification of newness appears as yet more banality.

In *May We Be Forgiven*, Harry's Internet ineptitude gives the text a way to mark mediation, because Harry thinks of the digital as a moment of difference ("he logged on"). But the indifference of the narrative more generally modulates the affective novelty of Harry. Homes's commitment to representing a real life in process, her commitment to narrative realism, becomes a way of burying novelty in the quotidian. The affective novelty of a life being lived with digital media is felt only as a series of commodity shocks for the reader (Wait, what? He has to spell out the fact he is using Google?) because the mediational condition is always already embedded. To read this condition is to actively encounter "real life" as always mediational.

Throughout *The Digital Banal* the representation of real life is not only a process of naming things in fiction that appear in the real world but also a process by which the mediation of real life in narrative reveals real life as a mediational condition. In chapter 3 of this book the act of "being real," as found in the constructed reality of Sheila Heti's novel *How Should a Person Be?* (2013) and in the reality TV show and film *Catfish* (2010–), reveals the mediational contingencies of "realism." And even the final chapter, which turns to novels about zombies and postapocalyptic futures, attends to the digital banal as a realist discourse. Despite their use of other genres, novels such as Colson Whitehead's *Zone One* (2012) or Gary Shteyngart's *Super Sad True Love Story* (2010) are near-future realist texts that reference back to the present, "assembling protagonist, antagonist, and witnesses who . . . make sense according to the larger social codes and moral systems of the real world to which the texts consistently refer."[17] The articulation of digital objects and processes as a realist everyday in *May We Be Forgiven*, and throughout *The Digital Banal*, throws into relief the banal mediation of the world to which the texts refer.

FACEBOOK EVERYDAY

In many respects, Facebook is the digital banal: it is a daily habit through which life is experienced mediationally. Founded in 2004 by then Harvard student Mark Zuckerberg, along with fellow students Eduardo Saverin, Andrew McCollum, Dustin Moskovitz, and Chris Hughes, Facebook has approximately 1.28 billion users who access the site daily.[18] It was perhaps the first Web 2.0 platform that made the web feel like real life for nonspecialist users. At its inception, Facebook was a site that verified users through their preexisting social networks and replicated those real-world networks exclusively. Since 2004 Facebook has become a default mode of social connection across the globe—85.8 percent of daily active users are outside of the United States and Canada.[19] As Kember and Zylinska argue, "With its constant flow of data, its shaping of human and nonhuman experiences and events, and its reworking of what we understand as a 'relationship' and a 'connection,' we could perhaps go so far as to suggest that *Facebook is a modulation of 'life itself.'*"[20] The banality of Facebook in the context of its users' lives—its everydayness—is both the means by which, and the block to recognizing how, Facebook becomes a modulation of "life itself." As an interface for social interaction, Facebook works by disappearing; it is a tool for connection. The affective novelty of Facebook is its uncanny re-presentation of your life, but this is effaced and appears instead as efficiency. In practice, Facebook is a program that determines the parameters and quality of "connection" as a reified concept, but in everyday life, it is mostly an icon that users tap to see what their friends and family (and not-so-close connections) are up to.

Facebook purports to be a neutral representation of sociality, of its users' social life. But, as has been consistently reported over the last few years, Facebook is not neutral, just effacing. Facebook's algorithms are a mode of social design that curates a user's access to information and communication; moreover, it produces conditions for connection that must be recognized as new affective modes of sociality.[21] Facebook is full of paradoxes: "eventalizing" the rote and ordinary, connecting without being together, being present in multiplex ways. Users of Facebook are always making their lives visible and present, existing in an unresolved present, where life can be called up and refreshed. This performance of an individual, sovereign life, to be witnessed by Facebook and its users as sociality, is also a making over of that life in ever more granular, quantified terms. The banal Facebook paradox is one of storage—the live present of Facebook is possible because data is stored elsewhere. The encounter with live Facebook subjects is possible precisely because subjects are always already interpolated as stored data. Facebook presents an unresolved subject who is becoming-with technology (perpetually in the present), while blocking from view the remaking of the sovereign subject as a software litany (the profiled subject found in directories, routines, archives, history), a neoliberal data subject.[22]

On Facebook we remain in the present, and in doing so fail to see the means by which we are present. In the words of Lauren Berlant, Facebook affords new ways to "eventalize the mood, the inclination, the thing that just happened—the episodic nature of existence."[23] Former Facebook employee Katherine Losse has described the kind of social relations afforded by Facebook as "noncommittal proximity, . . . a system devoted to potential connection, a way of being always near but never with the ones you love, a technology of forestalling choice in favor of the endless option, forever."[24] For many, the description of Facebook as "noncommittal proximity" is unlikely to capture their use of the platform, which can include intense personal and public commitment as well as drama. The presentness of Facebook is paradoxically both a heightened sense of being in the present, endlessly, forever, unresolving, and a stretched-out intimacy afforded by a mediational definition of what it is to be present. The very banality of life as it is lived on Facebook—breakfast photos and the funny things your cousin's cat did—is both the affective novelty of the platform and the means by which we are unable to see other material effects of the program. It is quite possible that in a few years Facebook will be an unpopular platform, but the mode of being it instantiates and the sociopolitical program it substantiates will remain, reiterated as yet another moment of human progress.[25]

Because Facebook appears as a banal aspect of everyday life, there is a risk of overlooking the profound ways that it is, and is always becoming, life itself. Throughout *The Digital Banal*, Facebook appears in various guises, signaling digital media interfaces and encounters in general. In chapter 1 I discuss at length a Facebook origin story as told by David Fincher and Aaron Sorkin in the 2010 film *The Social Network*. Rather than asserting that the historical account offered in *The Social Network* "tells" us about Facebook, analyzing the film reveals the ways Facebook is mediationally complex and an ongoing sociopolitical process. The depiction of a Facebook origin story on film also tests the limits of contemporary cinema's ability to represent its own digital medium, as code appears as yet another discourse of reading and writing. In *The Social Network* the foundational myth of Facebook is narrated as a revenge drama. A young man who is depicted as insensitive and unempathetic to those around him is nonetheless acutely sensitive to the ways he feels slighted in life—by women, by wealth and class and elitism—and sets about righting the obstacles to his proper flourishing by way of an algorithm, which will fix the glitches of human-to-human social networks. In the film the widespread attachment to Facebook is this: you will know if someone is single without even having to ask; you will know who is like you without having to work it out yourself, without having to risk a mistake. The film supplies a story to make sense of the Facebook ideology of connection-as-distance. The film also gives away its own unease with this narrative. It depicts the violence of algorithmically encoding social life, the white male patriarchy of proving the world's programmability. *The Social Network* is not especially historically accurate, but in its attention to reconstructing the appearance of historical authenticity, it reveals the digital banal. The affective novelty as described above (the violent programming of social life) is witnessed as a disturbance in an otherwise banal surface: Facebook as what will have become (that is, the audience's present); coding as just another discourse of reading and writing; and social life as always ostensibly about heteronormative romance and competition.

CONTEMPORANEOUSLY, COMPUTATIONALLY BANAL

In the context of a general fetishization of newness, banality—as we might associate it with boredom—reverberates throughout recent critical theorizations of contemporary culture. Ironically, we are in exciting times for banal theory. Since Fredric Jameson's diagnosis of the postmodern condition, we have been interested in disinterest, which is often attended to as affect. For Jameson, late capitalism brings about a waning of affect, a withdrawal from the presumption of a thinking, feeling historical subject. However, Jameson's goodbye to affect was the beginning of a critical turn toward it.[26] The banal as affect emerges particularly from analyses of late capitalism that draw on novelty as an overly coded encounter—novelty as an expectation rather than a disturbance. For example, in recent work by Sianne Ngai and Lauren Berlant, "minor" affective and aesthetic categories, such as irritation and flatness, produce scenes of potentially novel engagement that simultaneously block or hide the radical force of such engagement.[27] Ngai and Berlant offer a contemporary banal theory. Though Berlant is more particularly interested in affects, and Ngai aesthetics, both attend to culture that tropes repetition and seriality, exhibits narrative impasse, and elicits low engagement from the consumer, that is, scenes that are *barely* affective, or with little to no affective resonance.[28] Thinking about banal affects with regard to theories such as these allows for a deeper understanding of the critical potential of novelty within the confines of late capitalism. In other words, the banal surface emerges when radical, disturbing affective novelty is effaced by the commodification of "new" as a driver of the free-market logic of late capitalism.

In Sianne Ngai's work on "merely interesting" art we find a model for thinking about the banal. The merely interesting is at root "a feeling so low in intensity that it can even be hard to say whether it counts as satisfaction or dissatisfaction, feels good or bad to feel."[29] Like banality, the merely interesting is a modulation between "difference and typicality," a response to "novelty and change in a capitalist culture in which change is paradoxically constant and novelty paradoxically familiar."[30] For Ngai, the merely interesting is a postwar aesthetic, a result of globalization and late capitalism. As will be discussed throughout the following chapters, particularly with regard to computer programming in the films of David Fincher and Ellen Ullman's 2003 novel *The Bug*, the postwar period was also when personal computing and distributed digital networks were developed, and our contemporary software culture cannot be thought of as apart from the political forms of this history. Ngai's work touches on these historical computational conditions, arguing that the dominance of an "interesting" aesthetic coincides "with the growth of new media and communication technologies transforming the U.S. from an automated into an 'informated' society."[31] In today's new media culture this aesthetic is utterly common.

Similar to Ngai's "merely interesting" is Berlant's formulation of "flattened affect." Berlant identifies scenes of "underperformed emotion," or "flat affect," in the works of writers such as Teju Cole and Miranda July, in films by Gregg Akari, and in performances of actors Ethan Hawke and Greta Gerwig, performances you might also describe as *interesting*. In these performances, "worlds and events that would have been expected to be captured by expressive suffering ... appear with an asterisk of uncertainty."[32] For Berlant, then, a key aesthetic of the contemporary is one that modulates difference and typicality, as Ngai suggests of the interesting, holding on to the potential for affective investment, while blocking its materialization, its normative expression. The banality of this situation is the sense through which everything is *merely* present, a result of contemporary political formations in which underperformance or mere interest is an important refusal to do the anticipated affective, receptive work. Ngai's and Berlant's interrogations of the aesthetic possibilities of banal affects remind us that the banal incorporates the machinations of late capitalism. The banal, as read here, is another practice of effacement wherein the potential for culture to disturb is substituted for a posture of boredom, already-done-ness, but this operation keeps in play the potential disturbance to come—in Berlant's terms, the event that is becoming. It is not a surprise that realist narratives of contemporary life present the digital in terms of banality; the banal is a primary affect of contemporary life.

The banal, then, is a contemporary affect in which novelty cannot disturb the surface of the present. We experience this situation, in the words of Lauren Berlant, as an "emergent historical environment," or a "stretched out now."[33] Which is to say, we cannot apprehend our historical environment as such; we are not arrested as historical subjects, though we feel present. Instead, we occupy an unresolving present as a stretched-out now, which "merges an intensified present with senses of the recent past and near future."[34] Such contemporary affect circulates both with and *as* digital media. As Susanna Paasonen notes, studies of the affective dimensions of our digitally mediated lives contend that new media "are not merely about storing and sharing data but also about the spread, attachment, amplification and dissipation of affective intensity that help to shape and form connections and disconnections between different bodies."[35] In chapter 5 of this book discussion turns to Jonathan Lethem's *Chronic City* (2010) and Danica Novgorodoff's *Refresh Refresh* (2009) and scenes of users abiding with their computers—waiting for screens to load, watching eBay bids, clicking the "Refresh" icon in anticipation of a new e-mail. In these scenes digital media are generators of affect, spreading, amplifying, linking bodies. Banality is now a mode particularly associated with the use of digital media, through which intense emotions buttress "a circuit of lackluster feelings—think boredom, indifference, or listlessness."[36] More than this, though, the digital banal not only describes the situation in which digital media might produce banal culture or might lead to feelings of banality, it asserts that "banality" and "digital" are integral: digital media *is* banal.

The affect of banality-as-blocking is a logic of contemporary digital culture. By recognizing that the digital is banal, we can understand our banal interpolations—our distracted swiping, our protracted userness, our unresolving present—as a condition of the computational. This is most emphatically the case when we think about source code—the soft root of contemporary computational culture, which is also a mode of banal recursion. Thinking about code in terms of its mediational novelty is blocked by the common appearance of code in culture as yet another discourse of reading and writing. As will be discussed in chapter 1, with reference to depictions of code on-screen in the films of David Fincher, source code resists narrative representation as code and instead appears as a performance of writing code, of writing the future. To unpick the conceit of this cultural conflation, we need to find ways to apprehend code-in-process. The difficulty of this task is that code, as mediational, is a self-effacing form. If code is working, we can't see it; code-in-action is also a block on bearing witness to the action of code.

Code appears to function as an executable language. Writing code and pressing the "Enter" key appears to do things in the world, to execute action. In practice, code is multilayered. The processes that we might think of as writing code are not actually executable; programming languages must be translated into machine-readable instructions for execution. High-level programming languages are easier to write because they can be syntactically similar to natural human language. When programming code is input (usually in a high-level programming language), it is "source code." The programming command is then compiled as "object code"—machine-readable code, instructions that can be directly executed by the machine. In this way, and as Wendy Hui Kyong Chun has powerfully argued, despite the cultural propensity to view the act of programming as an act of writing that directly makes things happen, common programming languages are not executable.[37] According to Chun, "Some programs may be executable, but not all compiled code within that program is executed; rather, lines are read in as necessary. *So, source code thus only becomes source after the fact.*"[38] Code becomes source "through its simultaneous non-presence and presence."[39] If source code has been written effectively, it effaces itself; once compiled, it is instead "object code." Conversely, it is only once an action is executed that we can properly name source code as "source"—it is only in this action of effacement that we can identify what would have been the instruction. In execution, source code is an unresolved present—what it is and what it will have been.

The Digital Banal asserts that the digital *is* banal and that contemporary expressions of the banal may also invoke the digital. In Berlant's terms, many experience the contemporary as an impasse, as "an intensified present with senses of the recent past and near future."[40] This condition is expressed as the banal affect of underperformativity, flatness, and the merely interesting. The source of this culture—the source code that gives us our communications, our *expression*—is also a banal affect: source code as an unresolving present, a perpetual disturbance to come. If banality is a reification of newness, the execution of code is such banality par excellence: what is yet to be known is the executable, which is never read but rather reiterated as what has come to be known—the source.

Responding to what may be perceived as an anthropomorphization of code studies in the work of Alexander R. Galloway and of others such as N. Katherine Hayles and Adrian Mackenzie, Chun draws a distinction between source code and the execution of action (compiled by object code). The distinction is important for understanding the digital banal because it articulates certain challenges to thinking about power, sovereignty, and agency in digitally mediated culture. If all code is described as executable, then we add to the sense of magic that obfuscates the work of programming and the electro-mechanic operations of computation. This power conflates and mystifies the otherwise-rote labor of object code and the creative, but not executable, writing of source code. Source code can only ever be identified after the fact, but in being identified, it confers a sovereign power on the human (readable) program(mer) that belies the work of the machinic object code. Across culture, this sovereignty manifests as code procedures that reify what is yet to be known, and the reassurance that this "yet" is also a programmable future. Most users do not think about the presence of the code that runs their software. How could we get through a day thinking about such complex detail every time we messaged someone? But the durational logic of source code as an unresolving present, a disturbance to come, is felt in our daily encounters as the digital banal.

IMAGINING THE DIGITAL BANAL

The constellation of texts that make up the digital banal here reveals a mediational culture in which the digital banal is not just represented but enacted and perpetuated. The digital banal is an aspect of the effacing gesture of programming code, but it is distinguishable in films that presume to tell us stories of code, comic book panels depicting laptops and Yahoo! homepages, novels in which friends watch eBay bids, characters who glitch rather than forget, and narrators who authenticate their own voices through digital recorders. It is important to attend to instances in which digital media appear "beyond" the technological. As Erkki Huhtamo warns, "Singling out the code for exclusive scrutiny at the expense of everything else might not be the right way to go in an integrated digital culture, where technical, ideological and cultural codes are no longer separable from each other."[41] The tendency to think about digital media within the parameters of a clearly demarcated media or digital study is a worldview in which, in the words of Caroline Bassett, "the logic of information is offered *in the place of* the logic of the tale."[42] In the TV show *Catfish* or the comic *Refresh Refresh*, in the films of David Fincher or in writing by Sheila Heti, Jonathan Lethem, Jennifer Egan, Ellen Ullman, Dave Eggers, Gary Shteyngart, Colson Whitehead, and Mark Amerika, the digital banal is represented as the habitual practices of digital media in everyday life, effacing access to the new conditions and agency of that life. These works are structurally, narratologically, and affectively invested in what it feels like to be socially digital now.

The argument for the digital banal put forth in this book is organized into two distinct but related sections. The first half of the book is concerned primarily with the formal properties of the digital banal: code, commons, script. In this section I am particularly interested in software and the fuzzy edges of mediational interfaces—our screens, the platforms we write through, the ontological realities at stake in becoming-with digital technology. While the first chapter considers the production and representation of code on-screen and looks at programmers as key figures in new media culture, the second chapter turns its attention to writing with new media as a nonexpert user, of the potential for digital media—particularly with social media and Web 2.0 technologies—to function as a political commons. The third chapter moves the discussion on by considering how the platforms through which we write, and write our lives, determine the ways we have of living those lives, of producing new social realities. The second half of the book continues to interrogate the software of computational culture, but does so in tangent with discussion of material environment and situation. Turning outward, to places where software is made, to the lag of distributed digital networks, to server farms and underground cabling, to media infrastructure and environmental damage, these chapters look beyond personal digital devices and habits. Here I am concerned with digital media habitats: from the campus to the home, to networked urban terrain. The three chapters in this section move from the campuses of California, where software is "made," to living rooms where users wait and watch for connections to appear, to various iterations of New York City in which inhabitants are always already medially entangled. To investigate how the digital banal as an aspect of everyday life is represented, enacted, and perpetuated as literature and culture, this book breaks up what is technically entwined—the material and social concerns of the digital banal. This is not to suggest that one aspect comes before another, because there is no before/after: social networks precede the programming of Facebook, which paradoxically rewrites the social network *after* Facebook. Rather, splitting apart these aspects affords an opportunity for the kind of close attention needed to scrutinize conceits of seamlessness and operations of effacement.

Chapter 1, "David Fincher's Grammar of Codes," discusses the digital banal as a foundational aspect of digital culture: code. This chapter looks at the ways code is imagined and narrated in David Fincher's films *Zodiac* (2007), *The Social Network* (2010), and *The Girl with the Dragon Tattoo* (2011). In various ways these films are concerned with code, history, and sovereign agency in medial environments. I begin with work on screen media to posit the screen as a significant interface of our digitally mediated lives. As the book progresses it treats digital media in increasingly diffuse ways, but it begins by articulating how the big screen, as proxy for our everyday small screens, is a primary site for the obfuscation of digital media in everyday life. Working with Wendy Chun's writing on the "enduring ephemerality" of software, and with Mark Currie's work on contemporary narrative "presentification" and "depresentification," I argue that code, as seen in narrative cinema, offers a unique opportunity to apprehend the unresolving mediational present of digital media more broadly. David Fincher's drive for "authenticity" in his work produces particularly affective scenes of code as both a rote, everyday thing, and as a kind of "sourcery," able to perpetually present an event as becoming. I discuss these scenes in terms of what they show, but also attend to what they efface. Such scenes are opportunities to consider the way in which the material of digital media might always be receding from view, even as you throw light on it.

Chapter 2, "Jonathan Lethem's and Mark Amerika's Common Writing," continues with thinking about the root functions of digital media, but it does so through the framework of creative writing practices that use remix and plagiarism. New modes of plagiaristic writing undertaken by Jonathan Lethem and Mark Amerika function as performative commentaries on the commons, on ways of "being-acting-feeling together" in the networked realities of life after new media.[43] These writing practices elucidate a tension between bringing greater accessibility to cultural institutions and markets and the remaking of monetary and social value systems in terms of sharing economies. Both writers produce a palpably ambivalent intervention in this discourse, but their works make visible the operations of the digital banal whereby the prospects of new cultural practices are reified in pro-user culture, effacing the affective novelty of a new commons. In addition, the ways in which writing practices seek to know and narrativize the digital are always also ways of obfuscating what is complex and illegible about digital media. In the case of these literary remix writings, such same-old-literary-work-as-plagiaristic play potentially obfuscates what is newly happening, for example, new modes of writing with nonhuman agents or new global material conditions of expression (from data centers to rare-earth-mineral mining).

Chapter 3, "Being Social in a Postdigital World in *Catfish* and *How Should a Person Be?*," focuses on new instantiations of social life encoded in everyday mediational life. Through discussion of the documentary film and reality TV show *Catfish* and Sheila Heti's 2013 novel, drawn from real life, *How Should a Person Be?*, I argue that social media is a reification of new social conditions of becoming-with media and of being subject to media. *Catfish* and *How Should a Person Be?* pose as banal surfaces, but in doing so they gesture toward the affective novelty of this new emerging sociality. The discussion is routed through Alexander R. Galloway's work on the "interface" as the control logic of computational culture.[44] In Galloway's work the interface is the dominant logic of mediational living: it marks the appearance of a differentiation between one medium (IRL, that is, in real life) and another (computation). Conversely, Galloway argues that the *intra*face is a critical inversion of the interface that destabilizes difference and produces an effect much more akin to Kember and Zylinska's notion of becoming-with technology. Both *Catfish* and *How Should a Person Be?* banally mobilize these different modes and offer moments in which we can gain critical purchase on the ways in which sociality is being reimagined and reconstituted by new realist discourses. In addition, chapter 3 argues that the digital banal is especially suited to recognizing the mediational conditions of these new modes of being "real," which are overlooked by literary and cultural criticism that privileges a concern with sincerity in a post-postmodern era.

The fourth chapter turns its attention to a more historical question of knowledge: how does the way we "know" digital media shift and morph in relation to the digital banal? This chapter takes into account two novels that depict life as software company employees in Silicon Valley: Ellen Ullman's 2003 novel about programming in the 1980s, *The Bug*, and Dave Eggers's 2013 satire of a post-Facebook corporation, *The Circle*. I track the shifting political and historical attachments of these two texts via Richard Barbrook and Andy Cameron's 1995 critique of Silicon Valley, "The Californian Ideology." As software has become increasingly abstract, that is, as programmers require less and less knowledge of code in order to program, so the conditions of the digital banal have formed. The reification of programming knowledge that comes with its abstraction results in a fetish for power and sovereignty accorded to those close to the machine, but this condition effaces the new modes of living and working, more generally, that are instantiated in the "Californian Ideology" of high-tech capitalism. This chapter presents *The Bug* and *The Circle* as capturing different affective registers: from the agitated anticipation of writing the terms of new mediational conditions in *The Bug* to the affective co-option of using and the affective labor demanded to master those new conditions in *The Circle*. Although the two novels tell a chronological story—the first makes the conditions for the second—the historical period between them appears less as progression than as impasse: in both texts any interest in the novelty of digital media is modulated by an ambivalence that curbs radical engagement with digital media itself.

Chapter 5 is undoubtedly the most banal of all the chapters, offering close readings of scenes depicting waiting for e-mail and bidding on eBay taken from Danica Novgorodoff's *Refresh Refresh* (2008) and Jonathan Lethem's *Chronic City* (2009). Neither text is about the digital explicitly, but in both the computer is a present and ongoing concern in the daily lives of the protagonists. Both texts present the potential virtuality of the computer—delineated by the screen—as a frontier yet to fail. In other words, in both texts the computer represents the possibility of otherworldly connection and alterity, even as its stubborn materiality undermines any radical ontology. In these novels the computer is a mode of distraction: characters appear busy with some virtual other place, but are also at home, sitting in front of screens. The effacing gesture of media is a kind of distraction: the computational is often presented as distracting us from real life, a reintensifying of attention from one direction to another. Reading *Chronic City* and *Refresh Refresh*, we find that the bored banality of the computational encounter actually enables us to attend to cultural shifts that might be missed in action-packed event-based narratives. The chapter ends by considering how the digital banal is a condition by which digital media are overlooked by literary and cultural studies that are more focused on discrete historical events. Attending to the digital banal in a broad literary corpus enables us to see how multiple historical narratives are entwined and interrelated.

If chapter 5 discusses the most banal texts, then the sixth and final chapter is interested in novels that appear barely banal. Gary Shteyngart's *Super Sad True Love Story* (2010), Jennifer Egan's *A Visit from the Goon Squad* (2010), and Colson Whitehead's *Zone One* (2011) offer depictions of the mediational *after*life: these are postapocalyptic, futuristic, and zombie narratives. Chapter 6 attends to these novels through three concerns: the representation of the urban environment as media infrastructure; the condition of the digital banal that is shown as life *before*; and the condition of unmediation that defines the future imaginary of the novels' worlds. The moments of rupture in each novel produce the potential for affective novelty to disturb, but this is always a transient potential, which ends through the inculcation of a new normal. Through images of a future digital banal, each novel affords a way to attend to the digital banal in its contemporary mode. The digital banal is a mechanism of obfuscation by which the computational networks that define us as subjects are often made invisible to us. These novels' representation of media infrastructure, and life lived with and after digital media, is an affective investment in making visible the digital banal, the mode by which we don't see the digital conditions of everyday life.

Throughout the book I am concerned with what we can do with the digital banal: what are its limits and its exceptions? I mobilize the banal as a way to recover novelty-as-disturbance from texts that are, for the most part, institutionalized—mainstream films, literary fiction, elite university presses, major publishers, popular TV shows, and large production companies. The digital banal names the suppression of digital-media-as-politics in mainstream literary and visual culture. This book cannot offer a radical break from or destruction of the political conditions it describes—it is no manifesto and finds no real "outside" or future to turn to. As with the examples discussed in chapter 6, the future can be imagined as unmediational only to the extent that it is an imaginary that keeps us in the present condition of mediation. Instead, *The Digital Banal* looks to reveal—through discursive and descriptive methods—the uneasiness of the present and its digital mediational condition. The texts here that comprise the digital banal are offered as examples of that mode and as ways to read against it. When I think about how this book might be asking us to pay a particular kind of attention to the present, I hope that recognizing how we abide with the digital banal is an approach in conversation with recent takes on everyday political existence as a series of affective presents, of making ways to live from within, and of recognizing resistance within as already political.[45] In this mode, *The Digital Banal* reads normative cultural practices of representing everyday life—realist fiction, essay writing, reality TV, and barely speculative speculative fiction—for disturbances that might become ways to recognize and antagonize our new mediational conditions.

1

DAVID FINCHER'S GRAMMAR OF CODE

At the midpoint of David Fincher's 2011 film *The Girl with the Dragon Tattoo* are two very different scenes of filmmaking and film watching. First, Lisbeth Salander, played by Rooney Mara, films her brutalization of Nils Bjurman (Yorick van Wageningen), the legal guardian who raped her. In this scene the camera is set up on a tripod, and both the audience and the characters on-screen watch the playback as the action happens. The second scene shows Mikael Blomkvist (Daniel Craig) watching a movie he has made off camera: a slideshow of still images showing sixteen-year-old Harriet Vanger (Moa Garpendal) at a town parade on the day of her disappearance. The second scene is not visually connected to the first, but is positioned as a continuation through the sustained, escalating drone of Atticus Ross and Trent Reznor's score. These scenes draw our gaze toward processes of filmmaking; they are arresting performances of spectatorship within the film. These scenes emphasize the making, process, and procedure of film. In both scenes digital technology is a means of control, primarily control of information but also control of narrative—the "what will have become" of historical record.[1] In both cases, the "what will have become" is the point in the narrative when a likely outcome is justice for women who have been killed and raped by men. Together, these scenes are a turning point in the film and the catalyst for the investigation proper (when Salander and Blomkvist begin to work together).

We might also think about these scenes as touching on the workflow of the film itself. "Workflow" is a systems management term that emerged in the early twentieth century to refer to patterns of production and distribution and as a way to model efficient work procedures. Workflow is commonly used in media production to describe the movement and integration of data and people on a specific project.[2] David Fincher was one of the first Hollywood directors to use a fully digital workflow.[3] Not simply the path from input (recording) to output (postproduction), digital production workflows must take into account working with different file types and software packages, setting up the camera for a particular data set, working on nonlive action material pre- rather than postproduction.[4] Neither seamless and immaterial nor sequential and cut up, the digital workflow is itself an example of mediation in which labor is subject to both human and nonhuman temporal flows. In *The Girl with the Dragon Tattoo*, Salander's and Blomkvist's filmmaking and film watching position their performances, the narrative, and the audience as subject to the affordances of technology, that is, to the particular ways code might be experienced as a mediating operation. In other words, these scenes remind us of the ways that computation orders human time—the ways that we are subject to code.

These scenes both premediate later scenes of the investigation—the torture of Blomkvist at the hands of Martin Vanger and Salander's discovery of the timeline that links the murders to Martin's travels—and remediate acts of producing the film itself. They are digital events that narrativize digital processes.[5] The workflow model of editing is mobilized here as a procedure and as a metaphor. Workflow is a way to see and index those timed processes that afford the condition of real-time, processes that might otherwise be effaced in everyday experience and the culture that seeks to represent it. The workflow is an example of how mediational processes retreat from view as a condition of their working properly. These workflows also reference a kind of banal digital time: work(a)day images of code produce filmic images in computational temporal routines and registers. Fincher's films bring to our attention everyday digital temporalities. Through bringing into close discussion Wendy Hui Kyong Chun's writing on digital time and Mark Currie's writing on narrative time, I articulate such temporalities as the time of the digital banal, which is both the time of digital media and the narrative time that media can embody.[6]

For most users of digital technology, code is the hidden engine of their experience: silent, disguised, unknown, and possibly unknowable. In narrative cinema, code is produced as legible in a cultural frame: it is written and shown, described and depicted. In Fincher's films *Zodiac* (2007), *The Social Network* (2010), and *The Girl with the Dragon Tattoo* (2012), scenes of programming, hacking, and cracking code are sites of the cultural mediation of code. Fincher's direction of programming demands consideration of the effect of programming as writing and reading, which is seen on-screen, and of programming as an operation that complicates notions of real-time. Through the editing together of different narrative times—the story arc, the act of programming, the effect of programming—these films produce a performance of a present moment that will have been, while engaging with the complexity of code as a real-time procedure, which changes form in the before and after. The emphasis that the digital everyday places on real-time interactions has the effect—as with reality TV—of framing the experience of being present, so that presence, as such, is effaced only to become the desired liveliness of digital communication. As discussed in the introduction, the particular temporalities and effacing processes of computational code are the foundational iteration of the digital banal. It is necessary to work out how this condition appears *as* culture on-screen.

The screen mediates programming code—as the computer monitor—and it is also a site of our cultural mediations *about* digital life—as cinema. Within studies of digital media, the status of the screen has been challenged: screen-based media studies have dominated critical work on new media, perhaps at the expense of what Matthew G. Kirschenbaum has called the "mechanisms" of digital media.[7] New critical scholarship on media infrastructures also reminds us that digital media is never only an encounter that happens between a human and a screen; it is also data centers, cell towers, undersea cables, and rare-mineral mining as well as the human, animal, and environmental bodies living, working, and passing through these sites.[8] However, the site of the screen is a problem for narratives of code: what we see on-screen is an abstraction of computational process—no matter how data visualizations might lure us in with the promise of seeing "the digital event on screen."[9] If the digital banal is the process by which an encounter with digital media and computation as novel is itself reiterated as to be expected so that an engagement with the novelty of digital media is affectively obfuscated, then the screen is the first point of (non)entry. Rather than work from an assumption about whether the cinema screen can or cannot enable a way of seeing behind the computer screen, we can attend to the screen-ness of programming in films, watching the way computer monitors—and the bodies that sit with them, the hackers and programmers—limn the action of code. David Fincher's films, discussed below, offer up a visual grammar of code: a cinema that is attentive to the task of representing code in its material and symbolic state and as an effacing gesture that is also a political reality of everyday life.

GRAMMARS OF CODE

The Social Network depicts multiple scenes of code writing, particularly hacking, mostly performed by Harvard undergraduates, who are depicted as geeks in Gap hoodies, drinking light beer and doing shots. In a review of the film, Zadie Smith writes of the dilemma that director David Fincher must have had when deciding whether to include these scenes: "How to convey the pleasure of programming . . . in a way that is both cinematic and comprehensible? Movies are notoriously bad at showing the pleasures and rigors of art-making, even when the medium is familiar. . . . Programming is a whole new kind of problem."[10] Scenes of programming in *The Social Network* are not always pleasurable, but they are busy and hyper and engaging. They are also social, not just as the social media network-to-be, but as always-already socially and culturally embedded practices.

One of the first sequences of the movie shows the character of Mark Zuckerberg (real-life founder of Facebook, played in the film by actor Jesse Eisenberg) arriving home after being dumped by his girlfriend, Erica Albright (Rooney Mara), grabbing a bottle of beer and sitting down to write a blog post about the woman he was just dumped by. This scene takes place at a desktop computer, but the character also has a laptop next to the desktop screen (see figure 1.1). Open on the laptop is a Harvard website that shows student profiles. Zuckerberg's roommate jokingly suggests comparing female students' profiles to pictures of animals and rat-

FIGURE 1.1 "Let the hacking begin." *The Social Network* (2010)

ing them. Zuckerberg decides that rather than compare women's profiles to animals he should set up a program to rate women's photos against one another. This thought process is shown on-screen as Zuckerberg types it all in his blog, and it is simultaneously narrated by a voiceover (Eisenberg, playing Zuckerberg, reading the blog aloud). After Zuckerberg has hit on this idea, a quick-cut sequence of programming and blogging commences with his call: "Let the hacking begin."[11]

In the scene that follows—the making of Facemash—the voiceover continues to narrate the blog post, which describes the hacking sequence, while on-screen the film alternates between images of the two screens: the blog post and the code for hacking into the Harvard student profile sites.[12] The images of Zuckerberg in his dorm room are spliced with images of action taking place elsewhere on campus: female students arriving at a party in one of the exclusive members' clubs that Zuckerberg covets. The overall effect of the scene conflates the writing of code with the actions it will eventually effect. Through montage and compressed temporal gestures, Zuckerberg is shown to be literally rewriting the hierarchical nature of social networking (as it is represented by Ivy League institutions). In this sequence, iterability and executability are blurred by the edits of Fincher and his team.

The cuts that switch between the two scenes of action are violent. The women at the frat party are interpolated as data in the program, and this appears as aggressive editorial splicing. While the film offers a fictional origin story for Facebook—Erica Albright—it makes highly visible the exploitation of images of women, which *is* the Facebook origin story. As Melissa Gira Grant has described it, women "and their representations are [an] intentional . . . part of Facebook. . . . The unpaid and underpaid labor of women is essential to making [Facebook] go, to making it so irresistible."[13] Problematically, despite making this labor visible, the film still skews the historical record of women, particularly Asian American women, who worked at Facebook as programmers and customer service staff in its early incarnation. As Lisa Nakamura highlights, in *The Social Network* the depiction of "Asian women's labor as sexual rather than technical obscures rather than exposes the workers of color who 'make' social media."[14]

Alongside the construction of the social network played out in the Facemash scene are contrasting practices of reading and writing, which are represented on-screen as the blog post/voiceover and the programming code. In the scene, the depictions of writing flicker between writing plaintext with HTML (for the blog) and writing command code (for Facemash) (see figures 1.2 and 1.3). These are two different languages. Both are higher-level programming languages, but HTML is written in plaintext (natural language) with additional rules that are deployed to dictate the appearance of that text online. The code for Facemash is a structural layer below this (such as C++). The scene is soundtracked by pounding dance music, and within the same long scene (full of short edits) we see the instant "liveness" of Facemash as (mostly male) students in other dorms get sent a link to the site and begin rating the photos. The ellipses between Zuckerberg's blog text (readable) and his program text (code) serve to give an impression of fluidity to the procedures for writing structural code. The voiceover in this scene explains the procedures of code, framing the visually disconcerting switches between scenes and screens with a smooth technical narrative that performs the disciplinary norms of patriarchy in a manner that seems like algorithmic inevitability. The dialogue in this scene that refers to code is, for the most part, technically authentic—the only changes Mark Zuckerberg requested to be made to the script were those referring to the programs and algorithms he used to build the initial site.[15] The voiceover has the added effect of distinguishing between the two writing procedures, giving human inflection to the blog post, which in turn functions as a way for the viewer to understand what is happening in the representation of code writing.

DAVID FINCHER'S GRAMMAR OF CODE 25

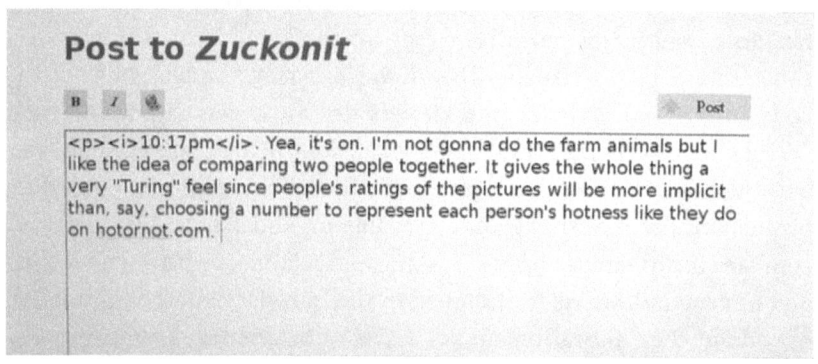

FIGURE 1.2 Mark Zuckerberg blogging Facemash. *The Social Network* (2010)

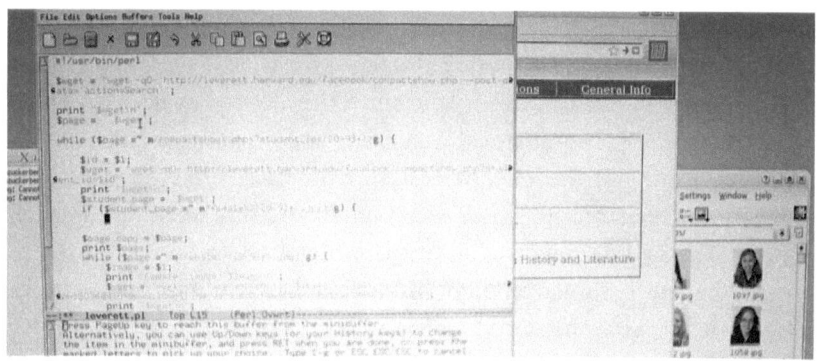

FIGURE 1.3 Mark Zuckerberg hacking and writing code for Facemash. *The Social Network* (2010)

The code is only named, and therefore technically understood, through the blog: "Definitely necessary to break out the Emacs and modify that Perl script." Its appearance on-screen is not legible—it is depicted as blurry lines of indistinguishable characters. The programming characters are lighter in color than the blog font; viewers are permitted to not know, or even to not see, this operation. In contrast, the blog text as seen on-screen is perfectly legible, and the audience can read along with the voiceover. The scene is fraught with the anxiety of distance between user and code. This anxiety is represented textually through multiple representations of reading, writing, and narrative. The counterpoint to these multiple depictions of reading and writing is one that epitomizes the difficulty in narrativizing code: in this section of *The Social Network* the blog functions as the narrative frame for that which resists narrative—code. This happens visually (the viewer can read the blog but not the code script) and verbally (the viewers do not necessarily know what "Emacs" or "Perl" refer to, but they can follow the context). And yet, even with such an accessible cinematic frame, this representation does not technically render the code readable or understandable; it merely conflates the difference between seeing and reading, or between viewing and understanding. As is discussed in the introduction, the production of code in the cultural imaginary as yet another mode of reading and writing is one way in which the executibility of code as machinic discourse is effaced. In the scenes of programming described above, the performance of the programmer is one of sovereignty: the programmer rewrites the world.

Such scenes narrativize code as constitutional. As Chun has written, the executability of code is not law, but rather "every lawyer's dream of what law should be: automatically enabling and disabling certain actions and functioning at the level of everyday practice."[16] Here Zuckerberg is seen to be constituting a new social order, and this constitution is depicted as latent with meaning. The programming frenzy we watch on-screen is energized by a dramatization of historical affect that was lacking in the actual historical architecture of Facebook: Zuckerberg was hurting.[17] The hurting leads to the hacking as a distraction (and as revenge), and the hacking involves scrolling through photos of women in Zuckerberg's social network. In tension with the performance of what could have been—the emotional frenzy—is the banal affect of what has become—our distracted swiping, our protracted userness, our unresolving present, our scrolling through Facebook profiles. In other words, these scenes exemplify the digital banal: they are meant to be exciting and show us the dawn of some new thing, but the excitement and energy is displaced onto and dispersed throughout old things (partying, heartbreak, misogyny), and the means by which the new is being constituted—hacking—appears as just another text in the process of being written. In these early scenes of *The Social Network*, the audience is presented with a benign avowal of the new order; or, to rework Apple's iPhone 4 slogan, the elite are changing everything, *again*.

TIME CODING

In the Facemash sequence of *The Social Network*, Zuckerberg is shown writing the script, the source. But what the audience knows to be the object—the reordering of networking through social media (Facebook)—can only be known in retrospect; as of the "present" within the film, it is unknowable. This scene, then, is one that performs code as temporal; the structure of this scene offers a reflexive gesture at its own conceit. The programming of Facemash, as performed, is also a representation of what will have been Facebook. The technological apparatus, as it is depicted, is cut up with, or is cutting up, the physical network as montage in such a way that draws attention to the time at stake: the film is a medium of a specific duration. The conflation of viewing and understanding is also a conflation of timelines. The montage sequence in a feature film is standard shorthand for compressing time. A regular film watcher knows that the montage signals a transformative moment, or a moment of transformation. The fact that this sequence is a montage suggests—through the language of filmic convention—that this sequence is transformative. Specifically, the future-orientation of the narrative in *The Social Network* is drawn out through the depiction of a transformative, future-oriented act of writing, *programming*. This is not an image of code for code's sake, but rather a situating of the programming act as social. Zuckerberg and his roommates and Ivy League members' clubs, these are the social networks of the film, and they constitute the Facebook that will have become.

Indeterminate temporality is key to the way *The Social Network* exemplifies the conditions of the digital banal. The complex timelines of the film and its production instantiate digital time: new media forms are reified as what is yet to be known, while what is reiterated is what is already known—the programmed future. The interplay of timelines involves cinema time (the duration of the film, the pacing of the film-watching experience), production time (the time of the total production from conception to the DVD release), and processing time (both the code on-screen and the code as screen). Fincher has described working on digital film as a process of addressing time; you look "at performance in kind of fractal time—time *between* time."[18] This fractal time, the time *between* time, is a generative way of considering Fincher's attention to time. In Fincher's films we are tacitly aware of the impossibility of making visible a between time of code, even as we watch scenes of writing and editing that recall the between time of cinema. The code procedures in these films are durational; there is no discrete moment when we can apprehend code. Simultaneously we are presented with the effacing move: as a cinematic text this duration appears in the guise of the banal ambivalence of programming as a timely progression. The following section of this chapter interrogates the digital banal of "fractal time" by bringing into dialogue Mark Currie's work on the "expansion" and "presentification" of time in contemporary narrative culture and Wendy Chun's articulation of digital culture as an "enduring ephemeral."

Unlike reading and writing in human-to-human communication, human-to-computer communication—as in programming or hacking—is enacted through what will have been executable language. Programming a computer involves inputting a string of characters that will execute action. This does not happen magically all at once, but by layers of code, each parsing the next layer, until a discrete switch is moved in a circuit. Human programmers usually work in high-level (abstract) programming languages, which are syntactically similar to natural languages; these are then compiled as machine-readable "object code." The source code—the code written by the programmer—is only source after the fact, after the code has been compiled and executed. Source code disappears and becomes object code; we can only retrospectively locate it as the higher-level code, the source of action. This trick of effacement is key for thinking about the way computational culture troubles a narrative. Code appears as a set of narratological clauses: if this happens, then that happens; find this term in this set, then return this object to this site. The mechanism of these processes is more stubbornly nonhuman; it involves acts that are not actionable by humans or by human language.

Code does not conform to a tensed narrative. Situating code as a representational encounter in narrative cinema is an acknowledgement of how popular contemporary narrative forms are driven by the complex temporal processes of code. From the presentation of code as narrative in *The Social Network*, we might begin to see what Mark Currie has referred to as the untensed "presentification" of contemporary narrative, which, I argue, is an effect of the untensed "enduring ephemeral" of digital media. Despite the assumption that programming produces the future, its status as source code after the fact means that it can only exist in the present. In programming, the present stands in for the future: "To program a computer is to produce a series of stored instructions that supposedly guarantee—and often stand in for—a certain action."[19] The capacity for digital technologies to store the past—in the form of data—is what produces the capabilities for computational programming of the future; this proliferates through culture as the assumption that digital media is an ever-expanding memory. Rejecting this assumption, Chun's articulation of new media as an "enduring ephemeral" unpicks the conceit of endless memory, the archival qualities of digital media. Rather, these types of capabilities are premised on a constant act of "refreshing," so that the past is not a stable linear sequence but a continual cycle of updating—it is constantly being rewritten.

Chun's description of code-time chimes with Currie's reading of contemporary narrative's attachment to an "expansive" present. In contemporary literary narrative, Currie witnesses an "ascendance of anachrony, and in particular the fashion for prolepsis," as "a performative function which produces in the world a generalized future orientation."[20] For Currie, this trend in contemporary fiction is reflective of the possibilities for narrative more broadly, in a culture that valorizes the documentation of the present in place of the present—a "depresentification."[21] More specifically, what distinguishes contemporary culture in terms of narrative time are technologies that decouple the presentation of narrative from the forward orientation of time, particularly the moving image: "Representation of a genuinely reversed temporality is one of the things that film can do that verbal representation cannot."[22] This logic of the present is the dominant temporal logic at work in *The Social Network*: splicing a past-present and past-past, to produce the former as what will come to mean the latter, in a perpetual present of the film. Court cases between Zuckerberg and Eduardo Saverin and between Zuckerberg and Divya Narendra, Cameron Winklevoss, and Tyler Winklevoss are the future, which is defined by the opening sequence of the film as a whole—Zuckerberg being dumped by Erica Albright. This dumping is a fictional plot device, which nonetheless is the moment the audience has been anticipating, the Facebook origin story.

The break that takes place between tense and the representation of time is contoured differently in the era of digital media. Instead of the reversal of time that Currie attributes to film, we encounter the enduring ephemeral of software. Culture functions programmatically, through the logic of software; code is a vital mediational ground of contemporary living. In the contemporary moment software "fastens in place a certain neoliberal logic of cause and effect, based on the erasure of execution and the privileging of programming that bleeds elsewhere and stems from elsewhere as well."[23] In other words, presentification and depresentification. When Currie writes about the expansive present that contemporary narrative genres attest to, he is also writing about the expansive present of digital media. For Currie, we record "the present as the object of a future memory, or live the present in a mode of anticipation of the story we will tell about it."[24] It is this untensed narrative time that appears in cinematic depictions of computation, which attest to a process that may itself trouble assumptions about how digital cinema presents time.

The Social Network offers two present narratives—rather than, say, a voice-over providing a sequential history—and their relationship in time is an effect of the editorial cut. This effect is amplified and made explicit in the fast edits of the scene in which Zuckerberg is shown writing the code for Facemash. In *The Social Network* the present-future outside the film—the present of the audience, which is the future of Facebook as it is represented in the film—always haunts the narrative of the film itself. Following Currie, this kind of dampened anticipation is one that extends beyond the boundary of fiction or of fictive texts; it applies to the ways we narrate life: "Whether this ontological boundary [between fiction and reality] is redrawn, blurred, or erased, the world of narrative is one in which the future has already taken place, and is not open."[25] The structure of *The Social Network* plays with a knowing audience's appreciation of its subject matter—it is by definition future-oriented in that it is telling a story about the past aimed at the present, the future of that past. Additionally, the temporal indeterminacy of the film is owed to its subject, Facebook. Facebook itself, particularly with the introduction of the timeline to replace users' walls, functions precisely as a tool to enable a future-oriented living in which the present may be experienced as a story we will tell about ourselves.[26] *The Social Network* mobilizes as narrative structure the distinct temporal effacement of the Facebook program, which follows the logic of the digital banal. The Facebook timeline presents an unresolved subject who is becoming-with technology (perpetually in the present) while blocking attention to the remaking of the sovereign subject as a software litany (the profiled subject found in directories, routines, archives, history). The film produces the present subject as a retrospective anticipation; this performance appears to be a process of subject formation (the becoming of Facebook), but it effaces the potential strangeness of this condition of time, reiterating instead a history that we need not bother with, the present ending of the film—an out-of-court settlement, our habitual status updates, the new normal.

The narrative present does not have a purchase on a temporal zone distinct from the past and future, and it folds into itself both past and future imaginaries. Playing on the present as refusing to be tensed is also an acknowledgment that the present is a site of tension. This could be Berlant's unfeeling present, which is remaining unresolved, holding on to the potential for affective investment, while blocking its materialization, its normative expression. As I have argued, such tension is also at stake in the processes of digital media, which elevate the condition of an anticipatory present. In a world where a trending video clip might be fifty years old, and "old email messages [are] forever circulated and rediscovered as new," our mediational culture is sustained by "a nonsimultaneousness of the new."[27] The compulsion to repeat and recirculate is an aspect of a culture "tied to an inhumanly precise and unrelenting clock."[28] Such unrelenting time is also a nonhuman temporality that we are always becoming-with, the mediational mode of contemporary living.

Paraphrasing Wolfgang Ernst, Chun notes, "Digital media is truly a *time-based medium*, which, given a screen's refresh cycle and the dynamic flow of information in cyberspace, turns images, sounds, and text into discrete moments in time. These images are frozen for human eyes only."[29] This is to draw a distinction between the way that humans see life through new media, in time, and the temporal operations of the computational processes that run new media. The difference between these durational experiences is bound up in the mediational as described by Kember and Zylinska, that is, the discrete temporal object—an MP3 file, say—is only discrete as it is engaged by the human. In its mediational mode, the screen's refresh cycle is an untensed duration. Our interaction with digitally mediated life is one of fixed graphical entities and fixed temporal incidents: text, video, or image, the thing we look at, watch, or listen to, is of a particular total duration, either static (text, still image) or time-coded moving data (video, audio). The hardware and software that run these graphic events are not still or fixed; they are continually updating, refreshing. The overall effect, when taking into account the operation of the technology and our interactions with it, is not a movement from past to future but rather a continually refreshing present. The persistent present of digital time is one in which the perceived ephemerality of digital media—the black-boxing of its operations—endures; that is, the past is not left behind and the future is never fully realized. Such presentification is a condition of contemporary narrative culture and also a condition of living with digital media. The conflation of these concerns in *The Social Network* is an exemplary operation of the digital banal. In scenes of programming we are presented with both the anticipation of retrospective moments and the unceasing drive of commands for recollections (a literal recalling of data); these are brought to screen by a reification of the ineluctable difference of this medium—the strangeness of code—which is reiterated as a banal program of writing what we already knew.

FINCHER'S PROCEDURAL

Zodiac follows the real-life story of the Zodiac Killer: a self-named serial killer who committed several murders in the San Francisco bay area between 1969 and 1974 that were never solved. The killings initially garnered public attention when the *San Francisco Chronicle* published coded letters that the Zodiac Killer sent in as clues to the next murder. The script is based on two books by Robert Graysmith, a cartoonist for the *San Francisco Chronicle* who continued a civilian investigation into the Zodiac Killer long after the police moved on from the case. *Zodiac* was one of the first Hollywood features for which the whole workflow was digital. The film is about an investigation, but it is one in which the outcome is known; there is no resolution, only the present of the film catching up with the real-time status of the case. Similar to *The Social Network*, *Zodiac* is a history film, but due to its subject and style, the procedural operation of the digital banal is emphatically effaced from the screen rather than ambivalently present. The suppressed future-oriented mode of *Zodiac* is recovered at the end of the film, when prior to the credits, we get a series of "where are they now" facts about the different people involved in the case. Because the Zodiac case remains unresolved, the film is much more about procedure and process than it is about outcome. As with Fincher's earlier film *Se7en* (1995), *Zodiac* is less about the serial killer than it is about the police detectives charged with solving the crimes; but much more so than *Se7en*, *Zodiac* is about the process of detection. The characters and the filmmaker labor over the daily detail of detection. Not simply a police procedural in the generic sense, *Zodiac* is also a journalism procedural, a forensic procedural, and a private procedural (that is, it follows the procedures of private life: family, work, ways of being). Embedded in the procedures of the film itself—the digital *thing*, the real-time making of it—and in the procedures depicted on-screen, is a film about time, routine, and the ways that meaning and outcome might elude action. *Zodiac* is also a film about networks. The procedural is always framed in relation to another procedural that functions as a network: journalists and police, the public and the individual, postal communications networks, US state and federal networks, cultural networks—the intertextual networks of other books and films and stories.

Zodiac produces these tropes—of time, network, and procedure—through the signifying object of the film: code. In the opening credits of *Zodiac*, the typewriter font that names the cast and crew fades into the graphic characters of the Zodiac code. In this way, the effect of encoding the names of those working on the film is also a performance of digital imaging, the working *of* the film. If the typewritten documentation is representative of the procedures and networks that write the official narrative, the obscuring of this text in the opening credits might indicate the complexity of coded utterances to follow. The film is primarily a story about the code the Zodiac Killer uses to attract attention to his crimes and the ways the legibility of this code influences the lives of those marked by the killer's actions.[30] As I have been researching for this book, it has been hard not to jump at every mention of the word "code," to see everywhere the patterns of our current digital culture. *Zodiac* is a film that can support the scrutiny of digitally inflected critical thinking, that hails it, even. Arguably, *Zodiac* represents the world it depicts as one already encoded with the formatting of digital culture, a premediation of things that will have been. Although the historical events that are the subject matter of the film take place in a world of typewriters, magnifying glasses, and print media, the film is also of its twenty-first-century techno-culture. In its attention to procedures of forensic data analysis, and in its representation of the protagonist, Robert Graysmith—played by Jake Gyllenhaal—as a gifted outsider who cracks the Zodiac's code and in doing so hacks the official networks (the police, the newspapers), *Zodiac* intimates that the subject matter of the film is more explicitly about digital culture. *Zodiac* is a digital film about older media that can be seen as a precursor to Fincher's later films that focus explicitly on digital culture as it is lived.[31]

Early on in *Zodiac* the interlinked subjects of code, procedure, and networks are explicitly framed in terms of everyday routine. The film itself opens with the first murder, but of particular interest here is the sequence that runs through the credits and segues into the film proper. This is a long scene that depicts Robert Graysmith's morning routine and arrival at the *Chronicle* offices. Shots of Graysmith on his way to work are spliced with shots of another journey to the *Chronicle* offices: the delivery of the Zodiac's first letter. Throughout the film this text, the letter, is continually asserted as the story, the action. The scene follows Graysmith getting ready for work at home, dropping his son off at school, and then walking into the *San Francisco Chronicle* building. When Graysmith enters the building, our view is tracked back to the street; the shot frames a postal van pulling up. We then switch back and forth between a series of shots of Graysmith's walk through the *Chronicle* building to the morning editorial meeting and shots of an envelope (the killer's letter) on its way to the morning editorial meeting. The envelope is identifiable by its handwritten, distinct form of address (the casual "S. F. Chronicle, *San Fran. Calif,* Please Rush to Editor!"). The sequence is underscored by the driving polyrhythms of Santana's "Soul Sacrifice." The music ends with furious strumming, drumming, and feedback over the arrival of the post and Graysmith at the morning editorial meeting. This marks the end of the credit sequence and the beginning of the film—a banal sort of climax.

At the meeting the letter and the code, which purports to reveal the killer's name, are circulated; Graysmith copies the code by hand, but when he is spotted he is sent back to his desk to get back to drawing the cartoon for the daily edition of the paper. After the close of the day, Graysmith goes home (walking past the bar where the journalists drink). The code is seen again in the following scene in the white-gloved hands of a photographic lab technician, producing the plates for the code to be printed in the *Chronicle*. This scene of mechanical reproduction is a return to the chain of dissemination that followed the letter's arrival. The audience watches Graysmith come in his front door and pin his hand-drawn copy of the code on a bulletin board. The following sequence depicts printed versions of the code—paper copies, transparencies for overhead projectors—being passed around various government and state crime investigation bureaus: the naval intelligence office in Sonoma, the FBI in San Francisco, and the CIA in Langley. The sequence is captioned to present the organization, location, and time lapse between each node in the network of dissemination: Sonoma, "12 hours later"; San Francisco, "6 hours later"; Langley, "5 hours later." Finally, "12 hours later," a couple in Salinas breaks the code while reading the morning paper over breakfast. The whole sequence might be subtitled "The Travails of a Text." Although the shots do not exclusively follow the Zodiac's letter, the sequence represents the letter, and more crucially the code, as a directive: the code-text creates the action for the operations around it. The workday is framed as the anticipation and execution of code.

In an interview for the special features of the 2007 DVD release of *Zodiac*, Detective George Bawart discusses the difficulties of 1970s police work: "One of the problems from the outset of this case was it was across multiple jurisdictions; departments didn't talk to each other that much. I think one of the biggest factors that would have solved this problem earlier would've probably been the advent of computers."[32] Key to thinking about the way code might function as a directive in the film is a critical move that relies on reading the communication networks of 1970s San Francisco (as they are represented in the film) as premediating digital networks: the digital material of the film itself brings into the viewing plane a ghostly digital presence, which in turn haunts the actions of a police procedural without digital aid. That this concern is generated by the movie itself seems to emerge not only from the imaging of code in the Zodiac Killer's letters but also from the way in which text more generally is made to be seen and communicated. In *Zodiac* procedures are encoded in text in the form of print newspapers, ciphers, letters, and police documentation. Of particular importance is the kind of text being shown: throughout *Zodiac* handwritten and typewritten text are visually contrasted and made to produce paradoxical connotations. The attention paid to typed and handwritten script is part of the way the narrative of the film hails the "what will be" of digital culture, not as its explicit subject, but as a haunting peripheral. As Jacques Derrida argues, typed or handwritten text does not precede the digital; it is always already technology. "When we write 'by hand' we are not in the time before technology; there is already instrumentality, regular reproduction, mechanical iterability.... And then on the other side what we call 'typed' writing is also 'manual.'"[33] The handwritten code is a precondition of the digital code, which is the material condition of the film itself. While Derrida suggests that computational processes remind us that, in the hand, we already have the digits of the future, there is something specific about the present that should not be deferred by thinking of it as predetermined. The uncanny code of *Zodiac* is a way to witness the precise effacement of computation through the production of the programmer as master. Graysmith comes closest to mastering the code because he makes it in his own hand, but his failure to fully comprehend it stands in for the present condition of the film, wherein complex code systems have autonomy and elude total comprehension.

The opening credits of *Zodiac* are all in a mock-typewriter font. The font continues to appear throughout the film, in particular to introduce different sections of the film by date. This aesthetic scheme highlights not only the historical setting of the film but also the thematic concern with typing and writing. Forensic evidence in *Zodiac* is preoccupied with identifying the handwriting of the Zodiac Killer (figure 1.4). The typewritten

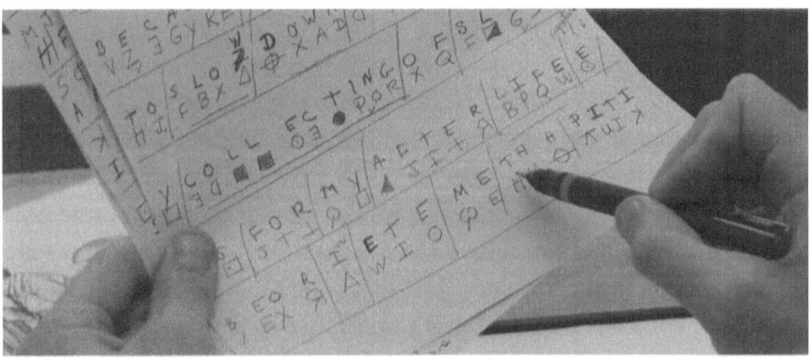

FIGURE 1.4 Robert Graysmith tracing the Zodiac code. *Zodiac* (2007)

documentation that forms the official narrative of the murders—the journalism, the police documents—is in opposition to the Zodiac Killer's communication by handwritten letter. The group identities of the press and police are both more and less anonymous than the utterances of the individual killer: despite the abstract font of the typewritten text, the viewer knows who the police and journalists are, whereas the killer has the handwriting of the "in-dividual," to use Friedrich Kittler's phrase, but not the identity to match.[34]

The emphasis on visualizing the act of writing runs throughout the film, with several scenes of journalist Paul Avery (played by Robert Downey Jr.) at his typewriter. Key to the current discussion is the way the film draws out Robert Graysmith's actions as an artist/illustrator. Graysmith's draftsmanship is visually connected to the killer's handwriting (see figure 1.4). Graysmith doodles and is the only character to copy, by hand, the Zodiac code. Graysmith's obsession with the code appears to carry his investigations further than those organizations working from mechanically reproduced copies of the code. Graysmith's pursuit of the killer long after the official investigation has gone cold is presented as an affinity between killer and investigator—perhaps an affinity of the hand. One of the key clues that Graysmith uncovers, and that has previously been overlooked (though it turns out to be a red herring), is the artwork on a set of posters advertising the upcoming showings of movies at a cinema, which is connected to one of the suspects. In the handwriting and draftsmanship of the posters, Graysmith sees the hand(writing) of the killer's letters. The possibility of narrative resolution rests on Graysmith's mastery of the source code, and his affinity with the source of the code, but this source turns out to be unreadable, unsupportable. The Zodiac Killer's code obscures his identity, just as the shot of the code—to be read (though not comprehended) by an audience—disrupts or obscures the watching of the visual sequence. Here the unresolved case returns to the viewer the unresolving digital time of code.

In the films of David Fincher, the appearance of a seamless narrative is persistently undermined by a multiplex system of representation in which time is played with to bring the work's digital operations to the surface. Digital rendering is used to represent, nostalgically, the material specificity of the recent past in *The Social Network*, and the more recognizably *past* of 1970s San Francisco. In *The Social Network* the actors typed in front of blue screens; replica web browsers—such as Network Solutions, the site where Zuckerberg registered the domain name "thefacebook.com"—were added in postproduction.[35] In *Zodiac* Fincher's team re-created crime scenes in the actual geographic locations of the particular crimes and then reversed the passage of time on the surrounding landscape in postproduction. The attention to historical detail sustains the image of seamlessness, a near likeness to history. For an audience that has never come across Network Solutions or registered a domain name, Fincher's attention to detail propagates the coherent totality of the narrative world and further establishes the look, the distinctness, of the historical moment. Digital entertainment is often associated with a particular kind of seamlessness, "a generic expectation of something new, a willingness to sever connections with fundamental laws of nature."[36] In *Zodiac* digital production methods are mobilized to achieve a certain performance of authenticity—an imagistic historical accuracy. But this retrospection is, as I have suggested by way of Currie's and Chun's work, not separable from all that is being anticipated. Both *Zodiac* and *The Social Network* undermine the presumption to history by calling forth the source code. While source code is never really so (it is only ever after the fact), its representation on-screen—as surface—makes visible the effacing gesture of the digital banal. Here code is not really seen, but it is given screen time as a ghost in the filmic machinery. Such time may still be a blocking of affective novelty by way of a reiteration of our expectation (the history we already knew). But in these films attention to the unresolved status of that history—the code never reveals the killer, Graysmith never masters the code, the fiction of Facebook as revenge for a failed romance reveals the black-box formation of Facebook—is an attention to slippage, a potential moment where encountering how we become digitally present is a challenge to the operations of the digital banal.

FROM OPERATOR TO PROGRAMMER

The Girl with the Dragon Tattoo tells the story of Lisbeth Salander, a twenty-three-year-old ward of the state living in Stockholm. Salander works as a freelance analyst for a covert firm that is employed to conduct private investigations, and she is a success at her job due to her skills in hacking and detection. Though Salander is initially employed to analyze the professional and personal life of the journalist Mikael Blomkvist, Blomkvist eventually invites her to work with him in solving the mystery of Harriet Vanger, who disappeared forty years previously. The procedure of the investigation frames both characters as outsiders (a journalist and an analyst, and not a police- or a state-endorsed forensic analyst), which in turn enables them to undertake ethically problematic actions (like Robert Graysmith, Salander and Blomkvist are unofficial detectives). In *Zodiac* and *The Social Network* it is the characters' mastery of code and programming that form the catalyst for action, but Lisbeth Salander is seen to be *always* online, and her physical, offline actions and thoughts are uncannily doubled in her watching and manipulation of other characters' digital lives.

Of the films discussed, *The Girl with the Dragon Tattoo* is perhaps the film that most clearly represents a subject delineated by the use of technology. Discussing *Zodiac* and *The Social Network*, I argued that in their status as "history" films, both produce a condition of the digital banal whereby the affectively distinct experience of contemporary life, a life lived with complex nonhuman agents (digital media), is reiterated as the to-be-expected future. In both cases the digital banal was discussed as a mode of presentification that is both the result of and an obfuscation of code. This process is seen on-screen as the reading and writing of source code (as origin story) in *The Social Network* and as a process of effacement in *Zodiac* whereby the source code of the digital film is returned to the screen as a premedial code, legible in the handwritten and typed missives of the Zodiac killer. *The Girl with the Dragon Tattoo* has no similar claims to history, but it does produce a similarly complex, difficult presentification of digital media.[37]

Before computers were machines, they were women who operated switchboards. The abstraction of computation—the move from hardware to software—produced the conditions in which histories of computing could ignore and neglect the first programmers: women such as the ENIAC girls (Adele Goldstine, Mary Mauchly, Mildred Kramer, Alice Burks, Mrs. Harris, Miss Mott, Miss Greene, Mrs. Seeley, and Mrs. Pritkin).[38] The work these women did was lost as programming shifted from an act of operating a machine to an act of programming a system. As Wendy Chun argues, this is more than a linguistic shift; it is the point at which programming becomes associated with mastery and sovereignty.[39] Although Lisbeth Salander has, on the surface, nothing to do with the history of women as computers, her role as ambivalent programmer is the residue of Chun's critique: by appearing masterful and also always subjugated, Salander is a figure in whom we can locate the banal obfuscation of power produced by the abstraction of hardware as software, as a reconstitution of patriarchal gender politics and as a lively, present concern.

After Blomkvist has been to see Salander at her apartment to seek her help in his investigation, Salander immediately starts up a program to trawl for data on the murdered women Blomkvist has so far identified.[40] The sequence is an authentic representation of "grepping," that is, using a command-line facility that searches for regular phrases in among plain-text data (figure 1.5).[41] Salander's digital searching is cut up with shots of Blomkvist's physical journey back to Hedeby Island. The sequence implies that in the time it takes Blomkvist to physically move about spaces, Salander is able to produce more work. The implication is made not by way of Salander's labor; instead, she inputs key phrases, hits the "Enter" key, and walks away. The success of the procedure is in the execution that she does not control: Salander waits for the computer. She gets up and walks away from the screen, picks up Coke cans to pack for her trip to Hedeby, chews her food, and watches the screen (figure 1.6). The omnipotence of the programmer is here being resisted in order to instead demonstrate the omnipotence of the programming machine: it dictates process, and we have to wait for it, but we anticipate its temporal gesture to produce meaning—albeit deferred. If the Facemash scene in *The Social Network* elides temporal constraints so that we can witness Zuckerberg as master of the social network (and of future social networking), no such power has been afforded to Lisbeth Salander, who must wait out the machine.

At various points in *The Girl with the Dragon Tattoo* the narrative cuts to a shot of Salander's laptop, where we see (and hear the ping of) a new e-mail from one of the accounts she is mirroring—Hans-Erik Wennerstrom's or Blomkvist's. Here the computer program is implied to be always on, always running. The computer itself is the background operation to Salander's life, and the code text is the background to the e-mails or websites she is watching. This is depicted literally: the window displaying the Unix OS is a background window on the monitor; the e-mail or website

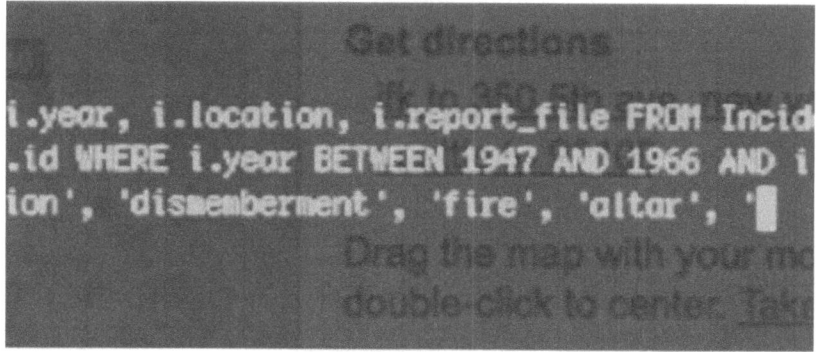

FIGURE 1.5 Grepping. *The Girl with The Dragon Tattoo* (2011)

FIGURE 1.6 Lisbeth Salander eating, waiting, grepping. *The Girl with The Dragon Tattoo* (2011)

window is foregrounded.⁴² After Lisbeth has been raped by Bjurman, a series of scenes shows her recovery and her preparation for revenge. These are spliced with Blomkvist's ongoing investigations into the Vanger family on Hedeby Island. In one scene Salander is at home in her apartment, laying out the tattooing equipment she has bought to carry out her revenge on Bjurman; the shot cuts away to a view of her laptop, where a new message sent by Wennerstrom has just appeared. After holding on the image of the laptop monitor just long enough for the audience to read the message, the shot cuts away again. Lisbeth is always anticipating the computer; there is no way of being in time that is not a computational time. In both *The Girl with the Dragon Tattoo* and *The Social Network*, representations of code and programming are delineated, visually and narratively, by the figure of the programmer/hacker. This character is implicated and constituted in the digital workflow. Code in action is distinct from the program that is written because source code only becomes source after the fact; the writer of code, the programmer of the machine, is at least partially constituted by what will have been. If the performative action or operation is one of presentification, an enduring ephemeral, then in the moment of execution, the subject who utters and iterates—the programmer—could be said to be refreshed, reconstituted, and in this way produced through the act of programming. The kind of subject produced through *The Girl with the Dragon Tattoo*'s attention to programming is one that is both governed by and intimately co-constituted with the computer.

In his director's commentary Fincher states that "the real thing that's actually subjugating Lisbeth is bureaucracy, and not . . . misogyny." I would argue that in the broader context of the novels and films it is a bureaucracy inflected with misogyny that subjugates Salander. As a ward of the state who is employed as an off-the-books hacker by an off-the-books investigation and surveillance service company, Salander is precariously positioned as a counterbureaucratic subject. When her laptop is stolen as she boards a train, Salander chases after the thief and attacks him. This event makes her once again a priority concern for the state—as represented by the figure of her guardian, Nils Bjurman—and is positioned, in the film, as the reason for the meeting that leads to her rape. The relationship between woman and machine is primary, the catalyst for Salander's actions; most significantly, it is catalyst for the act that puts her at risk of violent sexual assault. In the fraught scenes of the mugging, Salander is seen cradling her laptop, embracing it in an embodied sign of maternal and intimate attachment. Throughout the scenes of the mugging and the subsequent rape in Bjurman's office, Salander is seen as a hacker, an outsider, someone who must perform the normative discourse of subjugation. In Bjurman's words, "You do something for me, I do something for you, that's what normal people do." Salander is presented as someone whose construction of self is inextricable from her computer. Her subjectivity is inextricably linked to computation. Both the computer and Salander are "spectres that reveal the limitations and possibilities of user and programmer" as an "instrument and a symptom of neoliberal governmental power."[43] This governmental power is internalized and embodied as *both* a normative discourse and as the nonnormative affective attachment to digital media that makes Salander strange. Such attachment recalls the history of women and computing—which is to say the history of bureaucracy-as-misogyny—that hovers at the surface of *The Girl with the Dragon Tattoo*.

Though Salander can at times be masterful in the social milieu of the text, or more specifically, in comparison to the technical capabilities of her older male bosses, abusers, patriarchs, and patrons, she is never master of the computer. The computer, the black box, is the only thing that is more secretive than Salander herself. When Salander waits for the computer, she is framed as an operator. In the film the program-time of computation becomes the time of the film; those procedures dictate the labor of the characters, and computation calls the shots. This mode of subject formation happens in two ways: first, Salander is produced as a subject of the computational in terms of governmentality; second, Salander is shown as a subject affectively entangled with the digital media of her life—a mediational subject. Governmentality in its neoliberal form, that is, governmentality that "constructs the individual as both driven by and needing certain freedoms and desires that invisibly support a larger system," resonates with the computer as a distributed network of software and hardware.[44] While Salander's job happens outside the sanctioned spaces of Swedish social, cultural, and economic life, it is her position as a ward of the state, and the state's failure to adequately care for her, that determines Salander's reliance on her computer. This is in keeping with narratives of neoliberalism in the global North as a social program whereby an individual might overcome any gaps in social care left by a shrinking state, by leveraging access to distributed digital networks to better compete in a marketized, privatized social sphere. The computer represents the means for Salander to be an autonomous individual, a citizen, and it exists as an object that elicits risky affective attachments. The film presents the relationship between state and autonomous governance ambivalently, but overall is invested in Salander's right to individual freedom and meritocratic empowerment.[45]

Salander is the character in Fincher's films that most clearly embodies the programmer as a position formed through computational culture, revealing the position of the programmer to be a guide to new computational paths of neoliberal governance. Fincher conscientiously visualizes her digital identity and identification as being wrapped up in her status as an outsider. Salander's character is realized through her devices. As Fincher describes it, "Lisbeth would have her own kind of customized operating system.... Her computer is not gonna look like Blomkvist's computer." In the film there is, of course, a certain commodification taking place—a play with customizing product placement: "[Blomkvist is] operating OS X Lion and [Salander has] got her own weird custom skin interface."[46] Additionally, this is a gesture toward Salander as being a particularly contemporary subject who understands herself as always becoming-with nonhuman agents in her life. Throughout the film Salander is performed as a relational subject, formed through an entangled biotechnical environment. This performance is not—despite the cyberpunkery of her character—enthralled to a radical post- or transhumanism. Instead Salander emerges as an ambivalent computational subject through action (the act of programming) and subjugation (the passivity of watching the screen, of waiting for the program to return a result, an intimate attachment to the machine).

FINCHER'S BANAL

I opened this chapter describing scenes of filmmaking and film watching within *The Girl with the Dragon Tattoo*. I suggested that these scenes instantiate a particular set of temporal gestures: toward the fiction of realtime digital experiences, to the workflow of digital filmmaking, and to code as a workflow of everyday life. I want to end thinking about the opening credits of *The Girl with the Dragon Tattoo*. An artful 3-D animation sequence in black, this image presents what is to come as a posthuman, digital sublime, far away from the conditions of roteness and obfuscation, described in terms of the digital banal. And yet, in this sequence, Salander is again an ambivalent figure who embodies the potential radical newness of recognizing the self as mediational—in *time* with the computational—while simultaneously indexing an entrepreneurial subject, making itself in the image of computational governmentality. In the title sequence black liquid drips and falls over black leather and rubber objects; it drips in the gaps between the keys of a black computer keyboard. An animated black head writhes, gagged with black fabric. More black shapes morph in and out of view; power adaptors snake across the screen toward the back of a head full of machine parts—more cables, a fan. A lit match drops, and two bodies prize themselves apart from one another as the blackness is lit on fire. The sequence goes on; both bodies cast off the black, oily liquid, and a face that is recognizably Daniel Craig flashes crosses the screen. A (male) fist punches a female head. They kiss. They are gagged. They melt and morph again. From the outset Lisbeth Salander is *of* the machine, both mediationally and corporately. The opening credits practically cite Donna Haraway's work on the cyborg, as a posthuman figure morphs and melts into being. This credit sequence is graphically distinct from the film and might almost be considered a stand-alone music video (to Ross and Reznor's reworking of Led Zeppelin's *Immigrant Song*). If Donna Haraway is there somehow, in that first frame, what does she say? The women of the frat party and Facemash in *The Social Network*, Lisbeth Salander and her laptop-pet: these might be, for better or worse, the cyborgs Haraway conjured.

If we attend to Salander's actions over her inactions, we might see her machinic affinities as a feminist cyborg praxis.[47] Is her surveillance and hacking in fact a kind of cyborg writing, a resistant mode of being in the world? If so, then Salander's story is a making visible and a radical taking apart of the "phallogocentric origin stories . . . built into the literal technologies—technologies that write the world, biotechnology and microelectronics—that have recently textualized our bodies as code problems on the grid of C^3I [command-control-communication-intelligence]."[48] But the film never lets such a writing practice take hold: Salander waits, but Zuckerberg writes. Although *The Girl with the Dragon Tattoo* is a very different sort of text from *The Social Network* or *Zodiac*, I have treated them as being in dialogue as Fincher films and have argued that this dialogue reveals much about the politics of the digital banal. What at first appear as just a few isolated scenes of coding or programming across three distinct films are, when held together, a reflection of the way programming occupies the cultural imaginary. In these films we watch ourselves, produced in proximity to the digital material of our daily lives and the bodies that we presume master that material. It is then worth reflecting on quite what kind of figure the cyborg-Salander gestures toward in tandem with her Fincher other: Zuckerberg. While in *The Social Network* Zuckerberg is also a programmed subject, whose social idiosyncrasies are implicitly allied in the film with the unemotional operations of the programs he writes, Zuckerberg is masterful, and he is rarely shown to be watching, waiting.

Zuckerberg orders actions that establish social procedures inflected with misogyny. In *The Social Network* it is the women of the network who are visualized as programmed and programmable. Not as laborers for a burgeoning digital computing industry, but as objects of the male gaze.[49] Women are executed as command lines and effaced. Like the first programmers, these women are the source that can only be revealed after the fact, should anyone choose to pay attention. These women are digitized and mastered, and as a film, *The Social Network* is not committed to their voices.[50] Although the imagery and intimacy between woman and machine might present Salander as a posthuman figure, and since, arguably, Zuckerberg's work is to repurpose the "system," in the end, the films do not sustain such alterity. The digital banal is the incorporated capital of each film as much as it is the temporal, routine rhythms. Fincher is a commercially viable filmmaker, and his films are commercial successes. *The Girl with the Dragon Tattoo* and *The Social Network* are, in their different ways, both fantasies of overturning the flow of capital: both begin with a hack, both are performing—with more or less conviction—an antiestablishment posture. But both films are also corporate; all Hollywood films are. In this way, the banal imagery of programming in these films is echoed in the banality of the films themselves as they fail to do anything more radical with their digital material.

Fincher's films tell us the story of what will have always been our contemporary digital lives. They play with the affective novelty of this life: through scenes of frenzied programming, through the uneasy way we might wonder about how much Zuckerberg actually knows about what he is doing, through the intimacy of computer and user as performed by Salander, and through the handwritten code of the Zodiac Killer that anticipates its new media future. But such newness is folded back into the rhetoric of reiteration of what, in the future, is already known: the inevitability of social activity as always having been a program, a quantifiable, codable, controllable function.

2

JONATHAN LETHEM'S AND MARK AMERIKA'S COMMON WRITING

The digital banal is writ through the coded machinations of software and is enacted as so much remediation: our new soft reality is iterated as nothing new. We encounter this effect as the banal assertion that, in the digital era, everyone can be a master producer: music software puts us in the mix; photo apps help us make our best selves; platforms help us be the stars of our own TV channels, the writers of our own fiction, the makers of our own music videos. All these applications and practices rely on the remediation of discrete forms of culture as an openly accessible digital culture. No longer must we go into a record store and spend time finding the perfect cut; we can Shazam something we hear, Google the track, cut and paste the clip, drag and drop it into our own file. Easy. The expansion of the means of production is a good thing. But it is not a free thing, and the cost of all this free remediation of cultural production is our unpaid labor and our "private" interests, that is, as time, as data. The remediation of culture as a happy result of digitization elides what is also being remade in this moment: the social and monetary value of artistic production.

Here I am interested in writing that is formed through such tensions. The essays by Jonathan Lethem and Mark Amerika are possible because of new digital commons of culture and new creative platforms, but they are also commentaries on those platforms and seek to engender ways of noticing what broader social and cultural changes are instantiated in digitization. Lethem's and Amerika's writing exemplifies the condition of the digital banal in which we witness a rote program blocking affective engagement with novelty and the incorporation of that novelty as a rote aspect of digital cultural production. In this work, the rote, the banal, is essay writing, it is debates about authorship and plagiarism, it is citation and allusion. Such *same-old* literary work blocks affective engagement with what is newly happening: new modes of collaborative working with nonhuman as well as human others, the forever-corporate ownership of the materials of artistic production. Such novelty is internalized in the literary work as yet another way that the digital is inevitable rather than graspable: in the end, the essays gesture to, but do not realize, radical ways into and out of the banal. In addition, Lethem's and Amerika's practices make highly visible both the disjunction between writing and reading as social practices as well as the textuality of executable code. Such modes of authorship offer us a way to gain purchase on the complexity of understanding, knowing, and thinking through digital media.

COMMON COMMANDS

Writing about how we might recognize "the common" in "communism," Michael Hardt argues that images, code, ideas, and knowledge might be privatized and controlled as property, but that the policing of this control will always fail because these are "the common." The affirmation of the common is an "affirmation of open and autonomous production of subjectivity, social relations, and the forms of life; the self-governed continuous creation of new humanity."[1] The commons is multivalent: tangible and imaginary, historically contingent and precariously *now*. The commons is a felt, lived experience; it is a way of "being-acting-feeling together."[2] This togetherness is a way in which the self is recognized as being in common. This might be the kind of taken-for-granted commons that Jonathan Lethem describes in "The Ecstasy of Influence": "The silence in a movie theatre is a transitory commons ... constructed as a mutual gift by those who comprise it."[3] Positive ways of being-acting-feeling together drive the mediations on the commons that are discussed in Lethem's and Amerika's essays. Tracing the "circulation of the common" is to watch how "associations of various types, from tribal assemblies to socialist cooperatives or open source networks organize shared resources into productive ensembles that create more shared resources which in turn provide the basis for the formation of new associations."[4] In the works of Lethem and Amerika, plagiaristic cutting—a making visible and making more of the commons—is an act of assembly that creates a new resource for sharing. Reading Lethem's and Amerika's essays and poems is an act of asserting connections between cultural texts, unsettling the idea that histories of literature and art are formed from discrete entries of private objects.

A common language is, by definition, one that is widely distributed, known, and shared. Lethem and Amerika are making interventions in "the common"—literary commons, political commons, common digital texts—not via specialist, elite, or privileged creative acts, but by common commands: cut and paste, drag and drop, move here. Lethem and Amerika use practices of the remix to stage problems of authorship and speech in the digital age. These texts make cuts into culture, enabled by everyday new media protocols, but not necessarily sanctioned by cultural expectations or practices. Expressing and experiencing a commons now is to find a way to be both inside and outside the private territories of the Internet. This is what much post-Internet art grapples with: how to effectively use Facebook, or some other social media platform, to make work that is independent and public, and how to frame this act as subverting the directives of social media platforms that appear public but function in private ways. This creative work is not necessarily politically radical, but it is part of a conversation about "the common" and gestures toward a mode of critically making visible the banal operations of digital media.[5] In an essay for the *New Inquiry*, artist Jesse Darling writes of this position as a common compromise-come-creative-act that users everywhere must negotiate, and it is worth quoting at length:

> Like mall rats flipping tricks in a parking lot, users exhibit a feral fluency in the use (and transgression, as it is reimagined daily) of this common timespace: we tune out the ads and get on with the serious business of flirting, hustling, hanging out and talking shit. We *know* that this serious business is affective labor which produces capital for the custodians of netspace; indeed, meme culture (including but not limited to

YouTube parody, stock photo art, cut-ups and image macros) can be seen as the user asserting a subjectivity that exists and thrives despite (and beyond) her status as targeted marketing demographic. Like the Occupy movement, these activities amount to a kind of politics of the public (virtual) body in (virtual) space. We may never own the means of production as such, but will continue to assert, pervert and subvert the commons anyway: a gesture of post-corporeal territorial pissing which necessitates neither phallus nor spray-can nor html.[6]

In this poetic missive Darling claims the private capital of social media as a de facto public space in which users are always already implicated as transgressors committing transgressive acts. This might be done creatively, but also less conscientiously, as acting on an assumption that the Internet *is* public. The Internet is a commons because we behave as if it is. Although specific social media platforms may be more and less open, more and less exploitative in their mining of our affective labor, that labor contributes to the substantiation of a commons anyway, regardless.

Critical thinking about the commons has been taking place with renewed energy in recent years. The term moves across activist and cultural groups and refers to various socio-material gatherings, from "opponents of global capital seeking a vantage from which to criticise the 'new enclosures' privatizing of natural and social resources across the planet" to Lethem's cinema silence, to Lawrence Lessig's "Creative Commons."[7] In campaigns for public space and public resources, the commons signifies a specific opposition to private space, and to the privatization of social infrastructure and natural resources. It is a term that can be mobilized to undermine neoliberal rhetoric that claims markets serve a common good. In reference to distributed digital networks, the commons is a prolific concept used to evoke multiple industrial, social, and cultural practices, often paradoxically. As David M. Berry has argued, "Today, the basic category of *res communes* [common things] extends to or has been drawn upon by theorists and commentators to refer to the space of intellectual thought, conceptualising ideas and concepts within a digital arena as an 'ideas commons,' an 'innovation commons' ... an 'intellectual commons,' a 'digital commons,' inevitably an 'e-commons' ... , 'the public domain' ... or 'intellectual space.'"[8] Such categorization confuses more than it galvanizes. None of the kinds of commons listed by Berry really chimes with Jesse Darling's evocation of the commons, or the remixing undertaken by Amerika and Lethem. Rather, the commons, as it emerges through social media and the affordances of digital word processing and text-markup languages, is some kind of recalcitrant writing: a communication that, despite a private infrastructure, asserts a common materiality. Social media brings about the need to think in terms of the common, or about the commons. Social media capital is predicated on providing a common space that will always evade total capture and commodification. In other words, although social media might sell the novelty of new common spaces, while simultaneously reiterating the techno-capitalist consolidation of wealth and governance, it also does actually produce a commons, a new kind of affective encounter.

The creative remix-writing practices discussed here emerge from and draw attention to the common-despite-itself. Joss Hands describes this condition as the "absolute limit on social media platforms' capacity to control communication." The limit is what "provides the antagonistic space for what can be described as a natural language exploit; enabling communicative action and unforced affective flows to take place."[9] This antagonistic space is the home of Darling's mall rats, the site of postcorporeal pissing contests. The outcome of these contests is not always the point; there should be no new crowning of a newly rightful owner of language and social interaction. The point is, instead, to produce a writing that can make visible the disjunct between executable and natural languages, to reflect on and revel in the friction of the way language is resistant to such directives.

In many respects, Lethem's and Amerika's works elude literary-historical analysis or close reading; they require an approach that can account for common registers, trails of associations, and mediation as a condition of their work. In being so stuck in their recursive forms, these writings witness and reproduce the digital banal along with other, longer banal technics.[10] Remixing, copying, and plagiarizing are old, old modes of writing and artistic production. Hillel Schwartz calls this nothing-newness the "stickiness" of the culture of the copy: "Plagiarism in our culture of the copy is sticky with feelings of originality-through-repetition, revelation-through-simulation."[11] Considering our culture as being sticky with plagiarism reifies and subdues the affective novelty of communication today. Stickiness is now not just of repetition, but also of quantization, digitization. The very reach of software is predicated on its capacity to occupy, territorialize, and make common—through private means—the richness of everyday life. This becoming software is enabled by writing. The difference of code, its ineluctable strangeness, is obfuscated through its appearance in culture as writing, through its apparent readability. To qualify this statement: although code is executable, writing is nonetheless a cultural precondition for the digitization of everyday life. As media theorists such as Friedrich Kittler have long claimed, the praxis of 1s and 0s began "with the monopoly of writing.... Mouths and graphisms dropped out into prehistory. Otherwise events and their stories could not have been connected."[12] Amerika's and Lethem's writing produces connections as narrative and as digitization. They write new constellations of literary history *with* that history, while simultaneously executing new material connections. They are compelled to do so through the operative of the digital banal, which both creates the conditions for and blocks access to the common.

AMERIKA'S GHOSTLY INCANTATIONS

If the quantizing of data (digitization) makes that data common, of a common format, then such materiality instantiates particular kinds of writing practices. The conversion of much textual material to digital data and the iterability of code itself—premised on common executable language—are the conditions for all writing as remediation. In the essay "The Renewable Tradition (Extended Play Remix)," Mark Amerika calls attention to writing-as-remediation through his practice of "remixology." "Remixology is a way of intervening or hacking into the transmission of traditional media discourse and empowers artists to renew all discourse."[13] Amerika describes an aesthetic language of loops and feedback, where the new is always tied into the old because the old is an integral part of the new. This language finds fertile form in digital media through aesthetic practices of remixing. The art of the remix is predetermined to proliferate in digital culture, wherein processes of copying and re-versioning are fundamental operations of the technology. Digital culture affords a two-pronged practice of reappropriation. First, it is easier to create a seamless mix when the source material is already converted to a common material form. Second, processes of abstraction and conversion, as they proliferate, bring into the digital commons (the network of cultural materials made available by conversion to digital format) a multitude of histories and texts once thought to be discrete. Refined practices of the remix, such as Amerika's and Lethem's, continuously carve out a space between the material of the new—texts that now circulate in digitally networked commons—and the material of the old—the disparate previous iterations and inscriptions that circulate in a dispersed commons of culture.

In Amerika's writing there are two particular ways in which the notion of historical contingency is represented and played off against the digital as a *new* medium: repeated references to "enduring aesthetic facts" and the assertion of new writers "remixologically inhabiting" older writers and writings.[14] In Amerika's *remixthebook*, the "enduring aesthetic fact" seems to refer to a composition that persists through different literatures and histories, a "fact" that disparate texts have in common. An enduring aesthetic fact is not only this, but also a commonsense statement: it is the commons of our knowledge paradigm. Repetition of the phrase in Amerika's writing makes this a performative concept as the aesthetic fact endures through literature and through Amerika's own writing. He enacts this by reappropriating his own use of the phrase repeatedly. The phrase first refers to a conceptual connection. The realization of the enduring aesthetic fact connects Amerika's writing to others': "I realized / at age nineteen that I was now being *pulled in* / by Whitehead's *Religion in the Making* / . . . / focusing my attention on the experiential qualities of / my life story as an enduring aesthetic *fact*."[15] Amerika discusses reading Alfred North Whitehead's collected lectures of 1926: he is *"pulled in"* to Whitehead's book. The emphasis on this phrase suggests that Amerika finds reading Whitehead to be a kind of revelatory experience: he is taken in, is changed, and exits with a reconfigured relationship to literature. Here Whitehead's writing does not function as analogy or metaphor, but rather as a persistent indelible narrative. This is a narrative Amerika recognizes and reads as being not a coincidence but a revelation of the common. In *remixthebook* the enduring aesthetic fact is Amerika. He is technology and literature; he is made of these things; he speaks through these media that precede him:

> (... maybe I'm wireless
> an enduring aesthetic fact
> flying high on Tesla-like electrical conduction
> and whose remixological potential
> is the ultimate source for a renewable
> "Energy in the Making")[16]

Amerika rewrites his own earlier text and reappropriates Whitehead's book title (*Religion in the Making*). He performs a remix of the connection he made previously, but through the metaphor of wireless technologies.

Wireless technologies predate digital ones, but something of Amerika's grand statement also pulls a reader back to the malleability of digital text as it informs Amerika's practice. On the page previous to the above stanza, Amerika writes that he is a bad typist who has never really learned to use a keyboard.[17] He puts in the reader's mind the image of *remixthebook*'s production, the typing of a digital document. He begins to sculpt the idea of the author as a figure at play with sentences, phrases, gestures, already known, already written. Amerika's ineptitude at the keyboard is perhaps staged for the reader to demystify this process—this is not magic, just composition. Media history teaches us that typing is crucial in understanding how computers are discrete processes.[18] The act of simulation that a computer program performs is partly enabled by premediated writing—typewritten text that is homogenous, not in-dividual. Following Friedrich Kittler, Lucas D. Introna argues that as "always already encoded beings we are never authors, we are instead all skilful reusers."[19] Through the scene of typewriting, Amerika presents his process as mediational: the poetry is unutterable beyond the medium of production. For Amerika, for Introna, for Kittler, writing is inextricable from any process of digitization through its historical mechanical mediation. This knowledge is deeply embedded in the terminology used to describe digital media; for example, the way we speak of "writing" computer programs or code.[20] As is discussed in the previous chapter, there is a problem with understanding computational processes as writing, but one of the ways this problem is elided in cultural discourse is through media history that understands writing as a precondition of the computational process. The enduring aesthetic fact of writing is the enduring mediational given of the digital, type, dividuation. The abstraction of these givens as computational culture is the affective novelty of contemporary literary writing practices, which cannot be anything other than enduring. The recursive quality of Amerika's work attests to the digital banal at large—the reiteration-come-blocking of digital literary work today.

Amerika's process is "remixological inhabitation." Amerika doesn't quote other writers so much as he embodies them. The invocation of inhabiting other writers and voices is redolent of the idea that in parasitic media ecology we already utter through preformed semiotic structures. This status is heightened by the complexity of digital media—of writing as typing and text as cypher. In *remixthebook* some plagiarized passages appear in different font from the main text and are often graphically isolated on the page (boxed, indented). The layout of the main text is as prose-poetry, with large white borders. Amerika draws attention to the craft of the remix, writing the whole text as visually and textually unstable. The repeated hailing of his practice from within the text, and the graphical representation of his text that aligns it with poetry, prevents the common intonation that we find in Lethem's essay. Amerika's writing about remix practices is attuned to the ways that mode matters. His poetics disrupt their process of inhabiting. Instead they point toward the complexity of this act, a cultural discomfort with unstructured reappropriation. Amerika's remix is reflexive; it delves into the literary commons and borrows phrases from the history of writing, continually drawing attention to its approach. Remixology is a statement about the anxiety that goes with acts of plundering and the enduring way that these are not inherently progressive but rather a compulsion of the program.

Reuse, plagiarism, and plundering are not necessarily oppositional to the fetishization of newness as progress. Digital culture is foundationally reiterative. As Gary Hall has recently argued, "There is nothing *inherently* emancipatory, oppositional, leftist, or even politically or cultural progressive about digital piracy. The politics of digital piracy depends on the decisions that are made in relation to it."[21] The conditions of Amerika's work are the digital banal; Amerika's artistic intervention is to dwell in the affective specificity of those conditions. Amerika's work stages the way in which piracy, remixing, plagiarism, are not *inherently* emancipatory.

For all the literary play on influence, Amerika does not inherit a specific political attitude or mode. Instead the Amerika written about in the poetry views politics and an anxiety about politics *as* inheritance, as haunting.

> Taking on the stylistic writing gestures of
> other artists and then remixologically inhabiting them
> in some ancient form of "realtime" manipulation
> requires practice....
>
> Moving in and out of these "ghost tendencies" that
> mark the outlines of a body language once performed
> by another artist of the past also necessitates
> a certain amount of lived experience.[22]

The body of Amerika's writing persona strives to physically access those ghosts of culture that lurk around the literary commons. Such imagery functions as a useful metaphor for the ungraspable nature of so much accidental, barely perceptible reappropriation and remix, but more significantly it calls out the depth of contemporary processes of reiteration. This depth is not only as history (remix is nothing new) or time (there will have been nothing new, this is all real-time), but also as the computational: the digital as the condition we have always had coming. The turn to the necessity of lived experience in Amerika's writing is a way to recognize what is blocked and to reengage with what is affectively distinct.

THE THREE SPIRITS OF LETHEM'S ESSAY

In 2007 Jonathan Lethem published his essay "The Ecstasy of Influence: A Plagiarism Mosaic" in *Harper's Magazine*. It has been reprinted in several anthologies: in *Sound Unbound*, an edited collection on remix culture (2008); in *Cutting Across Media*, an edited collection on reappropriation art and copyright law (2011); and most recently in a collection of Lethem's nonfiction writing, titled *The Ecstasy of Influence* (2011).[23] "The Ecstasy of Influence" is about literature's ambiguous relationship to remix culture. It is a composition comprising borrowed texts, appropriated, reappropriated, mediated, and remediated, in order to riff on the notion of "influence" throughout the history of literature and art, particularly in relation to a general common culture elucidated by the Internet. The essay looks to wider cultural phenomena associated with the digital age (shareware, open-source, the Creative Commons) and brings them to bear upon literary practices. It also traces these phenomena associated with digital technology through other avant-garde histories of art, literature, and music to assert that these practices are not exclusively of the digital. In this way Lethem's essay hums with aesthetic concerns of its moment. Lethem's essay is engaged in the task of revealing and exposing, particularly of revealing commons and exposing hidden codes of literary influence. It does this by way of a performance of a kind of literary magic that, as with Zuckerberg's programming "sourcery" in *The Social Network*, simultaneously appears in service to the machine (in this case, literature), enabled by various intersections of privilege embodied by the person writing, and despite drawing attention to its act as source after the fact, it nonetheless appears to execute new modes of being in the world.

Lethem's essay attests to the ways that language demands and resists claims of individual authorship; it performs the familiarity of a voice and the commonality of sentiment. Lethem has spoken of the specific practice of writing "Ecstasy" as one in which he purposefully inhabits online spaces so as to better touch the textuality of common language. This is Lethem as Darling's mall rat: "Process-wise I find I do want to Google while I essay.... Chapters really do launch themselves, again and again, directly out of the immediate act of reading old reviews, research, blog entries, et cetera."[24] Lethem describes a writing process that fully makes use of the availability of much critical material through digitization. He uses that availability to cross hierarchies of critical material (blogs, reviews, research) and uses the source material to directly launch his writing. Whereas Mark Amerika tacitly borrows from a commons of literature, Lethem emphatically exploits the remediation of that commons within a digital environment—the plethora of digitized texts available across the Internet.

Throughout "Ecstasy" Lethem is haunted by the ghosts of Lewis Hyde, Lawrence Lessig, and Marcel Mauss, the three spirits of a gift economy. In his writing on the "gift," Lethem makes much use of Lewis Hyde's 1983 book *The Gift: Imagination and the Erotic Life of Property*, itself a reworking and reappropriation of Marcel Mauss's 1950 book *The Gift: The Form and Reason for Exchange in Archaic Societies*. (Re)turning to Hyde's text from Lethem's elucidates an alternative way of considering the "uncommodifiable surplus of inspiration" that forms its own cultural space, one comprising a barely tangible web of shared knowledge and understanding. Lewis Hyde writes:

> Works of art are drawn from, and their bestowal nourishes, those parts of our being that are not entirely personal, parts that derive from nature, from the group and the race, from history and tradition, and from the spiritual world. In the realized gifts of the gifted we may taste the *zoë*-life which shall not perish even though each of us, and each generation, shall perish.[25]

Hyde's "*zoë*-life" conjures a historical, religious notion of a common extralife, shared apart from the material day-to-day. Here the elision of difference between economies and worlds, the spiritual commons and an artistic one, informs and recalls the prevalent and slippery doubleness that marks Lethem's/Hyde's/Mauss's attempts to represent the gift as it functions in anthropological and cultural contexts. Lethem locates Hyde's *zoë*-life in a contemporary reading of the common. In "Ecstasy" Lethem states,

> A commons, of course, is anything like the streets over which we drive, the skies through which we pilot airplanes, or the public parks or beaches on which we dally.... The silence in a movie theatre is a transitory commons, impossibly fragile, treasured by those who crave it, and constructed as a mutual gift by those who comprise it.[26]

This section moves from the words of Lawrence Lessig to Lethem's own words—or at least a phrase scripted by Lethem, the origin of which remains unacknowledged. Here Lethem elides the political implications of doubleness in a concrete sense—how it might actually function across economies, across geopolitical territories, across history—to invest his ideological practice with a permissively broad encounter with the common.

Through complex literary interplay between Hyde, Lessig, and by extension Mauss, Lethem enables a later version of a text (Lessig's *Commons*) to intervene in a precursor or antecedent text (Hyde's *Gift*) with implied multiplicity (other texts, Mauss's *Gift*). The two reappropriated texts remediate each other's forms and concerns through this intervention—and the interventions they inherently refer to—and yet also retain the impression of a historical logic that allowed the earlier texts to influence the later ones. This practice is close to the way Mark Amerika defines remixology. For Amerika, writers expose the space in which they channel or use other writers' gestures as "an embodied praxis / where the vocal intonations of / the artist are used as source material to discover / new aesthetic facts."[27] As is previously suggested, the act, or more particularly the performance, of embodiment that Amerika asserts is problematic. In his own writing Amerika seems to undermine the extent to which this actually occurs. But the broader image it produces is of a commons of previous writing that persists. In Lethem's production of the section of "Ecstasy" on the gift, he seems to fully plunder the enduring aesthetic fact of the gift—as it persists as an idea in literature and in the anthropology of writing, in opposition and relief to capital economies—to intimate a new aesthetic fact, or at least the enduring fact, remixed. Lethem uses his process of remixing to demonstrate his own prioritizing of the ideas of the gift and the commons, his practice reverberating (literally, so many voices) with the sense of his argument.

The folding together of Lessig and Hyde is a problematic political move. Within the literary gesture of the mix, much is at stake, and so Lethem's work here requires some glossing. Lawrence Lessig is a lawyer, author, and professor at Harvard, who has been influential in highlighting issues of law and technology as they affect copyright. He is, perhaps more famously, a founding board member of the nonprofit licensing organization the Creative Commons. Lessig's own work, and his work as part of the Creative Commons group, implements legal ethics and terminology drawn from a gift economy. The Creative Commons enables many artists and producers of cultural matter, who have no other recourse to influence the trajectory of their work, to retain control of how their work is used. Most of the licenses are based on ideas of sharing, and of giving credit to producers of original source material. In this way the Creative Commons critiques Hyde's *zoë*-life. Instead it applies more of Mauss's earlier argument for a balanced gift economy, which is suggested in response to the problem that a "gift that does nothing to enhance solidarity is a contradiction."[28] For Lethem, the Creative Commons' interpretation of a gift economy does not go far enough, reinstating an authorial claim by another means: "As much as I admire [the Creative Commons], in a way that project was actually a little too disciplined for what I wanted to say at that moment because most of the creative commons licenses involve clear reciprocity."[29] Lethem's folding together of Hyde, Lessig, and Mauss creates a literary impression or sense of the gift that does exceed the constitutional boundaries of the Creative Commons. Arguably this resistance to constitutional boundaries also serves to problematize the concept of the gift, representing it as a chimera. Lethem's later nuancing of his stance reflects a more critical mode of thinking about copyright and "copyleft" issues. Attempts to commodify content under the auspices of a commons might be a concerning remediation of the commons as the subjectivation we share. As David M. Berry describes it, "The commons has been transformed into a 'Creative Commons,' which is a distorted and diminished concept of the commons, predicated on a system of private rights codified in intellectual property rights."[30] In this way it is possible to consider the Creative Commons as perpetuating the digital banal. The Creative Commons reifies novelty (the open access of cultural production and consumption), affectively blocking the potential to experience the commons otherwise; it reiterates the quantified inevitability of reciprocity, which is to say, remuneration by means of cultural capital.

In "Ecstasy" Lethem follows Barthes, for whom the "'I' which approaches the text is already itself a plurality of other texts, of codes which are infinite or, more precisely, lost (whose origin is lost)."[31] It is worth tracing Lethem's "I" through a particular passage to observe how a common register is intoned and how plurality appears as singularity. In the opening section of the essay, titled "Love and Theft," Lethem tells the reader a story. Mediating on the way all art might be said to constitute a paradox that "urges us not to look back" while it "encodes a knowledge of past sources," Lethem writes:

> I realized this forcefully when one day I went looking for the John Donne passage quoted above ["All mankind is of one author"]. I know the lines, I confess, not from a college course but from the movie version of *84, Charing Cross Road* with Anthony Hopkins and Anne Bancroft. I checked out *84, Charing Cross Road* from the library in the hope of finding the Donne passage, but it wasn't in the book.[32]

This story is not Lethem's. It is an extract from Jonathan Rosen's book *The Talmud and the Internet* (2000). The quest for the Donne lines led Rosen/Lethem/the-"I"-of-the-essay back to the book *84, Charing Cross Road* (where the quotation did not actually appear), and then to an Internet search (which proved difficult, as the lines spoken in the film were abridged), on to the Yale Library online catalogue (which, at the time, did not have the sophisticated search facility required to turn up these lines), and eventually (after altering the search terms) to a personal website of someone who just really loved Donne. In turn Rosen/Lethem/the "I" discovered that the lines they sought to attribute belonged to one of the most well-known of Donne's passages, "containing as it does the line 'never send to know for whom the bell tolls; it tolls for thee.'" Rosen/Lethem/the "I" states, "My search had led me from a movie to a book to a play to a website and back to a book. Then again, those words may be as famous as they are only because Hemingway lifted them for his book title."[33] This passage contains many authors and many texts, as well as many representations, all fragmented, reappropriated, and in many cases altered. There are Lethem, Rosen, Donne, the website manager, the scriptwriter of the film *84, Charing Cross Road* (Hugh Whitemore), and the actor who spoke the lines in the film (Anthony Hopkins). Then there are all the texts that these authors produced. The actual story is seemingly seamlessly integrated into Lethem's essay while reflexively drawing attention to its status as seamful text.

Rosen's *The Talmud and the Internet*, from which Lethem lifted the story, begins with Donne's poetry as a response to the death of Rosen's grandmother. The story itself testifies to the common, and its reiteration in Lethem's voice further unsettles any claim of the individual's narrative. The story remains personal even when it is revealed to be lifted, and so it might make a claim to a communal experience of the personal instead of the uniqueness of the individual experience. As the context of Rosen's book implies, this is a story of digital times. The figure "I" is able to search for fragments of text and achieve a near-instantaneous result, an ease that effaces the hyper-mediacy of the technology and the conversion of Donne's text to digital data. Inherent in the text that is this section of "Ecstasy" is a structural fluidity, a movement across multiple temporal and spatial instances. The text exists as multiple versions over time, as the figures in different periods who enabled the preservation and interpretation of the text. It simultaneously exists at multiple sites across space as it is stored as data, and it is encountered as material texts.

Whatever is new about Lethem's kind of work—the seamlessness of reappropriation, the ease of access enabled by the structural composition of the medium—must be balanced against what is continuous—the literary practice of forming texts from others' words through tropes such as allusion, plagiarism, and quotation. The critical point of entry for reading the digital banal in Lethem's essay is that it is not possible to separate the old and the new; rather, the reader has to apprehend the relational processes through which the writing operates. This could be remediation: the ease of the essay's authorial voice, its immediacy, is an effacement of the hyper-mediacy, the hypertextuality, of its material form. However, as with Amerika's enduring aesthetic fact, the affective resonance of the essay is in its mediational mode, the sense in which the voice comes into being with the technology—writing, computation—rather than as a set of discrete objects in time. The fact that the essay does not easily give up its mediational mode—that it disguises it and simultaneously gestures toward it—is the digital banal. The already-embeddedness of digital media in everyday life—present here as the processes of launching an essay from Google, of cutting and pasting text—can be witnessed in tension with the blocked affective novelty of becoming-with digital media. The conditions for the essay are digital: culture has been digitized. As Bernard Stiegler argues, networked society "has more or less systematically grammatized its social nets," and "by this fact organizes technologies of transindividuation in an industrial context."[34] Remix, as a practice predetermined by linguistic laws, is itself determined by a contemporary condition that sees the "long circuit" of language (to use Stiegler's phrase) as being short-circuited by the technics of digital distribution networks.[35]

THE AUTHOR AS OPERATOR

In this context Lethem's essay asks, if the individual is a contingent subject category and the notion of an individual creative act—an act determinedly distinct from others—is undermined, what kind of "I" can be constituted? Following Bernard Stiegler's work on transindividuation, we can read Lethem's essay as a short circuit of the long process of individuation by literature. In Stiegler's theory of technics the human is not subject to history, and technology is not a set of discrete objects that change in time; the human *is* technics. Man emerges as a technical being, and time has always been technical.[36] In Stiegler's work, technologies—reading, writing, forks, spoons, discourse, education—are instrumental, but the instrumental is not separate from or after a first human. Rather, Stiegler insists on the "insertion of technics into a fundamental order of temporalization."[37] As an aspect of technics, literature is fundamental to the long circuit of individuation. In other words, literature is not the reflection of the human, but rather is co-constitutive of the human coming to know itself as such: "You individuate yourself by reading this book because reading a book is to be transformed by the book.... You individuate yourself by reading the book, if you are in the process of individuating yourself."[38] Individuation is a relational procedure. Reading is not a way to know the self, but rather a process by which a reader and a book are individuated. Stiegler states, "You can individuate through my discourse by adherence with my discourse, but it's also equally possible to individuate oneself by its contradiction, its negation."[39] Stiegler's attention to discourse is useful for thinking through how Lethem reproduces some fundamental ways of being conscious as a literary exercise. Lethem's essay makes visible the contingency of an individuated consciousness formed through the long-circuit technics of society. As Irit Rogoff surmises, in relation to Stiegler's work, "The value of something is actually the capacity for trans-individuation that determines entry and continuation of those circuits..., a circuit to which others can add themselves by building on it."[40] To this end, transindividuation "does not rest with the individuated 'I' or with the interindividuated 'We,' but is the process of co-individuation within a preindividuated milieu and in which both the 'I' and the 'We' are transformed through one another."[41] Lethem's acts of reappropriation, whether acknowledged or not, are not in themselves radical or new. The "I" of Lethem's essay is preindividuated literally, a kind of prepackaged "I" that has been uttered before. "I" is also a presumed "we," the commons; this "we" is not discrete but always contingent upon "I."

I turn to Stiegler—as Kember and Zylinska do in their work on mediation—to understand such commonality as not only a human-to-human constitution; it is also a mediational mode in which the nonhuman gives the human agency. Lethem's essay short-circuits the technic of literature and writing. The essay testifies to the inextricability of co-individuation, to the impossibility of unbraiding "I" from "we," and the already-said from the will-be-said; in addition, the saying is not attached to a particular subject, but is instead technical. The technical here is also the digital banal: the short circuit is attention to reification as an affective block to being aware of our mediated condition. Today we are less likely to handle the texts we (mis)use; we cannot read their medium, and the work we create is shaped by the particular contingencies of that process. Out of this emerges the sociocultural program whereby our textual communication resides precisely at the point where public space is privately owned. The digital banal of Lethem's essay links thinking of the limits of speech as digital material to thinking of the limits of the human as an autonomous subject and to thinking of the limits of the individual as an iterable subject.

"The Ecstasy of Influence" is formed from the common commands of everyday digital culture and reveals the ways these commands work on and in everyday culture. This is not to say that "Ecstasy" is an everyday artifact. Lethem's aesthetic strategies are permitted by the specificities of the essay's cultural frame: a well-respected writer, addressing serious issues, in respectable literary magazines (*Harper's*), and in books by respectable university presses (Duke, MIT), and mainstream literary publishers (Jonathan Cape). Writing about creative plagiarism and plagiarism-detection software such as Turnitin, Lucas D. Introna observes that the detection algorithm "detects similarity when a *sufficiently long string of consecutive characters* from the original is retained in the copied version," and so, conversely, "*originality becomes encoded as undetected fragments or copies.*"[42] Creative plagiarism is defined by the extent to which the original text is recomposed for a new context. This kind of practice would not be caught by plagiarism detection software. In this way, what is being advocated by the detection software is, technically, not original writing per se; rather, it is a practice that successfully obscures the original format of the text. The common commands of Lethem's essay might not pass the plagiarism detection software. In an academic context,

Lethem may need to justify his reappropriation before a committee. Perhaps Amerika's reconstituted poetics would turn up as a false positive, an original text by way of being a more sophisticated remix. Introna's reading of plagiarism detection highlights the important role that platforms of publication play in affording opportunities to subvert, and to read subversions of, common software commands. Lethem's essay is sanctioned by the literary press. These organizations are part of the protocols that the writers discussed here worry at, but they are not necessarily undone by the creative practices they support.

Although Lethem's common commands might not fool the algorithm, it is entirely possible they will mislead the reader. In "The Ecstasy of Influence" others' words are mixed and mashed, but the tone and the authorial voice *seem* consistent. In this way the essay parodies the leveling, smoothing ability of digital media to present all information evenly. Despite the title's giveaway, "Ecstasy of Influence: *A Plagiarism*," unless the reader has already come across the texts Lethem samples, it is possible to not fully comprehend the vast stereophony of the piece. It is Lethem's seamless narrative aesthetic that marks this work as distinctly *of* a digital culture. To achieve this, Lethem mediates his source material to varying extents, not least so that the piece reads with a single, consistent authorial voice. This voice glosses over the multivocality of the piece, instead representing a univocal narrative. On the page is a seamless expression that is instantly recognizable by, and accessible to, the reader; the essay has a strong authorial voice and a strong cultural position. The consistency or seamlessness achieved by Lethem in a work of reappropriation may be in part due to the nature of the continued cycle of remediation, that is, the notion that the sentiment and expression remediated in Lethem's work are themselves remediations of centuries of writing. Literature is a feedback loop of other literature. When literature is openly ransacked and made to work without a distinct authorial "I," our normal reading practice gives it one. We assume from the text a surprising consistency at the level of the written language. Within the text and the reader, remediation has already (re)produced some kind of common tone. Which is to say, Lethem's essay is a tonal manifestation of mediation; it is an aesthetic strategy of co-individuation.

The author-who-is-not-really is a kind of enduring aesthetic fact, a literary instantiation of co-individuation, certainly in the present moment when they have always already been Barthes's "scriptor," always replacing the dead author as a producer of a text. Lethem has not authored "The Ecstasy of Influence." The text has a myriad of other authors. Lethem has composed the text, and it is in this process of composition that the "Jonathan Lethem" who is the "author" of "The Ecstasy of Influence" comes into being. This construction is practiced throughout Lethem's essay and is, perhaps, an explicit version not only of Barthes's scriptor but, more particularly, of the kind of author associated with digital text. Such an author does not leave the personal trace of handwriting, and experiences a more complex idea of the act of "writing"—from hand to type to code to interface, with no authoritative manuscript. This act of authorship, which is not authoritative, reveals the operations of the common through manipulation of distributed digital networks, as well as how these operations can be undercut by attention to the long circuit of intragenerational and intramedial knowledge and experience.

The whole of Lethem's piece is presented without quotation marks. Like Barthes's imagined tissue-text, all quotations, direct or inferred, are unmarked in the mix. Printed at the end of the piece is a key that comprises some of Lethem's notes and citations. Barthes's own lifetime was not within the pervasive digital culture that we associate with the contemporary; yet his formulation of the author, and of textuality, seems indelibly written into the consciousness of new media and literary critical theory. In Amerika's terms, these critical structures are enduring aesthetic facts.[43] But despite the lingering aesthetic fact of Barthes, the author is not the figure of interest here. Lethem's work sets up these investments in history as to be expected. The formulation of the digital banal—which can account for the machinations of code as potentially blocking ways to connect otherwise—is key to understanding Lethem's work, because the remix is the *only* way to write now. In other words, the agency of the writing needs attending to more than the agency of the author to reveal the common agency of all users-come-authors.

Lethem's essay is an argument as to why writing after new media—writing through remix—is always already like literary writing and is inevitably an argument for this kind of writing as a good thing. The essay practices a particular method of remix writing, one that disavows formal citation in favor of a kind of affective attachment to culture. The nascent ambiguity about the genre of this text is precisely the work of remix instantiated by the text: a mixing of categories that is always, conversely, a revealing of the commons. We can account for this sort of writing politically as a way to speak through the commodification of communication in the digital age. Such creative endeavors ultimately signify the limits of commodification. Paraphrasing Franco Beradi, Joss Hands calls such acts "poetry as hacking." In both Lethem's and Amerika's writing we encounter the possibility that "the antagonism through which the human brain has eluded the real subsumption can be re-invigorated by linguistic forms such as poetry."[44] Amerika and Lethem are self-conscious hackers. In trying to think about a creative writing after new media, a writing that might attend to and cut through the abundance of writing in new media, Lethem's and Amerika's acts are curatorial, contouring art from an already-noisy media or literary environment. In the context of the digital banal, in the context of what is at stake in Lethem's and Amerika's writing, the hope for such a method is a kind of cutting into communicative capitalism in which, as Jodi Dean describes it, "we confront a multiplication of resistances and assertions so extensive that it hinders the formation of strong counterhegemonies."[45] That is, these essays are writing the common, against the commodification of such. Yet this critical move also assumes the privilege of being identified as a producer who can disavow the method of production as a disguised avant-garde or antiwork gesture. Such privilege enables Lethem's "Ecstasy" and is registered anxiously as Amerika's ghosts.

THE DIGITAL COMMONS

Digital platforms, particularly social media platforms, are restricted as sites of common experience by the private ownership of data at a protocological and software layer and by the long circuits of discourse that amplify and privilege some subjects and suppress others.[46] Writing about the digital is, as has been said elsewhere in this book, always itself mediating a range of material concerns: device, body, intelligence, and it mediates these as hardware, software, user, programmer, and something more diffuse, the culture of this digital moment. We must be attentive to the ways in which critiquing the social instantiation of platforms is not only critiquing software and protocol, it is also critiquing the social. This is not to argue that the social is technologically determined, but rather to trace the inflections of the social as algorithmic operations through the social as it is being narrated—a process of co-constitution. As Joss Hands argues, with digital media "there is also a natural language layer and an affective layer of such platforms that remain relatively vulnerable."[47] This vulnerability is the limit point of capital, "because capital still relies on the revenue generated by users as the core of its business," and in so doing it relies on the affective layer of social media as a perceived autonomous, public sphere.[48] The Internet is of common commands in a way that, as it stands, has nothing to do with the social commons and everything to do with control and protocol. And yet the Internet and social media bring about an affective common in which people do participate in and produce a common space and, to some degree, a common register of social participation.

For Jesse Darling this affective layer is an antagonistic encounter necessitating artistic intervention. In Lethem's and Amerika's remix writing, the essay's gift to us is in how it speaks rather than whom it cites. The essay witnesses the enduring aesthetic fact of the singular as indelibly plural and the individual voice as a framing device rather than a given position; it gives away the difficult recognition that a work of individual, private authorship is also a work of affective labor—a commodity in waiting—by another name. Beyond the essay, Lethem has tested the protocological limits of social artistic practice by giving away his other work. Around the time of the publication of "Ecstasy" in *Harper's*, Lethem's website featured an area titled the Promiscuous Materials Project.[49] Via these pages, Lethem offered up stories and song lyrics for others to steal and reappropriate. There were limits: users could not reproduce the texts in whole or in anthologies or publish adaptations in book form (as this would breach Lethem's publishing contract). On offer was the opportunity to adapt the lyrics and stories into songs, stage plays, or short films. Lethem did not demand any monetary reimbursement; it was all to enable creative plundering of "the language of culture" as "map-turned-to-landscape."[50] For Lethem this project contributed to a "commons of cultural materials," insistently creating art that is all intertwined and infinitely reusable.[51] One of the artworks that came out of Promiscuous Materials is a collage by American artist Aaron Wexler. The collage is based on one of Lethem's Promiscuous stories, titled "The Collector." The story is an anecdote on the habit of collecting, featuring a protagonist who is drawn to the sense of control and order that collecting, as a process, can provide. Eventually the collector realizes that his obsessive wanting to contain and archive the world around him has left him isolated. The story is a parable from a pre-Facebook age, before living for and in an archive became a rote social operative. Through the story we can potentially recuperate the banal operative of the Facebook timeline—the underperformance of reciprocity of feeling—as a site of affective disavowal that is paradoxically also generative of diffuse engagement. The promiscuous travels of the collector are an attempt to recuperate the limits of writing for a platform, to instead generate other modes of engagement.

In the collage Wexler directly represents things collected in the story—baseball cards, birds, butterflies, and so on. There is no clear narrative to the collage, but still the elements represented maintain their integrity as figures from Lethem's story. In an artist's statement Wexler describes his collages as adapting a traditional "cut and paste" technique to produce, in part, a "seamlessness equally redolent of digitized media."[52] In Wexler's work he takes images from the world around him (magazines, the Internet), and then adapts them by redrawing, Photoshopping, painting, cutting; he paints the new image he has created onto canvas and then cuts up the new canvas, finally repiecing his cuttings together to form the final canvas.[53] In this process there is an interesting tension between the acknowledgement of reuse and the determination to create a personal distance from the original source through a multiplex system of adaptation. Wexler writes of his own work, "I think a lot of artists have become savvy about reappropriating subject matter and imagery. One has to really transform information—or even run it through a filter, you might say, in order to make something new. I consider myself someone who mis-reappropriates."[54] Wexler's term, "mis-reappropriates," reformulates an idea of a derivative art practice—one of reappropriation, of borrowing or stealing—as an active, creative practice, or at the very least as something willfully confused. W. J. T. Mitchell argues that art now must leave space for confusion and for forms of mis-reappropriation if it is to survive as a culture critically distanced from technologies of power: "If we are indeed living in a time of the plague of the fantasies, perhaps the best cure that artists can offer is to unleash the images.... A certain tactile irresponsibility with images might just be the right sort of homeopathic medicine for what plagues us."[55] A tactile irresponsibility can be traced through the various calls to act (together) discussed above: from Darling's mall rats to Amerika's facts and ghosts, to Lethem's gifts. But if there is a tactile irresponsibility configured in Wexler's collage of "The Collector," it is not as a misuse of Lethem's story, which is a permitted encounter, but rather as putting into play a coded aesthetic that mishandles its material: making digital art with paint and canvas, making a digital text into a digital image.

It is difficult to frame the Promiscuous Materials Project as successful. Quantifying success in this instance is a challenge, but across the three categories on which we tend judge the success of art and entertainment—popularity, critical acclaim, monetary value—none of the work that has come out of the project can be said to have really succeeded. This might be due to the dry nature of working with material given away so easily. The nonsuccess of the project might be due to the general way in which a permitted transgression is an oxymoron. The being public of private social media is a transgression most people make unknowingly; the taking of material from Jonathan Lethem's site is the endpoint in and of itself that comes with the "owner's" blessing. The author/reuser dynamic is never questioned as people using the Promiscuous Materials site are likely already fans or followers of Lethem's and have purposefully sought out his material. Lethem echoes the banality of commercial enterprise as it eats all the counterculture and regurgitates it as "counterculture." Lethem's participation in thinking through new modes of writing and artistic production in computational culture once again draws us into the operative of the digital banal. By permitting transgression, the transgressive act is reappropriated as a banal one; the potentially new encounter is reified as some old new condition we always have coming.

The Promiscuous Materials Project is less radical than the essay, as it makes less of a claim and it feels that less is at stake. But it does signify an action that matters, and it, like the essay, draws attention to the way in which the common is not always to be found or enabled by thinking of the Internet as a de facto common terrain. With both tongue in cheek and genuine concern, Lethem has suggested that the success of the Promiscuous Materials Project was always going to be temperate:

> Here I've set up this tiny little area of communism within capitalist society and contradictions immediately arise, you can't have both all the

time.... For a lot of people, especially with a film or a play, getting the source material free doesn't mean that they've suddenly, magically been enabled to make everything else happen for free; they are still existing in the real world where films and plays are very hard and expensive to put together.[56]

Lethem's promiscuous materials might be given away, but that is not to say that whoever receives and uses them is enabled to realize the creative intervention they want to make. The project resides at the limits of the relationship between capital and gift. The gift is given, but this gesture is seen to be one-way and not enough. If it is not enough, it is because success here is always already judged by means of capital and exchange value; use is not in and of itself a value. Although the project might produce a particular version of "being-acting-feeling together," this is in relation to distinct commodities—the *texts*—and a distinct community—Lethem's.

If Lethem's essay is in the mode of the digital banal, then the literary criticism that the essay demands its reader undertake is a kind of literary banal. It is important to keep acknowledging the commonplaceness of Amerika's and Lethem's actions; it is also necessary to acknowledge the commonness of mine, as a literary critic. To talk about authorial presence, influence, and literary plagiarism is, of course, not new. Key here, as throughout the book, is thinking about the very particular inflection that such modes of representation hold in the contemporary moment. Sameness and repetition, and the methods for making those qualities visible—reappropriation and remix—are proximate to the affects and operations of what Amy J. Elias terms "the digital planetary commons." In an essay that traces recent histories of the term "commons" alongside work in affect theory and "the Planetary Turn," Elias outlines how we might model digital commons that will inevitably end up on a "planetary scale" in order to substantiate "good faith values" and conceptions of "human agency, ethics, law and optimism," rather than a "hive or a sweatshop."[57] While the work discussed in this chapter may not imagine a digital commons on the planetary scale that Elias describes, they certainly attempt to model, to worry at, to ask questions of, or less dramatically, to iterate "good faith values" and protocols of digital culture. In the next chapter an anxiety about the sameness and the cliché of the digital commons appears as a desire and a command to be visible as an individual and in relation to the limited ways digital culture can engender such an individual. In both this chapter and the next, the claims made by the artists and authors considered go some way to deconstructing the operation of the digital banal as a mode of unseeing the many and minute political and social compromises we make, as individuals and collectively, in our everyday digital interactions.

3

BEING SOCIAL IN A POSTDIGITAL WORLD IN *CATFISH* AND *HOW SHOULD A PERSON BE?*

Whereas postmodern culture posits the authentic subject as a problem, postdigital culture is predicated on an authentic subject that performs as such. In Umberto Eco's famous formulation, it is not possible to say "I love you" without hearing the statement as simulacrum. Instead, it is better to acknowledge the construction from the outset, to say, as "Barbara Cartland would put it, I love you madly."[1] On Facebook, Twitter, Tumblr, we like and love and hate each other with emoticons and caps lock and pictures of cats, with this and that sentiment in Impact font, and the platform treats these statements as authentic utterances—valuable precisely because they tell it something about the subject speaking. This chapter traces the connection between postdigital and post-postmodern representations of sociality and subjectivity. Here the operations of the digital banal are used to critique the idea that a "new sincerity" provides a way out of the banal indifference of cultural life under postmodern conditions. I turn to an articulation of the digital banal—which I will make via Alexander R. Galloway's work on the "interface effect"—to argue that post-postmodern and postdigital conditions do not necessarily trouble the reification of sincerity that postmodernism has diagnosed. Rather, we need to address the cultural worrying about sincerity as a recursive command of software. In the previous chapter a similar concern was discussed as remix writing: the recursive mode of the remix, reified as the iterable commands of software, becomes a site at which we can encounter a new commons—ourselves as authors-come-users-come-labor. This chapter discusses the film and TV show *Catfish* (2010–present) and Sheila Heti's novel *How Should a Person Be?* (2013). Both texts are explicitly concerned with being sincere and with validating social subjectivity in a new media age. The anxieties of these texts manifest differently, dependent on the political assumptions each text makes about how mediation works. Both texts, in different ways, attempt to understand the social as mediational, not to block an encounter with sincerity but to better map the conditions for it.

As categories of the new sincerity, post-postmodern and postdigital presume to describe an aesthetic and political imperative of North American art and literature in the twenty-first century. As Lee Konstantinou has suggested, these terms circulate in relation to others: "globalization, cosmodernism, metamodernism, altermodernism, digimodernism, performatism, postpositivist realism, the New Sincerity, or, for more lexically austere analysts, the contemporary."[2] What is at stake in which term you turn to, and how you use it, is the question of what kind of cultural break has or has not been enabled by the ongoingness of late capitalism and the dominance of neoliberalism. In the particular geopolitical conditions of the wealthy, liberal democracies of the global North, this question often manifests in art as an issue of expression, authenticity, and mediation: how do we work with or move on from our mediated subjectivity? Writing about a new sincerity in the films of Wes Anderson, Warren Buckland suggests, "In a dialectical move, new sincerity *incorporates* postmodern irony and cynicism; it operates in conjunction with irony."[3] Similarly, contemporary Internet art practices, such as Jesse Darling's or Jennifer Chan's, are also contending with the constraints of medial commodification. For Chan, "This particular cultural moment is defined by digital identity formation that vacillates between two extremes: careful self-curation and 'indiscriminate over-sharing.' . . . Initiative is both self-interested and ideological."[4] The social context of these art practices is one in which the largest platforms of the Internet confidently assert, "[We are] a community where people use their authentic identities. We require people to provide the name they use in real life; that way, you always know who you're connecting with."[5] This is both a cultural-political demand and a technical one: if "false" code is input, the program will not run, or it will run, and in the process, become something else. Looking back on chapter 1, we might consider this codified sincerity and authenticity part of the ambivalence of Fincher's *The Social Network*; the film can contain an irony that its subject cannot.

The digital banal is the condition by which new media appears as everyday, rote; under the digital banal, the ways in which new media estranges us from or brings us closer to ourselves, each other, and the nonhuman are elided. By reifying what is new, reiterating what is known, the material and political conditions of digital media are effaced; the experience of novelty is affectively blocked, and the opportunity to address our shifting terms of how to be is suppressed. In *Catfish* and *How Should a Person Be?* we find scenes where this act of blocking is quite directly witnessed. In both cases there is something to be overcome, but while *Catfish* can only negotiate this from within the norms propagated by social media, *How Should a Person Be?* refutes the norm and so remains unresolved—the title itself is a question.

To work through these texts' engagements in the digital banal, I turn to what Alexander R. Galloway terms "the interface effect." For Galloway, the allegory for our society of control is the interface. The interface is an agitation between two modes, between the edge and the center, and it is *the* status of culture and politics in the contemporary moment. In Galloway's model of the interface, the center is the transparent point of an interface. If you are playing a video game, the center is the terrain your character is travelling through. The periphery is the point at which mediation shows itself, say an energy bar at the edge of the image or a clue or instruction that is visible in the corner of a screen. More obliquely, the edge might be a pop-up reminder that your controller battery is getting low or a message notification from another application. The critical mode of the interface effect is the "intraface": An "imaginary dialogue between the workable and the unworkable, . . . the intraface is within the aesthetic. . . . The intraface is *indecisive* for it must always juggle two things (the edge and the center) at the same time."[6] I read the intraface as, to some extent, the sincerity *and* irony of post-postmodernism. It is also the digital banal. The difference between the interface and intraface is one "of coherence versus incoherence, of centers creating an autonomous logic versus edges creating a logic of flows, transformations, movement, process, and lines of flight."[7] Galloway's critical turn to the interface/intraface is a way of making the effacing logic of digital media palpable. Digital media suppresses the limitations of the program (we see the interface, not the work), but simultaneously represents those limitations as a disturbance (the program is always also vulnerable, unworkable; it can be made visible as intraface). The effacing gesture of the digital banal—to substitute what is new or unworkable for what is known, the interface—can be witnessed. Galloway's schema generates a way to identify the mechanism of the digital banal as it takes place uniformly, but also as it fails, as the unresolved perpetual present of digital media creates a condition of indeterminacy, a surface of questions and critique.

THE SIGNS OF A SOCIAL NETWORK

The 2010 film *Catfish* documents the story of Nev Schulman, a photographer based in New York, who begins an online relationship with Megan after Megan's younger sister, Abby, sends Nev copies of paintings she made of his photographs. The film follows Nev and his filmmaker brother, Ariel Schulman, and production partner Henry Joost as they travel to Ishpeming, Michigan, to try and meet Megan and find the answers to some inconsistencies in the budding romance. But Megan is not who she has appeared to be. The TV show, produced by MTV, follows a much "wiser" Nev as he helps to connect people who have met a partner or friend online who refuses to meet in person. This section of the chapter moves between discussion of the film and the TV show. In both cases I am interested in the way sociality is performed, not only as a sequential narrative of proving authentic identity and authentic affectivity, but also as an animated graphic overlay; icons and pixels limn the borders of everyday digital experience, making up an image of sociality today. The signs of social networking overlay, underwrite, and get entangled with the "reality" of the traditional diegetic space—the TV show or film—making their own visual case for the online social network as *the* diegetic scene. The reality TV show and feature film that trace the "actual" lives of those involved are the nondiegetic, the periphery, the edge. *Catfish* is not explicitly about the material properties and forms of digital media, but it is entirely about how digital media mediates human engagement. *Catfish* is about the people, but the screen is always in the way: the screen is a site of the social.

Catfish (the film and TV show) is full of images of pointers scrolling and selecting, shots of text as it is typed and as it appears in message boxes, screens-within-screens, and Photoshopped pictures. *Catfish* posits the graphical language of digital technology as a wall between the viewer and the technology, a barrier to their understanding and access to the truth. This is a narrative of surfaces and boundaries, of borders and mediations. The numerous shots of screens, within the frame of the screen the viewers encounter, serve to emphasize the way the human subjects of the film are delineated by their position in front of a computer screen. The camera in *Catfish* continually zooms in on the various screens that represent communication between the subjects, but this zooming in can only make more visible the surface; the camera cannot take the audience past the pixels that comprise the image on-screen (see figure 3.1). A digital image only contains so much information; you can keep making it larger, but it will get less legible, not reveal more information.[8]

Catfish fetishizes the modes of visual representation that computer coding produces. It pays attention to the graphics that make up the surface of digital media (the point of human encounter). The network that the computer substantiates (the Internet) and the network that it symbol-

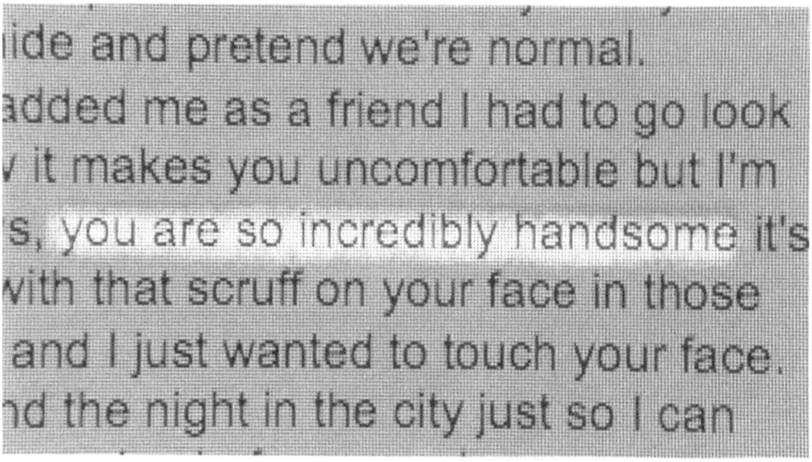

FIGURE 3.1 Reading through the screen. *Catfish* (2010)

izes (friends through Facebook) are pointedly obscured by the screen. Repeated images showing screens as pixels suggest digital communication as mediation. In *Catfish* code is not the subject, but the artificiality of digital communication is. This artificiality is, in fact, a representation of the nonhuman computer and the nonreadability of code. The aesthetic of the film is also, unwittingly, its ethic. This is what Kember and Zylinska term an "ethics of mediation." In *Life After New Media*, Kember and Zylinska suggest that "media ethics," predicated as it is on a distinction between embodied human and media agents, must give way to an "ethics of mediation" as an "expanded understanding of mediation as a vital process, a way of being and becoming in the technological world, or a way of emerging through time."[9] *Catfish* makes the visual surface of digital communications into the visual surface of the film, and in doing so offers a kind of mediational intraface, an image of being and becoming-with(in) a technological environment.

The intraface of *Catfish* is a precarious critical mode; the destabilizing effect of the surface is constantly blocked by the conservative drive of the format and narrative. The graphic media objects in *Catfish* are partly the edge appearing in the middle. For example, an edge of the frame of *Catfish: The TV Show* is the pop-up at the bottom of the screen telling you which song and artist is featured in the show; this information presumes an online-active spectator who will immediately act on that information. The social media graphics within the narrative of the show are a corollary to this social media reference outside the show (but on the screen). Despite these oscillations, the interface is never really disrupted; *Catfish* as interface is coherent, and we understand that the love stories we watch are inextricably stories that are commodified and reproduced as marketable in typical ways. Within the TV show, we watch particular bodies and agents interact in ways that confirm a workable, rather than unworkable, digitally mediated social life. The workability triumphs through the "reality" of Nev and his friend/cameraman Max.[10] Max is, in all but name, the cohost. Max is always visible on-screen filming Nev, but his footage is rarely cut to. Max is there to testify to the authenticity of Nev: Nev is someone who understands the way constructed reality works, and who is accompanied by a "real" friend, substantiating his claims to an embodied, honest reality. In *Catfish* the film, Ariel and Henry authenticate Nev in a similar way. The conceit of the show and film is that, for the subject and the "catfish," the honest, true reality is the narrative that Nev unveils. In the show this is also always a mediated reality. Each episode ends with the couple in a Skype group–video chat with Nev and Max. In *Catfish*, particularly in the TV show, the precarity of the social script is also shown to be at risk or at stake. This is not just in the chase for a happy ending but also in that the authenticity of the social is here constructed through the model of social media, wherein friends are attachments that not only make the self a social being, but are the only way to attest to the authenticity of the individual's existence at all.

FINDING FRIENDS

The question of location is perhaps the overriding ontological crisis at stake in the *Catfish* universe. Nev is always locating the catfish. Often on *Catfish: The TV Show*, and certainly in *Catfish* the film, vast geographical distances support the lie of the intimacy provided by the social media interface: the stories the users tell about themselves are plausible because they are physically apart. More obliquely, *Catfish* is concerned with locating where a true body resides. The concept of an authentic social reality becomes the prize at the end of a road-trip movie—it is a locatable point on a map, a journey of locating selves, an image of locative media, and a nonengagement with the geographic, environmental, and political influences of social media. In the second half of *Catfish* the film, Nev goes to visit Abby. Nev, Ariel, and Henry fly from New York City to Vail, Colorado, for a filming job, and then decide to drive a detour to Ishpeming, Michigan, to pay a surprise visit to Abby. By this point in the film, the seeds of doubt as to Abby's authenticity have been sown for the audience, and so the film moves, at least temporarily, along the lines of a traditional road-trip thriller.[11] The scenes of the men's road trip are composite images combining "real-life" footage from the car and graphics from Google Maps and Google Street View, a journey "illustrated with jaunty blue arrows that yank us around Michigan."[12] In *Catfish* being present is being presented by GPS. The impact of these composite images is disconcerting. Rather than a sense of travel and movement, of perspective that pulls the viewer's eyes to the horizon, the audience is shown a flattened map—not a landscape. In scenes such as the road trip the digital is shown to augment the reality being documented. The representation of Google Maps might lead us to rethink cinematic representations of the road; this is an intervention in the genre of the road movie, an explicit representation of the banality of always being *on*-road, *on*-grid through GPS. We might also consider the Google graphic not so much an augmentation as *the* mediational process of being present.

Catfish: The TV Show deploys many of the same techniques as the film, but here the giveaway has already taken place—the TV show is up front about the fact the "catfish" is not presenting an honest identity. In the TV show the road trip is documented, but it is no longer anticipatory in quite the same way; the imaging of finding the catfish is compressed into encounters on doorsteps. It is also displaced onto the on-screen graphics representing content from the subjects' various social network profiles, instant messages, and e-mails. Because the audience already knows these will be lies, or at least partial truths, the encounter with social media communication is the primary site of anticipation, expectation, and interpretation. The text boxes and photos for the most part replicate or reproduce the visual format of the actual social networking sites they refer to; they signify the multiplex versions of reality being represented by the program (see figure 3.2). The messages and photos are all part of the subject's reality (and the reality of the catfish), but they are not authentic in the sense of what a viewer expects from a reality TV show. They function as a giveaway of unreality. They communicate not-truths and are postproduction graphics—evidence of the production/construction of reality. This unreality presumes the narrative possibility of its opposite, which is not reality per se, but reality as "the truth." Each episode presents a new couple. In keeping with reality TV convention, there are reunions and wrap parties that both extend and shore up the edges of distinct seasons and ultimately the *Catfish* world.

Episode 6 of season 1, "Kya and Alyx,"[13] opens with Nev and Max messing around in a hotel room, and then Nev turns to his laptop to see what is in his inbox. There he has a message from Kya explaining how she is in love with a guy she met online called Alyx, and she wants to meet him, but they can't get it together. Nev reads the message aloud. The scene cuts from Nev reading the message from his laptop to Max watching/filming Nev to graphics of black text on a white background shown as a screen—as

FIGURE 3.2 Tagging Sunny and Nev. *Catfish: The TV Show* (2012, season 1, episode 1)

if the monitor Nev is looking at is being filmed. The text is large, and a cursor highlights various phrases that Nev also emphasizes as he reads aloud. This opening is typical. Often we happen upon Nev and Max in some unspecified hotel room, as if they spend their lives on the road, documenting catfish. This mobility is part of the ethic of social media and digital capitalism; it is not only a model of fluid living, where we can be at work anywhere, all the time, it is also a documentation of the dispersal of social community. Nev and Max are usually in a twin room, and it is implied that they stay together in this room. Max and Nev's physical closeness points to the way that the show uses their relationship as a false mirror for the broken relationships it exhibits: these two are in the same place and are therefore more real.

Max and Nev are always framed as homosocial rather than homosexual. Given that many of the stories featured on the show are about nonnormative and queer relationships and identities, Max and Nev's platonic friendship is a significant counterpoint. Max and Nev tend to signify various apposite states. For example, despite the performance of Nev as someone who believes in new media romance, Nev and Max, as presenters, only ever articulate an anxiety about online romance. They also assert that nothing is real until people are face to face. Talking to Kya about the journey they will go on for the show, Nev tells her, "I look forward to maybe watching you guys fall in love for real." For real, which means in person. But as far as Kya's own claims are concerned, she and Alyx are already in love, *for real*. When Max and Nev later discover that Alyx's Facebook profile contains images from another Facebook profile, they determine Alyx's to be the fake one because the other profile has about five hundred friends, whereas Alyx has only ten, making it a "much more legitimate profile." Max concludes that the other guy is "a real person." The show is not a critique of sociality as mediation; it is rather subtly suspicious of it. *Catfish: The TV Show* is a kind of testimonial to the complex ways we are co-constituted with media, but this is in terms of what the production is, rather than what it says. In *Catfish* Facebook becomes the primary interface used to validate existence, despite the show's premise that Facebook is easy to misuse. Although Max and Nev privilege meeting in real life as the true form of friendship and romance, they themselves feature as tagged image-entities and as a simulation of a friendship acted out on camera. The film and TV show attest to us as entangled human-technological beings, not in some spectacular sense, but through the optic of banal, predictable stories of romance and dating. The format of the show, and the narrative genre of romance that structures its logic, is the effacement of what might be affectively different about relationships today. The film and TV show demonstrate an anxiety about this difference by incorporating the interface into the diegetic space. Graphic images from Facebook suggest that the show knows that romance IRL (in real life) is romance online, that we are mediational, but the presentation of Nev and Max blocks the novelty of this recognition.

SOFT SCRIPT

In *How Should a Person Be?* Sheila Heti is on a mission to work out how to be. The awkward open-endedness of this question is an unheard final downbeat: How to be . . . what? The novel works through different versions of the question. How should a person be . . . a good artist, an authentic individual, a social and socially responsible person, famous, known, unknown, a woman, a man, sexual, serious, friends, alone. The novel offers no answer, but is a meditation on the question itself. It is always mediational:

that is, the *being* that Sheila investigates is always becoming-with other agents and agencies. The narration flits between an "I," who is presumed to be Sheila the character, but who also might be Sheila Heti the author, and a third person, who is a character in a play. In various interviews to promote and discuss *How Should a Person Be?*, Heti emphasized that her book was not influenced by the form of the novel; rather, she was "thinking about movies made by Werner Herzog and TV shows like *The Hills*. Other mediums are doing this kind of thing more."[14] By "this kind of thing" Heti refers to forms of "constructed factual" or "fictional reality." One of the conditions that digital culture reifies is social interaction as an endemic aspect of cultural production; sociality is an integrated function of consuming and producing culture. For example, Nev and Max are researcher/detective *friends*, always simultaneously hanging out and working in the text; and then, of course, their working *is* the text. Heti's novel interrogates this condition.

At the 2013 BAFTAs (the British Academy of Film and Television Arts awards) the TV show *Made in Chelsea* won the award for best "Reality and Constructed Factual" program. According to a BBC news item on the introduction of the BAFTA category, "Constructed reality shows are a cross-pollination of soap opera and documentary, following real people going about their daily lives—but some storylines are constructed or initiated by producers in advance."[15] In a debate over the BAFTAs' topic of constructed or structured reality, Claire Faragher, the producer of *The Only Way Is Essex*, describes how the cast and crew work from a "soft script," which prepares the narrative and sets up situations that guide the "actual" stories of the cast.[16] The soft script is to some extent the "construct" of "constructed fact," at least in the sense that these shows differentiate themselves from the genre of documentary and declare some scenes to be scripted. Whereas the constructed reality shows recognized by the BAFTAs present to the viewer a constructed reality that effaces its mediation—cameras, lights, runners, and makeup artists are hidden—Heti's novel instantiates a medially constructed reality. Heti frames her book through the genre of constructed factual narrative, but this does not quite encompass the workings of the novel. The genre of constructed factual clearly signals the constructed nature of the narrative in production, but within the narrative itself, no such intervention is signaled. In shows such as *Made in Chelsea* and *The Hills*, each episode is presented as if no production crew accompanied its stars, who are just themselves and not acting. Heti's novel incorporates the signaling within itself.

Within the first two pages, *How Should a Person Be?* declares an interest in fame as a way of being registered, seen, taken into account: "How should a person be? I sometimes wonder about it, and I can't help answering like this: a celebrity."[17] But in this book celebrity is not notoriety so much as it is an intrinsic cultural value: "Everyone would know in their hearts that *I* am the most famous person alive—but not talk about it too much.... It is the quality of fame one is after here, without any of its qualities."[18] Heti is invested in the mediation of reality TV, in the constructed fact, more than she is in the medium. The distinction between the quality and qualities of fame might transpose onto a dichotomy of mediation and medium. Fame refers to a quality of becoming-with media, but not being subject to it. It is no surprise that a newly personalized media culture, producing multiple ways for users to undertake self-surveillance, is paralleled in popular culture by reality TV. As Mark Andrejevic argues, reality TV is "surveillance as a means of self-expression and a shortcut to fame and fortune."[19] Such a means of expression and shortcut to being known is amplified on social media where, as Rachel E. Dubrofsky and Megan M. Wood note, "Similar to what occurs on reality TV, people who appear authentic despite surveillance are valorized as the most authentic."[20] The novel *How Should a Person Be?* is careful to pose the question of self-expression as self-surveillance via its material construction. The title's question gets at this in that it is a command for self-expression that is also a monitoring of and a checking in with the self. In addition, the novel refuses to settle into its realist prose. Instead, it turns to scripts and e-mails as material markers of the ways in which the character Sheila is known: she is being communicated with, she is being performed, and we are watching/reading her.

The first act of the book describes Sheila's recent divorce and establishes her friendship with Margaux. These events are told in retrospect. In the second chapter of act 1 the narrator-Sheila is describing her wedding when she relates how, several months before the wedding, Sheila and her fiancé watched another couple get married.

> Then I saw and heard the lovely bride grow choked up with emotion as she repeated the words *for richer or for poorer*. . . . As my fiancé and I

walked away, I said that I thought it was a pretty vain, stupid, materialistic part to get choked up on—but we admitted that we did not know her financial history.[21]

The next paragraph describes Sheila's own wedding:

As I said the words for *richer or for poorer*, that bride came up in me. Tears welled in my eyes, just as they had welled up in hers.... It was a copy, a possession, canned. The bride inhabited me at the exact moment I should have been most present.... I felt ever uncertain, thinking back on it, about whether my marriage could truly be called *mine*.[22]

A bride welling up over her vows is *that feeling when*—it is the performance of a social script. This can be read as the performance of a particular bride or the performance of being a bride in general. Given the generality of the novel's question, it seems that Sheila's marriage is not hers in the sense that no marriage is owned; it is always also a meditated social construct. I highlight this section not because it is particular in the novel, but because it is indicative of a general tone and anxiety that carries throughout the text.

ON MEDIATION AND BEING

How Should a Person Be? is a novel in flux: Sheila is recently divorced, commissioned to write a play she cannot seem to focus on, and in the midst of forming new friendships that influence her creative practice. The novel is a mediation on these processes, but is also mediational in the sense for which I have been citing Kember and Zylinska; throughout the novel Heti considers the way she is becoming a person—a social, identifiable being—*with* technologies. Heti's novel is a fictional work that plays off the conditions that create *Catfish*: social media indeterminacy. The novel stages this indeterminacy as a process, neurotically and obsessively; it is always on the verge of undoing itself (literally, it is barely a novel) as it registers the anxieties and processes of selfing—of constructing, working on, and producing a recognizable social self. In the novel these processes are not always digital technologies, but rather technologies of self-production and expression: art and literature as genres, typewriters and voice recorders as tools, friendship as constitutive of individuals. Overall this is a novel that is conspicuously nondigital. Aside from a few transcribed e-mails and a couple references to checking e-mails, seeing something "on the Internet," there is no sense that Sheila and her friends think of themselves as having differentiated digital lives.[23] In *How Should a Person Be?* digital media appears as a surface of the text; the text itself seems barely aware of it. As with Berlant's flat affects, the flattened agency of digital media is not necessarily a nonencounter. The anxiety of mediation is present in lieu of the media device itself: "The other night out at the bars, I learned that Nietzsche wrote on a typewriter. It is unbelievable to me, and I no longer feel that his philosophy has the same validity or aura of truth that it formerly did."[24]

Heti's novel is littered with the detritus of technologically mediated social interaction—e-mails, recorded conversation—and the anxieties associated with the absent presences that such documents connote. In a mostly glowing review of Heti's book, James Wood writes off these communications as red herrings, luring a reader away from Heti's art of fiction: "Heti may include real e-mails and recordings of actual conversations, but, of course, her book is shaped and plotted (however lightly), and uses fiction as well as autobiography."[25] However, Wood misreads the function of the e-mails and recordings. For Wood these are by-products of processes that remain in the novel as a kind of misdirect, diverting the reader from the authorial labor of fiction. In contrast, I argue that these other media are at the center of the way Heti's narration works at the titular question. The e-mails and recordings are there to testify, not to some fake documentarian impulse, but rather to processes of mediated self-construction in general. *How Should a Person Be?* is discursive, chatty; there are constant shifts in form, from play scripts to transposed e-mails, from descriptive prose to allegorical asides. This is one way in which the novel is banal; it invokes common communication rather than literary exceptionalism.

The banal investments of *How Should a Person Be?* gesture toward the banal as the registering of a refusal to register novelty; the banal marks the place where surprise might have been. In various ways Andy Warhol is the banal figure with whom Heti is in dialogue—as Wood also suggests. At the Basel Art Fair in Miami, Sheila observes a banner over one of the entrances featuring a quote from Warhol: "Everybody's sense of beauty is different from everybody else's." Sheila asks Margaux what she thinks it means. "Oh yeah," Margaux replies. "It's saying you can be rich and stupid about art. You're all welcome."[26] This exchange establishes Warhol's legacy to Heti's work in terms of a posture of ambivalence that troubles Sheila. Sheila does not respond, because there is nothing left to say but, "Several hours later, growing tired from the art and the cold, we left."[27] Warhol figures throughout the novel in complex ways. While in the end Heti's text speaks to the particular conditions of the digital banal, it puts the banal technic in proximity with a prior banal culture. One of the key technical and mediational subjects of the novel is Sheila's digital tape recorder. The appearance of this shiny object disturbs the novel and defines the kind of literary mode—a social literary mode—that the work will eventually take. The recorder is an allusion to Warhol's art practice. As Pat Hackett explains in the introduction to Warhol's diaries, which were themselves transcribed from phone conversations and tape recordings, "From the mid-sixties to the mid-seventies, Andy was notorious for endlessly tape-recording his friends."[28] I am interested in how the tape recorder does something quite specifically contemporary in Heti's novel, instantiating a way to engage in social life *after* new media. It is through the ambiguous allusion to Warhol that such a particular contingency can be witnessed.

Warhol's work is a candidate for the category of "merely interesting." As discussed in the introduction, the merely interesting is characterized by "its low or minimal affect, its functional and structural generality, its seriality, its eclecticism, its recursiveness, and its future-oriented temporality."[29] In Sianne Ngai's work the merely interesting is about a tension between "difference and typicality," a response to "novelty and change in a capitalist culture in which change is paradoxically constant and novelty paradoxically familiar."[30] The most recent historical flashpoint of the merely interesting is the "postwar information aesthetic of cool."[31] Although Ngai does not explicitly describe Warhol in this context, he haunts her argument in various ways. In a footnote to a discussion of Gertrude Stein's *Tender Buttons*, Warhol and Stein are described as similarly working toward reproducing "commodity's culture's positive affects without necessarily becoming affirmative." They methodically and methodologically test the line between "the appropriation of an existing aesthetic and participation in that aesthetic."[32] Ngai's reading is proximate to Hal Foster's work on Andy Warhol's repetitive artistic practices.[33] For Foster, the repetition of images of death—car wrecks, electric chairs—in Warhol's series "Death in America," punctures the banality of the image *as* repetition, producing a schism between where affect has gone and where it might be produced and felt anew.[34] The undecidability of Ngai's merely interesting is produced when feelings about an artwork are so low in intensity that we can't be sure we feel anything. This is also the slippage in Warhol's repeated images, where our investment in the aesthetic is so minimal (because we have seen it all before) that we are more disturbed by the surface than the subject.

For Warhol, the tape recorder was a method of ambivalently capturing the "noise" around him.[35] Warhol worked with as little intensity as possible. In terms of the banal, we might say Warhol practiced a mode of structured unfeeling in the production of art. Warhol's works that used a tape recorder, for example the novel *a, A Novel* (1968), produce a "kind of intransigent unproductivity in that they distend the present and incur a feeling that we should already have left the moment at hand, yet have not."[36] This is a description that has a lot in common with Ngai's interpretation of the merely interesting and Foster's description of Warhol's visual art. Warhol epitomizes the recursive propensity of the banal that does not simply repeat but almost-not-quite-entirely effaces the possibility of new experiences in its paradoxical commitment to novelty. Heti herself might be merely interested in Warhol: he is an ambivalent figure in her work, paradoxically signaling something old and also an investment in the new and now. *How Should a Person Be?* is written in a historical moment when such banal propensity is the structuring logic of dominant modes of communication and artistic production, but also a moment when we are inclined to still want to say something new about life, to express what Lee Konstantinou has described as "post-ironic belief."[37]

In the second chapter of act 2 Sheila meets her new love, "a silver digital tape recorder." It is mutual love at first sight: "It has long been known to me that certain objects want you as much as you want them."[38] This object is one of the few conspicuously digital items in the novel, and its digitalness is almost beside the point. And yet, because it is one of the few conspicuously digital items in the book, and because it is a reified interface for the digital society of control in general—a recorder—it can be read emblematically and allegorically as an ontology of the digital banal. For Warhol the cassette tape recorder was a way to remove his subjectivity from the social situation; as a prosthesis, it marked Warhol as a listener. The playback function was crucial in Warhol's work, where such recordings were never really about the record, the archive; they were about the social, about amplification. For Warhol, "the appeal of sonic scale was its potential for undermining the private containment of the listener's interiority."[39] For Heti, the recorder is also a social mechanism, but more significantly, it is a way to encounter her own mediational agency. After purchasing the recorder, Heti goes into a coffee shop.

> I whispered low into my tape recorder's belly. I recorded my voice and played it back. I spoke into it tenderly and heard my tenderness returned.... I wanted to touch every part of it, to understand how it worked. I began to learn what turned it on and the things that turned it off.[40]

The machine verifies Sheila as herself, and so Sheila is becoming a person with the machine. Sheila falls in love with her machine and confirms her presence through it—*I must be real, I can hear myself.*

The chapter after Sheila buys the recorder describes the moment when she presents Margaux with the recorder. Margaux is her best friend, the book's main subject. But she hates the idea of the recorder: "Don't you know that what I fear most is my words floating separate from my body? You there with that tape recorder is the scariest thing!"[41] Sheila has been trying to write a play, but she is stuck. She believes the recorder will get her creativity going. It works. The chapter after Sheila buys the recorder is the first chapter presented as a script; the script describes the moment Margaux is presented with the recorder. Rather than understand this scene as solely a metafictional conceit—where the novel presents itself as a work of art in construction—this scene is an encounter with the intraface. The digital recorder, and its mobilization as embodied agency, temporarily makes the novel itself unworkable. For a moment, Margaux refuses to make or be the novel; subsequently the novel becomes a play script. The intraface is a mode that resists, or at least makes visible, the digital banal, which demands more seamless integration of discrete ways of being than Heti can keep in play. Here, digital media is reified as a shiny new thing (the recorder) blocking the affective novelty of digital mediation (the condition of being recordable). The destabilizing of the novel at this point allows us to see this process at work: the novel is all of a sudden a play, and the reader is confronted with the transformative mediational novelty of the digital recorder.

The recorder is an allegory for personal digital communications. Through it, Sheila substantiates herself as a social being in the world. It is a tool, a word processor, and as Margaux's reaction suggests, it is a medium that estranges an utterance from the body and simulates that body as itself. The recorder is a mechanism for Sheila's script, which is both digital and analogue material, and both a fictional and nonfictional occurrence. In the novel the appearance of the recorder, and the script, is a material metaphor for amplification, but this is a mediational rather than effacing process. The recorder signifies a moment when voice is iterated as distinct from writing, and this happens through a shift in the format of book itself (the change in layout to script) as well as through the introduction in the narrative of a voice-recording device. No longer is the novel only narrating to us, it is also performing voices; this is marked by Margaux's comments and by the fact that characters now speak independently of Sheila's voice. Characters' names appear before they speak.

MARGAUX
Well, *of course* there are people here that are really truly great! But how could you see that? Like, for instance, if Takeshi Murakami had just one of his sculptures here, you wouldn't know how good it was.[42]

Corollary to the script in the novel are the e-mails represented on the page as numbered lists, in smaller font, graphically distinct from the general narration. Heti attends to the difference of e-mail as a distinct medium within the novel—something other than the novel: "*One morning, Sheila finds an email from Margaux.*"[43] The novel is undone by the e-mails and the scripts because they are not within the constraints of the fiction; they attest to Sheila Heti's social life, mediation as becoming-with, and Sheila Heti's work as author.

NEW MEDIA LITERARY STUDIES

Discussing the game *World of Warcraft*, which features various graphic overlays that provide vital paratextual data to the player (energy bars, a compass, and the like), Alex Galloway argues that the "existence of the internal interface within the medium is important because it indicates the implicit presence of the outside within the inside." For Galloway, "'Outside' means something quite specific: *the social*."[44] It follows that if "the nondiegetic takes center stage, we can be sure that the 'outside,' or the social, has been woven more intimately into the very fabric of the aesthetic than in previous times."[45] For Galloway, the interface inside the game is an "intraface," which is a useful term because it engenders analysis that can take into account "parallel aesthetic events [that] reveal something about the medium and about contemporary life."[46] The operation of the social, instantiated through the interface, indicates an intraface, and by extension, this operation in a novel can be seen as, or in relation to, a general condition of contemporary media. If the novel is an intraface, it must be posing its own edges as questions within the text, and in doing so pose itself as a momentary instantiation of a system of "a logic of flows, transformations, movement, process, and lines of flight."[47] In Heti's novel the e-mails and scripts are conversation. Conversation is the social. In the novel Sheila wants her work to be social, she wants it to be *this*, the conversation.

In act 2, chapter 6, Sheila has a dream about her play and calls her Jungian analyst, Ann: "I went to my computer and made it gently ring."[48] The analysis session is presented in script form. After Sheila recounts the dream, Ann suggests that Sheila is anxious, because she keeps quitting things she thinks might be dangerous: her marriage, the play. To this Sheila responds:

> (*defensive*) Wait! I want to cancel the play not because it's *dangerous*, but because life doesn't feel like it's in my stupid play, or with me sitting in a room *typing*. And life wasn't in my marriage anymore, either. Life feels like it's with Margaux—*talking*—which is an equally sincere attempt to get somewhere, just as sincere as writing a play.[49]

Here is the question of how to be social as it is posed in the novel. It is also the edge of the novel, the point at which the novel is not itself but rather a general iteration of the status quo. This is not just a mediation on the literary work in the manner of something typed versus something verbal, or a solo authorial project versus a social one. It is also a moment in which the novel recognizes the work of the social. There is a precarious indistinctness of work and social life endemic to workers in the creative economy and to everyone as social media users in the contemporary moment. The edge of Heti's novel is where her sociality is also the material of her labor. This edge is fully incorporated *in* the text, as intraface, in those passages that are, and reflect on, Heti's social work. The barely perceptible but ubiquitous presence of digital media in the novel blocks the apprehension of new modes of artistic production and social life instantiated by digital media. In the intraface this process of effacement is critically made visible.

Describing the "informalities and ethics of new media culture," artist Jennifer Chan identifies the post-Internet condition as that "which is as much about the existential and ethical dimension of making art online and the creation of surplus value around its affects, as it is about the politics and anxieties that exist around so called post-Internet art practices."[50] Today artists "write, curate, blog, chat, comment. With every interaction, your playtime is the corporate network's goldmine. Under post-Internet conditions artists must capitalize on boredom, busyness, and procrastination."[51] This command/condition is a function of creative labor within what Jodi Dean names "communicative capitalism" and Tiziana Terranova figures in terms of "immaterial labor": processes by which conversation—sociality—is creative work.[52] This condition is writ large through *How Should a Person Be?*, but only if the novel is understood in terms of mediation and the digital banal rather than a literary category apart from everyday technoculture. James Wood writes of *How Should a Person Be?* that "Heti never pursues that solitary note with the rigor that it deserves. It is easier, more charming, more hospitable, more successfully evasive, to bring in the gang of friends and get a 'vaguely intelligent' conversation going."[53] For Wood, the sway of the social is a problem; it is an evasive maneuver that gets Heti out of her authorial duty. I argue that the social is, in fact, *the* work of the novel, and to follow Galloway, it is its intraface. Heti's use of constructed conversation instantiates the social of the nondiegetic space (the world outside of the text that is being made into something else in the text) within the diegetic (which is the artwork as a social production). This agitation is an aspect of the digital banal, which makes over the social as work and the social script as a digital mechanism.

The published novel, authored by and credited to Sheila Heti, is testament to the compromise of how social a novel can be. It can be a conversation to the extent that it incorporates the transcription of conversation, of sociality, so long as it remains marketable as a novel. In order to fully address what is to be gained from situating this novel beyond its literary milieu, it is important to consider what is at stake in reading this text as a meditation on the digital banal instead of as a literary work of post-postmodernism and the new sincerity. This is, after all, a novel, and as described, it stages various scenes of thwarted writing that result in Sheila Heti's social methodology. On the back cover blurb, Miranda July calls this work a "new kind of book and a new kind of person, . . . a major literary work"; Lena Dunham describes it as "a really amazing metafiction-meets-nonfiction novel." These frame the book as literary. It is not only in discourse with the constructed nonfiction of reality TV, the banal postmodern gestures of Warhol's artwork, and the social work of art in a post-Internet market; *How Should a Person Be?* also exemplifies the post-postmodern discourse of contemporary literature as it attempts to document a new kind of subject, one that is both invested in the authenticity of emotion (nonfiction, sincerity) and skeptical of modes of representation (metafiction, irony).

The new(ly) sincere encounter is with the problem of the person; how might we be a good one? In recent scholarship on post-postmodern literature and the new sincerity by Nicoline Timmer, Stephen J. Burn, Adam Kelly, and Lee Konstantinou, the post-postmodern is understood as having a renewed interest in character.[54] Whereas postmodern literature and art decentred the human subject, post-postmodernism addresses and produces a thinking, feeling, "interpersonal" human subject.[55] The category of the interpersonal is where my interest in the social of Heti's novel as mediational intraface meets a literary critical interest in how the novel engenders characters who think and feel in relation to one another. This interest is a response to postmodern literature's experiments with ahistorical, fragmentary, holographic networks of characters; it is also a result of the commodification of social life in ever more banal ways.[56] As Konstantinou notes, in "our post-postmodern moment, the social transforms itself into what Mark Zuckerberg calls the 'social graph,' generated on a digital platform owned by some friendly, for-profit corporation."[57] Literature is a site in which the processes of capturing social life (which I argue are computational and mediational) can be made visible.

Discussion of post-postmodernism understands itself in response to the "information society" and is cognizant of many of the sociopolitical aspects of a new media life.[58] However, little attention is paid to how, within computational culture, software might be the layer at which interpersonal, authentic subjectivity is delimited. In other words, what is identified in literary criticism as a problem of sincerity is actually codified in ubiquitous, obfuscatory, everyday mediational systems as a computational logic of verification. As posthuman and nonhuman studies have made clear, the thinking, feeling, interpersonal subject is always mediational.[59] Under the conditions of the digital banal, this mediational mode is not perceived as a new experience but as the inevitable progression of human-computer society. In work on the post-postmodern, this banality is represented as the assertion that artists are still in an ongoing debate with some previous moment. Whereas a post-postmodern analysis might suggest that Heti's novel is about the viability of the interpersonal, feeling subject of literature *after* postmodernism, I suggest that it is a novel about the ontology of the social being in conditions of the digital banal.

In Nicoline Timmer's account of post-postmodernism, one of the dominant critical investments of this new literary genre is sharing: "In the post-postmodern novel 'sharing' is important; for example sharing stories as a way to 'identify with others' (and to allow others to identify with you)."[60] Timmer frames this in terms of writing by Dave Eggers and David Foster Wallace, which conscientiously, but anxiously, presents the act of voicing others' stories as ethically vital. For Timmer, in the post-postmodern novel "a desire for some form of community or sociality is highlighted"; there is "a structural need for a we."[61] Reading *How Should a Person Be?*, we encounter a similar investment in community and a belief in the power of sharing stories. As Sheila tells Ann, her life "feels like it's with Margaux—*talking*—which is an equally sincere attempt to get somewhere." But if sharing is a demand of communicative capitalism, and moreover is an algorithmically determined and determining social action, then a contemporary aesthetics of sharing is also always mediational, banally so. Timmer posits literature as the genre that is being contested and challenged from within; how do we make the solitary novel a "we"? Heti's novel exemplifies how talking is a common command of digital culture, and even as it appears in a novel, it is contesting the very right of literature as a genre, and the novel as a dominant expressive medium, to exist. Heti's digital tape recorder and her e-mails remind the reader that there is no separate space in which we encounter the literary object and no alternative medium through which the writer speaks.

In the previous chapter I discussed how the contemporary "we" is complex. Any "we" now is likely to form through, and speak as, a corporate platform, a proprietary program, or nonhuman agency. In the end the answer to Heti's titular question is that we should be empathetic, a friend, a participant. The novel knows that these are not simple things; it is itself a commodification of these things. The novel has a life beyond itself, in the offline and online bodies of Sheila Heti and her real friends. As we see with Nev and Max and the catfish, the indeterminacy of sociality today can be offset by having social media authenticate your networks. *Catfish* does not want to undermine the digital banal as it reiterates the ways normative society works. In the film and TV show, your public status is your social capital (if you can't be "true," then you must be faking it, and you forfeit value). *How Should a Person Be?* does want to query what constitutes a social life today. It does so by drawing attention to the edges of its mode and to the ways these edges are also blocking new affective resonances. I will next be primarily considering the ways that several novels represent encounters with digital media through the terms of the digital banal. None test the very possibility of this action so much as *How Should a Person Be?* Heti's novel incorporates its own concern about the value of the novel today, not as a newly sincere invocation of literary value, but as a digital recording device that destabilizes the authorial work of construction and effaces the individual creator while it reifies the "transparency" of recording.

In the first chapter I discussed the representation of code in David Fincher's films as a way in which the effacing procedures of digital media—code disappearing, the past persisting as an unresolved present—can appear on-screen and be critically witnessed, if only fleetingly. Close attention to *Catfish* and *How Should a Person Be?* is repaid with a related reveal: sincerity and authenticity are uncovered as stubbornly refusing incorporation into new media agencies, despite their incorporation as computational checks. Today, policies and algorithms determine us all in terms of a sincere identity; this is a significantly new mode of identifying and being identified, which is perceived to be a banal reproduction of institutionalized identity practices (full name, photo, school).[62] The graphic overlays of *Catfish* draw attention to the authenticating procedures while the narrative flirts with more open modes of being and being together. *How Should a Person Be?* refuses to resolve its own problem, disturbing the operations of the digital banal, holding on to a sense that there is emerging, in Miranda July's words, "a new kind of person."

The first four chapters of this book were about working through the program of the digital banal: it asked how this logic is writ through digital culture and how we encounter it in the artworks that seek to narrate it. In the next few chapters, this work is mobilized and dispersed across engagements with various scenes of digital media in and as everyday life. From fictional tech campuses of California to a broken future in New York City, the digital banal defines the way contemporary American literature represents its mediational condition.

4

TWENTY YEARS OF CALIFORNIAN IDEOLOGY IN *THE BUG* AND *THE CIRCLE*

About halfway through Ellen Ullman's 2003 novel *The Bug*, the protagonist Berta Walton begins training as a programmer, initially at summer school and then independently. In her previous role as a software tester, Berta knew code only as obfuscation, but now Berta is excitedly inculcated into the pleasure of *knowing* the computational: "This information had a startling effect on me.... For the first time, I understood there was a mapping between the symbolic words of the code and the physical existence of the machine."[1] Describing the work of the program, Berta's account breaks down into discrete units of information, revealing processes that have been hidden from her. These units of information are strung together as the procedure of the program; simultaneously, Berta is making this procedure a narrative, a story of how things happen. At times Ullman's language strays toward the procedural, the instruction manual, but it also writes the procedural as in some way narratological: "I began to understand their chiseled workings, how each path had been created by these careful statements of condition."[2] Berta is engrossed in her new education:

> June turned to July. I began staying later in the evenings. I stopped calling friends altogether.... I stopped listening to the radio, watching the news. I was learning about functions.

```
display _ count (count)
int count;
{
  i = 0;
  while (i <= count)
  {
    printf ("count now = %d\n," count);
    i = i + 1;
  }
  return;
}
```
... A chunk of code that when completed—done executing its own statements, done with all the statements in all the functions *it* had called—will eventually return to the caller.[3]

The chunk of code is indigestible but for the narrative. The play on the word "call" throughout this passage suggests the flux that exists between knowing that the computer performs only *its* commands and undertaking the human work of programming the source instructions. The chunk of code will always return the call—until it doesn't and becomes the glitch, the bug. The tester-turned-programmer, who now sees how the function might fail, cannot see her own functionality failing; she misses the glitches in her everyday routine. The returned calls of the code are rendered poignant by the programmer's phone calls left *un*returned. Berta's engagement with the machine resembles the engagements of other programmers and hackers described throughout this book: Lisbeth Salander, Mark Zuckerberg, Mark Amerika, Jonathan Lethem. Their actions, practices, and relationships all occupy digital time: the presentification and enduring ephemeral of digital media. In the persistent present of digital techno-time, the past is not left behind and the future is never fully realized; the present is a rote command to refresh, banally, to recur. And yet, because Berta's body does not return her social calls, the human body becomes a glitch in the emerging social fabric, a difference between digital and other kinds of social script.

Describing the development of software as function and industry over the last few decades, Wendy Hui Kyong Chun has argued, "Higher-level programming languages, unlike assembly language, explode one's instructions and enable one to forget the machine."[4] Here Chun references the way in which today's programming is not an act of working on the machine, or with the machine, as it has historically been. Working in higher-level programming languages is writing code that is parsed and executed by other assembly and object code. Programming today requires a programmer to forget the machine and to communicate with other (and others') code. This historical trajectory of working with code is a useful metaphor for the distance between *The Bug* and Dave Eggers's 2013 novel *The Circle*. While both novels are set in software companies, the earlier novel is about the work of programming and the later novel about the work of unseeing the program. While one references the obfuscatory language of code and the physical and intellectual labor of programmers, the other juxtaposes a rhetoric of transparency with the immaterial labor of user-consumers—the latter condition enabled, in part, by higher-level programming effacing the machine.

In relation to the digital banal, both novels are interested in the everyday ubiquity of digital media, which simultaneously effaces the deeply embedded ways that the computational affects daily life. *The Bug* is the story of programmers who are so far involved with the system that they forget where the human ends and the machine starts. In the words of Ullman's memoir, the characters of *The Bug* just want to get "closer to the machine."[5] The potential of this radical mediational future that *The Bug* is oriented toward is alarmingly curtailed in *The Circle*. In *The Circle* the condition of being closer to the machine is generalized to the point of near invisibility. The program/system is a way of life, but it is also the place of life; the protagonist of *The Circle* actually lives inside the company, in a dorm on campus. Not just close to the machine, but living in it, there is no life that is not work. Both texts continue previous chapters' interest in how new ways of working and being are reified into expressions of freedom under the logic of sharing. In this chapter I explore this situation in relation to the appearance of time and work in both novels, and with reference to Richard Barbrook and Andy Cameron's critique of cyber-utopianism, "The Californian Ideology." In that 1995 essay, and in Barbrook's return to it twenty years later, we can locate the ambivalence that is the structuring logic of both Ullman's and Eggers's software imaginaries.

WAITING IN TELLIGENTSIA

Although it is framed within a story set in the early 2000s, most of the action in *The Bug* takes place in 1984: the narrative is of the daily grind of writing code for a still-nascent Graphical User Interface (GUI) and the emergence of corporate programming culture. *The Bug* is the story of two employees of the fictional software company Telligentsia: Roberta (Berta) Walton, an exiled academic with a PhD in Philosophy, working in quality assurance (testing for bugs), and Ethan Levin, a programmer who trained in front-end programming and is employed to write intermediary code for the mouse and GUI of Telligentsia's new product.[6] The novel begins in the early 2000s as Berta is waiting to have her passport checked at San Francisco airport. Berta reminisces about her time at Telligentsia and her work with Ethan, and this reminiscence is the main narrative of the novel. The novel is written in the third person and implies an omniscient narrator, but it begins and ends with Berta's point of view. During the mid-1980s Berta and Ethan were drawn together at Telligentsia after Berta identified a bug, UI-1017, in one of Ethan's programs. The bug proves near impossible to resolve. As Ethan's personal and professional lives unravel, he imagines that the bug is not just a glitch in software but that its power is out in the world: he and his colleagues nickname the bug the Jester. While Berta learns to program and works toward resolving the bug (and her own personal troubles), Ethan is utterly derailed by the bug. He commits suicide. In that action his life *is* the program: "He should go to hell. Yes, now he knew what he had to do. . . . Go to hell. Goto. Ha! Unconditional. Jump."[7] In *The Bug* programming is a process and a lived experience, a way of thinking and a mode of being.

At the airport Berta waits for an immigration agent to check her passport. The scene begins with Berta waiting for the response of another human, but the prose quickly turns its attention to the nonhuman agent that both the airport staff and Berta are technically waiting for—the computer program validating her passport data. "And so we waited. Ticktock, blink-blink, thirty seconds stretched themselves out one by one, a hole in human experience."[8] Waiting is figured as a pause in human-time. The computer "has filled our lives with little wait states like this one, . . . little slices of time in which you can't do anything at all, . . . the sort of unoccupied little slices of time no decent computer operating system would tolerate for itself."[9] Berta, perhaps because she is so close to the machine, refuses to wait absentmindedly. She worries at the pause until the root of the wait is revealed: the immigration agent is using a program that she herself worked on at Telligentsia years ago. Given the novel's year of publication, perhaps we can draw from this airport scene an anxiety that marks the emerging historical environment of the United States at the time. For many literary histories of contemporary US literature and culture, 9/11 figures as a turning point, but for Ullman the affective root of the airport scene—albeit a scene occupied by a wealthy, white US citizen—is not 2001 but 1986, when Telligentsia was "going to 'revolutionize' international arrivals with [its] database."[10] From the *then* of the 1980s—which presses on the present *now* of the airport—the computer revolution spread "like a virus to the world: human beings everywhere learning to suspend themselves."[11] Before Berta is recalled to herself and confirmed as present, she remembers Ethan: "Through the time tunnel of the long pause came his name. Ethan Levin."[12] Eventually—really only thirty seconds later—the immigration agent calls her back, "Welcome home, Ms. Walton." But the narrative never fully returns, and a few paragraphs later the story proper begins: "March 5, 1984, a day full of error."[13] The waiting induced by the program is also a production of a present that will not resolve. The pause in the present becomes the condition for the recounting of memory: narrative analepsis. Berta's "time tunnel of the long pause" is another way of marking digital time: the presentification of the what-will-have-been of the programmed future.

The Telligentsia database is the program of the past enacting the future it has enabled. The immigration agent embodies the wait as presentification rather than as presence. Standing, waiting for the computer to let him know if Berta is okay, his posture has adapted to computer time: "A certain suspension of himself; an unattractive slackness in his body, his mouth; a gone-to-nowhere look in his already vague eyes."[14] The agent's slackness, nowhereness, nothingness, is witnessed by Berta as a disturbance in the present rather than an event in the present. The agent disavows the expectation to look lively and appear as present; instead, the power to recognize presence is deferred to the computer. In other words, the airport scene narrates a mediational present whereby the human characters experience a situation through its computational qualities, occupying a present that will not resolve, as the past is never left behind and the future is never fully realized. The novel never returns to the airport scene, but neither does it ever leave this scene: the Telligentsia-future is, to borrow Lauren Berlant's phrase, the "stretched-out now" of the novel's narrative.[15] Right at the end of the novel, after Berta has worked out the error that is causing UI-1017—when it is too late to keep Ethan alive—she comes to terms with the fact that the machine's time is not only not human time, but it does not even have purchase on such a time: "The machine seemed to understand time and space, but it didn't, not as we do. . . . The notion of the 'moment' itself is the illusion."[16] The stretch of time in *The Bug* is so much recursion: a bug (the lag programmed into the immigration database) brings back a bug (UI-1017/Jester), which brings back a bug ("the ancient mystery of time").[17] The reoccurring unknown allows for the characters' withdrawal from life, but in the end the text pushes back on this, and Berta announces the newly emerging conditions of the present: "Between the blinks of the machine's shuttered eye—going on without pause or cease; simulated, imagined, but still not caught—was life."[18]

Roberta and Ethan's programming graphically breaks out of the narrative; it needs to be seen to be processed: "`if ( (coord->row >= region->startrow).`"[19] The novel materially instantiates the complex intelligibility of its own critical investments—a concern made clear in the pun-come-workplace, Telligentsia. Software conflates an event with a written command, shifting the word "program" from a verb to a noun.[20] Code can be executable: a programmer inputs an instruction, which is then relayed across layers of other code, and if all the clauses are in agreement, there is action—the code runs. Once executed, the code is a noun, the thing that has happened. To program (with code) is a verb, but a program is also the name of the executable, and of the larger system. In Ullman's writing we witness the interplay between "program" as verb and noun: sometimes human action, and sometimes machine process; "program" is also the name of Berta's object of study, the thing that Ethan is making, and eventually, the Jester. The naming of the Jester resides at the fault line of programming between verb and noun. The Jester is a category between software as a language that "*wants* to be overlooked" and software as unlike language—as source code *and* as executable code.[21]

The figure of the jester has always been one representing the domestication of play: the jester makes nonnormative or risqué behavior legible within normative social structures. The performance of the Jester works because difference is amplified rather than suppressed. In the cultural imaginary the transgressive performance of the jester is associated with the ability to speak truth to power; jesters and tricksters are characterized as "provocateurs and saboteurs who dismantle convention while occupying a liminal zone."[22] In the context of the novel, the naming of the bug is crucial in affectively apprehending its difference. When Berta and Ethan are working on the bug, Berta—ever the philosophy graduate who researched linguistics—cannot let go of the structural indeterminacy of the language they must use: "malloc" (that is, "allocate memory"). "Can't you tell just by the sound of it, she'd said, that no good can possibly come from something called *malloc*?"[23] And Ethan, repeating Berta, intones: "*Malloc, Moloch, malocchio.* . . . Malloc. Malice. Malaise. Malign. Malinger. Mala suerte. Malkin. Malcontent. Malevolent."[24] The naming of UI-1017 is a deconstruction of various binaries that are effaced in the execution of code: programmer/program, human/machine, inanimate/animate. The Jester is a figure that stands in for the complexity of the program.

FROM ASPHALT TO SOFT GREEN HILLS

Early desktop personal computing was a culture of tinkerers; you had to program the machine to get it to do stuff. Today's personal computing is one of black boxes: devices are conduits, not meant to be unpacked by the user. The differences between *The Bug*'s and *The Circle*'s representations of software are an effect of the digital banal, the way the digital has become unremarkable. The novels reflect and produce their present cultural conditions, which in one moment reify the computational, and in another demand seamless integration. The indeterminacy set up in *The Bug* becomes the ambivalence about knowledge that marks *The Circle*. The historical shift—from worrying at complexity to worrying about complexity—that these two novels might mark is figured through the relation that the characters of each novel have to the program. It is worth comparing the scenes where Berta and the protagonist of *The Circle*, Mae Holland, arrive at Telligentsia and the Circle campus, respectively, in order to consider what kind of programmed subjects are called into being.

> The parking lot at Telligentsia, the wasted feeling of having driven through traffic to arrive nowhere: a lake of asphalt in Fremont, California. The workstation in a cubicle. The morning begun not with hello but with a system prompt. Everyone's day begins like that now, but on that morning of March 5, 1984, only programmers and testers lived that way. . . . In 1984, it was still possible to find it strange, and hate it: the monitor that showed me my face in its blank glass stare, the system that beeped at me when I mistyped my password, the machine whine that rose up from everywhere, like being sealed in a roomful of mosquitoes.[25]
>
> My God, Mae thought. It's heaven. The campus was vast and rambling, wild with Pacific color. . . . The walkway wound around lemon and orange trees and its quiet red cobblestones were replaced, occasionally, by titles with imploring messages of inspiration. "Dream" . . . "Participate."[26]
>
> [Mae] entered an elevator of glass, tinted faintly orange. Lights flickered on and Mae saw her name appear on the walls, along with her high school yearbook photo. WELCOME MAE HOLLAND.[27]

The arrival scene in *The Bug* is the day full of error, the day Berta finds UI-1017. The scene at the Circle is Mae's first day of work after she has left her old job at a public utility company that was housed in "a tragic block of cement with narrow vertical slits for windows."[28] In between the two scenes, software has become ideology. In *The Bug* it is through Berta's recollection that Ullman attends to the strangeness of new media life. Because of the retrospective point of view, Berta's accounting for her daily life is also always an account of the emerging conditions of life *after* new media. Ullman explicitly calls this out—"everyone's day begins like that now"—but she deliberately unsettles the expectedness of this condition by introducing the idea that being recognized by a computer is strange. More implicitly, we find some quality redolent of our interaction with screens now: smartphones that materially privilege the portrait as a mode of capture, platforms that are always asking us who's in the picture. When Berta sits down in front of her monitor, her own face stares back at her *as* a monitor—its blank glass stare is *her* blank glass stare. This reflection is not so much before mine as *with* mine when I look at my smartphone screen, which is camera, compact mirror, and interface.

Any blankness is quashed in the elevator at the Circle campus by a wall-sized projection of Mae, a photo that she hasn't seen in years; she "had been happy for its absence."[29] Instead of a surface reflecting the present, the hailing of the user by the machine is archival. Everything about the campus—from the garden to the naming of each area after a historical era, to the user you are becoming—is designed to make all that is new appear not new, appear familiar. When newness does surface in the narrative, it is explicitly as a better present. Annie (Mae's best friend, who is senior staff at the Circle) plays a joke on Mae on her first day by decking out her workspace *exactly* like her old office cubicle at the public utilities company: "grey and small and lined with a material like synthetic linen."[30] But it's ok because it is a joke! The future doesn't look like this! As Annie explains, the setup took her ages to find online, "We honestly had nothing on the entire campus ugly and old enough."[31] Rather than argue that *The Circle* dates *The Bug*, I suggest that both occupy an open present moment defined by the mediational conditions of the digital banal. *The Bug* looks back from the early twenty-first century at the emergence of everyday personal computing and renders this moment to be source after the fact. Despite the affective novelty of new rote procedures and protocols depicted in that novel, its future is programmed. The technological determinism and digital-utopianism that characterize Mae's life in *The Circle* are made tenable through the effacement of the affective strangeness that such shifts in media infrastructure manifest; the effacement is modulated by the historical as parody.

The open present of both novels is also the becoming historical event of Silicon Valley. Late twentieth-century digital cultures emerge from the two-pronged instantiation of sanctioned knowledge and counterculture experimentation in the San Francisco Bay area. Slacker-turned-cyber manifestos expounded by magazines such as *Wired*, *Mondo 2000*, and *Future Sex* shared a geographic proximity to Silicon Valley. Alternative lifestyles, corporate product development, and science and technology research at Stanford University (often funded by the US military) put into play a peculiarly localized ethos of the potential future of digital technologies that underwrites many of our contemporary encounters with that technology.[32] The proximity of these various cultural, economic, and academic concerns defined an idea of the digital—and specifically of online environments—as that which could be a fully immersive virtual reality; and as that which would be a de facto *better* reality. In deference to the lure of the new, early cyber studies pivoted on the "Internet-as-frontier" metaphor.[33]

The history of personal computing and home digital entertainment is full of promises of effacement. While such future imaginaries were popular, the cyber-utopianism that surrounded digital culture studies at the end of the twentieth century has been critiqued for as long as it has been preached. In the 1995 essay "The Californian Ideology," Richard Barbook and Andy Cameron tell the story of what will have been the digital banal. The essay was first written and published in response to the unfettered cyber-utopianism of media platforms such as *Wired* magazine. Caroline Bassett has written that *Wired* magazine's role in cyberculture was "boosterish": "As an early edition of *Wired* magazine put it, computer technology was bringing about a 'peaceful, inevitable revolution.'"[34] Looking back twenty years later, we can consider how Barbrook and Cameron's intervention articulates the conditions for what I term the digital banal: the computational of today was a set of structural and affective relations and knowledge paradigms that were emerging in California and were reified into newness as inevitably technological progress. Barbrook and Cameron observe the status quo that has come to pass: the "digital future will be a hybrid of state intervention, capitalist entrepreneurship and d.i.y. culture."[35] Like Ullman's writing, "The Californian Ideology" is a working out of ambivalence. The ideology that Barbrook and Cameron identify may appear to be unchecked enthusiasm, but it is paradoxical in nature: "A new faith has emerged from a bizarre fusion of the cultural bohemianism of San Francisco with the hi-tech industries of Silicon Valley."[36] This new faith is politically ambivalent about the future—about the social and environmental impact of the virtual/plastic future—even as it proselytizes that the new future will save us from the worst excesses of humanity. The "amalgamation of opposites" represented by new media corporations and new technological cooperation was "achieved through a profound faith in the emancipatory potential of the new information technologies."[37]

Citing "The Californian Ideology" is a way to once again agitate the tension between the historical continuities of living with technology in general and with digital media in everyday life now. There is a relationship between what Barbrook and Cameron describe as the burgeoning "virtual class," who comprise "skilled workers ... tied by the terms of their contracts," for whom "work itself [is] the main route to self-fulfillment," and Jennifer Chan's description of the precariousness of cultural production in a postdigital economy, but they are not the same working life. The movement from "The Californian Ideology" to the exploitative limits of creative work today is not inevitable. As Richard Barbrook argues in an anniversary reprint of "The Californian Ideology," we need to attend to the computational as an unresolved present. Ambivalence means we may always be coming into something else: "Computer-mediated-communications isn't inherently neoliberal in its social implementation."[38] Both *The Bug* and *The Circle* demonstrate this openness of time, if not of political agency. Published ten years apart—set even further apart, in the recent past and near future respectively—the novels speak to each other's historical moments. Together they occupy a stretched-out now. The political ambivalence of programmers Roberta and Ethan in *The Bug* is substituted for the naïveté of customer service operator Mae Holland in *The Circle*; the programs that they all work on/in go from being an open process to a black box. This situation is not so much a change—a before of open systems and knowledgeable users and an after of closed boxes and lemming-like producer/consumers—as it is an abstraction. While Ullman and many others from the 1980s and '90s were vocal about the socio-environmental impact of new media, more often "the rhetoric of peer-to-peer informationalism ... actively obscure[d] the material and technical infrastructures on which both the Internet and the lives of the digital generation depend."[39] The ambivalence that marks our lives *after* new media—the banal recursion in place of the novel encounter—is a trace of this paradoxical abstraction of the digital technic.

The rhetoric of new digital technology in the 1980s and '90s proffered a virtual utopia, "a more natural, more intimate state of being," as it effaced the new conditions that such virtuality depended on and produced.[40] As Fred Turner has argued, writers such as Kevin Kelly, Esther Dyson, and John Perry Barlow, who were all associated with emergent digital technologies in the 1980s and '90s, "deprived their many readers of a language with which to think about the complex ways in which embodiment shapes all of human life ... and about the effects that digital technologies and the network mode of production might have on life and its essential infrastructures."[41] In *The Bug*, Berta's outsider status grants the reader access to a critical take on the new media horizon. When Berta learns to program, the reader learns about programming. *The Bug* is written at the limits of programming as power and knowledge. It also tips over the edge of the human-computer interface and drops into the machine realm, where procedures are executed. Ethan's suicide is an encounter with the limits of what we can't really see of computation—the space in between the location of each new action. The "here" of Ethan's program is not habitable for the human programmer. This limit exposes the limit of knowledge of code that bothers Wendy Chun and gives us the kind of openness toward the future that Barbrook redeems as he turns back to his own earlier writing: unresolved new complexities. The programmers in Ullman's and Eggers's novels are all subjects of and subject to software. Their sovereignty is an aspect of thinking with code, and it is contested regularly by representations of code that appear as illegible or untenable or that disappear from the surface of the text altogether. In this way the texts embody the material complexity of digital media. A condition of the open present is unresolved complexity. In *The Bug*, and as I will go on to suggest in *The Circle*, the ambivalence of the digital banal and the attention to surfaces effaced by the mediational condition of software are ways of marking the presence of complexity.

RED BOXES IN BLACK BOXES

In our black-box society the relations we live by are algorithmically determined. In our mediated daily lives, "the values and prerogatives that the encoded rules enact are hidden within black boxes."[42] Barbrook and Cameron imply this in "The Californian Ideology." In black-box culture private corporations run complex proprietary algorithms, which a very small number of people understand and which are all but illegible in plain English (and which, in fact, are only source after the fact). The preconditions for this culture are the attitudes and praxes of hobbyists and tinkerers who gifted their labor and their creativity to each other in the guise of shareware.[43] The paradoxical legacy that informs our contemporary moment is that open source is ironically the foundation for the black box of software today.⁴⁴ The gift of Roberta and Ethan's love for the machine is reciprocated each time they are called into presence by the machine: "Here you are, Ethan. . . . Here you are. Ethan. Here."⁴⁵ This reciprocity has imploded in *The Circle*: the good feeling that accompanies sharing has been incorporated into the program as the capital of new media systems. Today our devices return a simulation of the good feeling that accompanies giving, through recognition. This recognition is not good enough in *The Bug*, it cannot keep Ethan present, but in *The Circle*, being hailed by the program is a primary moment of affective identification. Paradoxically, again, openness is a reified affect, while being open is effectively prohibited.

The Circle begins when Mae gets a job at the Circle, a market-dominating technology company—a Google-Facebook hybrid. The company was founded by the "Three Wise Men": Ty Gospodinov, who is "the Circle's boy-wonder visionary," a reclusive programmer who wrote the Circle's source program, TruYou; Tom Stenton, "the world-striding CEO and self-described *Capitalist Prime*—he loved the Transformers"; and Eamon Bailey, the public face of the company, who is "twinkly-eyed, happy and earnest."⁴⁶ TruYou is a program that links all online activity to a verified real-name account.⁴⁷ Although Ty is a programmer/hacker, his work in developing TruYou is rarely discussed as coding; rather, he is an "inventor," a "genius," who "devised the initial system."⁴⁸ *The Circle* is not interested in knowing how the program works; it is invested in thinking about how such a program might operate in the world. As such, the novel both critiques and performs the control logic of today: it is an interface that presents a seamless ideology by effacing material work. When Mae joins the Circle as an employee in Customer Experience, the reader follows her transformation from excited user to zealous convert. The reader is invited to situate Mae's embodiment of the Californian ideology as hyperbolic and "terrifying."⁴⁹ The novel offers a shrill satirical imaginary rendering of the real-name future we already inhabit, but it is an ambivalent book that conforms to the digital banal. In *The Circle* digital media is reified as well-meaning but youthful wrongheadedness, effacing the potential affective novelty of the mediational condition by presenting it as an unwanted mode of alienation. Mae marks the relationship between the virtual class, as Barbrook and Cameron describe it—a deregulated highly skilled corporate class—and the precarious condition of cultural production as interpersonal communication that constitutes aspects of service work today. For Eggers, then, the Californian ideology remains unresolved.

As an unskilled, newly employed service worker at the Circle, Mae understands the product of the company she works for only insofar as she understands the way it engenders social relations and individual being. Mae does not need or want knowledge of the material systems that she serves and that serve her. Mae's role is to participate in, appease, and develop relationships inside and outside the company. Her cloying naïveté is performative: Eggers's narrative can only rarely disclose its fear of a company that preaches absolute transparency and an end to privacy because Mae is silent witness to the logic of software ideology. Despite the problematic whimsicality of both Mae and the working environment in *The Circle*, we can read in this novel something of a contemporary culture of computation—even if what we read is the project of effacement. Similar to *How Should a Person Be?*, *The Circle* exemplifies the way the digital banal is a condition of nondisturbance, or flatness. The radical ways in which the character of Mae renegotiates her relationship with her own body are first displaced and then effaced across the novel. At first this takes place in the narrative as a series of incidents in which Mae reorients her sense of self in line with the demand to be social on campus and the command of the program to be social. We also witness the ineluctable strangeness of Mae's new media condition reified as a kind of pathology— a sort of sexualized fascination with the self so perverse that it almost (*almost*) takes over Mae's desire for sex with other humans.

In *The Interface Effect* Galloway suggests, "Whenever a body speaks, it always already speaks as a body codified with an affective identity (gendered, ethnically typed, and so on)."[50] And in addition, given the "postfordist colonization of affect and the concomitant valorization of affective difference, a body has no choice but to speak. A body speaks whether it wants to or not."[51] *The Circle* explores such a life to the extent that it satirizes affective identity politics by playing on the way software can make a body speak, whether it wants to or not. Early on in her time at the Circle, Mae is invited to attend a Portugal-themed brunch. She is not aware that she was invited, does not attend, and as a result upsets Alistair, her coworker who organized the event. Because the Circle is a social media company, Mae's lack of engagement and lack of awareness is treated as an employment issue and is dealt with by way of a meeting with her boss. Reflecting on the episode with Annie, Mae's friend who holds a senior post at the Circle, Mae can't understand why she was even invited in the first place; as far as she is aware, she has not professed a love of Portugal. Annie asks Mae if she has ever been to Portugal and whether she took photos, to which Mae answers yes; she went to Lisbon years ago and took some photos. Annie explains:

> Then that's probably it. If they were on your laptop, now they are in the cloud, and the cloud gets scanned for information like that. You don't have to run around signing up for Portugal interest clubs or anything. When Alistair wanted to do his brunch, he probably just asked for a search of everyone on campus who had visited the country.[52]

These are the banal recursions of the cloud: the past as ever present; socializing as a command to be social; automated categorization of personality. More insidiously, here is a way that Mae speaks without agency; or rather, here is the way that the novelty of having a program be social for you obscures the novelty of being socially programmed/programmable.

The narrative of *The Circle* is propelled forward by Mae's giddiness at her new understanding of how she should be and Eggers's handling of his prose, which reflects the abstract, isolated, speeded-up time of the corporate tech industry. Whenever Mae can't sleep or can't concentrate on some issue at hand, she doesn't pause or wind down, but goes to her desk and puts in Customer Experience time, "knowing there she could be useful, and that there, her efforts would be appreciated, immediately and demonstrably."[53] Because the novel is not invested in the real-time labor of software as software, just in the real-time soft labor of Mae, there is little friction in its prose style, no gesture of alterity. Unlike the disruptive quality of lines of code that are incorporated in the body of *The Bug*, the management of Mae's body and time in *The Circle* speaks to Eggers's concerns about affective labor and the material conditions of everyday transparency, but does not render visible how this labor relates to the machinic labor of digital media. There are few opportunities to mark out the hybrid, multiplex nature of being-with digital media in addition to an ambient concern about being around digital media. Circle staff are "busy, just short of overworked."[54] Their downtime does not count as work, but it is accounted for via monitoring of participation. Mae is chided for her lack of participation in campus events:

> "Listen. It totally makes sense you'd want to spend time with your parents. They're your parents! . . . I'm just saying *we* like you a lot, too, and want to know you better. To that end, I wonder if you'd be willing to stay a few extra minutes, to talk to Josiah and Denise. . . . They'd love to just extend the conversation we're having, and go a bit deeper. Does that sound good?"
>
> "Sure. . . . I'm all yours."
>
> "Good. Good. I like to hear that. Here they are now."
>
> Mae turned to see Denise and Josiah, both waving, on the other side of Dan's glass door.
>
> "Mae, how are you?"[55]

In one line spoken by Mae's manager, Dan, the activity that begins the scene has shifted, moved on; there is no pause in action, or dialogue. The passage conveys a kind of claustrophobia. Despite the spacious grounds of the campus and the open-plan work practices, the Circle's planning of every move—its micromanaged politics of the individual—is repressive, propelling the narrative forward.

The affective novelty of the Circle is visible in the novel, but not in terms of Mae as a thinking, feeling subject. The affective novelty of the mediational condition is witnessed through Mae as a desiring subject. Problematically, this desiring female subject is, in the manner of bad stories about lively women, punished for her agency. By the end of the novel Mae is a zealous advocate for the Circle. She is utterly monstrous, and the reader is absolved of all responsibility to think about her as a complex subject. Mae needs those around her to "acknowledge the incredible power of the technology at [her] command. . . . She knew she couldn't give up until she had received some sense of . . . acquiescence."[56] As with *The Bug*, acquiescence is the cost of life. In *The Circle* Mae has three men with whom she is in various states of intimate relationship: Mercer (her ex-boyfriend and an anti-Circler who dies resisting the reach of the Circle—Mae's conversion is at the cost of Mercer), Francis (a total Circler), and Kalden (a mysterious man whom Mae meets at the Circle and who knows about the Circle, but whose skepticism about the Circle is unlike other concerns voiced in the novel). Sex is a problem both in and for the novel. One of the most horrifying images of life after privacy is a scene in which Mae accidentally live-streams her parents having sex; the primary feeling attached to this moment is shame. Likewise, Mae's own sexuality and sexual activity is often presented as unwanted or as troubling: Mae's "curves . . . brought the attention of men of myriad ages and motives"; if Mae were to get tipsy, "bad decisions would ensue."[57]

Of all Mae's relationships, the illicit meetings with Kalden are the most intense. Their encounters are both sexually and socially charged: Kalden's anonymity—Mae can't find his profile when she looks him up—is a departure from a program premised on verifying the TruYou. The second time they meet, Kalden leads Mae to a hidden underground cave. Kalden's access to this space suggests to Mae that he is someone important, but she has been warned by Annie to be wary of someone who can't be found on the program. In the cave,

> They entered a large room, about the size of a basketball court, dimly lit but for a dozen red spotlights trained on an enormous red metallic box, the size of a bus. Each side was smooth, polished, the whole thing surrounded by a network of gleaming silver pipes forming an elaborate grid around it.[58]

Mae does not know what she is looking at; Kalden tells her, "It's a storage unit." The metallic box is one of the Circle's servers, and this is one of the few moments in the novel where the material conditions of Mae's work are made visible to her. It is telling, then, that this is not an algorithm but rather the ultimate black box of our everyday digital lives: data storage.[59] Mae struggles to keep up with Kalden's basic explanation of the server. The server is, however, sexy, powerful, and Kalden, the master who partially reveals this power to Mae, is sexy by proxy. Mae "wanted to kiss Kalden again, and she took his face again, down to hers, and opened her mouth to his. . . . He hissed into her ear. 'Mae.' She couldn't form words. 'Mae,' he said again, as she fell apart all over him."[60] Mae is turned on by Kalden, but moreover by the proximity to electronic energy and digital might; in the words of Ullman, Mae is finally close to the machine.

A few pages later in the novel Mae is given another task for her job: she is one of the lucky few who will be answering CircleSurveys. Should Mae find herself with any downtime, she will be able to turn on CircleSurveys and help the Circle give much-valued feedback about various products to their clients. As part of this process Mae is fitted with a headset, which will notify her when a survey is waiting for her attention. The Circler who is installing her headset suggests various notification sounds—a chirp, or a tri-tone. Or there is a "random one that people sometimes choose.... Here it goes." Then, "Mae heard her own voice say her name, in something just above a whisper. It was very intimate and sent a strange swirling wind through her.... Mae was flushed, bewildered."[61] Mae's own voice whispering her name to herself is "seductive, thrilling."[62] The eroticism of hearing the machine speak her self back to herself writes over the eroticism of Kalden whispering her name to her; or, the intimacy of the moment with Kalden lends its affect to the computational moment. Here is the affective novelty of becoming-with digital media, embodied as Mae's intimacy with the Circle. Eventually Kalden is revealed to be Ty, the creator of TruYou, and by extension the Circle. Mae's desire for Kalden is a desire for Ty, who is the human agency of the nonhuman program. Being turned on by the Circle (hearing herself speak her name to herself), in lieu of a physical encounter with Kalden/Ty, is a recognition of the affective novelty of becoming-with digital media. However, that this relation appears embodied as unruly female behavior—Mae is tipsy with Kalden and she ignores Annie's warnings about anonymous men—classifies the strangeness as something not to be celebrated. As with the narrative cut that links Lisbeth Salander's rape to her attachment to her laptop and with Margaux's suspicion of Heti's new love, a recorder, so Mae offers a way for the user to recognize herself as everyday mediational subject, provided she is always already alarmed by her subjectification.

AMBIVALENCE

In *The Circle* the operation of the digital banal keeps novelty in check. New things happen, but in ways that obfuscate complexity. The novel satirizes Silicon Valley's obsession with simplicity: "Secrets Are Lies";

"Sharing Is Caring"; "Privacy Is Theft." Satire here does not make visible complexity; instead it ambivalently conjures a world in which knowledge is forsaken but knowing is all. The novel's distance from the material histories of software is emblematic of the digital banal, which by default discourages knowing software better, but which by way of effacement proclaims to offer us invisible tools to know each other better. Like Mae's discovery of the server, *The Circle* functions as a revelation of a black box rather than an encounter with what may be inside of one. This is a novel about the culture of software, which does not explicitly say anything about the culture of software. In this way it mimics precisely the contemporary condition of living with digital media; we live our lives with and through systems that are "difficult to 'know' in the traditional sense, due to the sheer scale and velocity of their complexity."[63]

The question of knowing how software works, and how the industry that sells it to us functions, links to key questions about the ethics of contemporary writing practices: how do you write originally in a saturated media culture; how do you write politically in an atomized entertainment culture? Dave Eggers's work has long been engaged in such questions, and *The Circle* is no exception.[64] When *The Circle* was published there were claims of plagiarism from the author Katherine Losse, whose memoir of her time working at Facebook, *The Boy Kings*, had been published the same year. Writing for *Gawker*, Nitasha Tiku suggests that while there are resonances between the two books, there are also significant differences.[65] Although Eggers's novel has been lauded, it is consistently naïve.[66] This is not bad writing, per se, but rather a posture of outsiderness that Eggers is keen to take credit for in interviews: "I've never visited any of the Internet companies that exist, and didn't interview anyone who works at any of these companies. I really wanted the Circle to be something else entirely."[67] At stake here is a more pervasive banal issue: Eggers's novel, supported by a prestigious literary publisher and the literary media, is touted as *the* statement on a topic. As Katherine Losse explains, "To be treated like you can't represent a culture, you can only represent yourself is really disturbing—to have a man have a female character and then take it as the representation of the whole culture."[68]

What concerns Losse most particularly is that by not taking her claims of plagiarism seriously, Eggers performs again the sexism of the industry he lampoons in *The Circle*. For Losse, "It's not just about this book. It's about the whole industry."[69] In the end, the proximity of Losse's and Eggers's work might have less to do with plagiarism and more to do with the Californian ideology. The paradoxical tenets of the new medial liberal control society are embedded in the culture of San Francisco, where Eggers and Losse have both lived and worked. Rebecca Solnit has called this the "monoculture" of San Francisco.[70] Losse is aware of this context, and her book is a memoir about a particular iteration of that monoculture. However, Eggers is unconcerned with the material and protocological instantiations of that culture. In *The Circle* we don't see any of the structural behaviors that define the tech industry. As Tiku writes, in *The Circle* there is no "privileging of the hacker/engineer over all 'non-technical' employees," no "frat-like cliques perpetuated by hiring white males from a certain background.... We don't see a den of programmers until the end of the book."[71] *The Circle*'s focus on Mae repeats, rather than critiques, the male gaze of social media; it makes Mae the nightmare-to-come of governance-by-Facebook in place of narrating the much-documented sexism of this industry, which continually exploits "the unpaid and underpaid labor of women."[72]

In *The Bug* and *The Circle* interest in knowledge and novelty is modulated by various modes of ambivalence. In *The Bug* Berta reflects from a position of substantial wealth, accumulated by way of knowledge of the industry, which distracts her from reflecting on what she knows about becoming-with digital media. Berta capitalizes on her knowledge but is only later able to articulate what she may have always known about the digital lives she was making. Despite *The Bug*'s critique of programming and code as material procedures, the overall novel is—in keeping with the Californian ideology—paradoxically both libertarian and liberal, and the efficacy of each cancels the other out. In *The Circle*, representing the general mediational condition of the contemporary—technology as life, Mae's becoming-with—is paradoxically an act of effacing the particularities of the culture that determines these conditions. Such paradoxical conditions mark the aesthetic mode of the digital banal. In both novels the digital banal is both dominant operation and critical mode because the structure of unfeeling, the *interesting* that marks where commitment should be, is always open to other interpretations; it operates ambivalently.

Citing Michael Warner's work on counter-publics, and Stuart Hall's on encoding and decoding, Christina T. Wolf argues, "Exposure to novelty is not only important for new knowledge acquisition, but can also be instrumental in shaping the self—'reading' or watching media involves active processes of interpretation and imagination, processes through which audiences or publics are created."[73] In both *The Bug* and *The Circle* the problem of ambivalence emanates from subjects defined by their exposure to, rather than comprehension of, novelty. In *The Circle* problems between staff are referred to as glitches, and the operations of software are exported to the labor of participation.[74] This is in lieu of these operations being subjective concerns in the narrative; rather, characters and their actions are of concern. If, in *The Circle*, software appears as character— but not as a character—then this chimes with other strategies of the digital banal discussed throughout this book. In much of the fiction discussed, the digital banal registers as thinking digitally and as uttering through metaphors that gloss technological infrastructure and software as common proxies of human experience. The digital banal is the common, recurring, rote ways in which digital technology is unseen in everyday life; the language of these novels is attuned to that condition and reifies it. In the next two chapters I will consider more explicitly how the digital banal hovers as a kind of feeling toward—and of—the contemporary moment. Reading fiction by Jonathan Lethem, Benjamin Percy, Danica Novgorodoff, Jennifer Egan, Gary Shteyngart, and Colson Whitehead, I argue that the digital banal is a mood or posture that delimits representations of digital media in everyday life.

5

REFRESH, UPDATE, WAIT, OR, LIVING WITH THE DIGITAL BANAL IN *CHRONIC CITY* AND *REFRESH REFRESH*

When Berta waits for the Telligentsia database to recognize her at the airport, she begins a reflection that carries the reader through the entirety of *The Bug*. Her wait-state is an unresolving present that occurs in digital time—the presentification of the computational meets the presentification of contemporary narrative modes. Berta's reflection is also a kind of distraction. Distraction is broadly understood to be an affectively distinct aspect of contemporary culture.[1] Distraction is a type of perception we associate with digital media—digital media as a set of objects and platforms that distract us from our real lives, or social interaction as something that we now do distractedly. Distraction implies that a subject is barely engaged. Such subjects are not fully attentive to the action of distraction or the act they are distracted from. Distraction is a way of modulating attention in terms of visibility. To be distracted is to be embroiled, to some degree, in a mode of effacement whereby attention is pulled in one direction, blocking or suppressing the viability of an alternative. Being distracted presumes "a strategy of disappearance or invisibility. Distraction allows a second event to take place behind or 'to the side of' the first one—it enables a close approach."[2]

Writing about distraction in the digital age, William Bogard argues that we must attend to the "material scene" of distraction and understand it as a scene of "proximate relations." Distraction is "a social-machinic assemblage, ... a machinery that generates differential rates of flow of matter and energy."³ Distraction, then, is not only mediational but is premised on the mediational encounter, or scene, as one of differential kinds of perception that are more or less visible. Distraction is not so much about moving attention from one path to another but about increasing attention in one direction and decreasing it in another. Boredom is a quality of perception that determines distraction. Describing the "generational shift toward hyper attention," which "can be understood as a shift in the mean toward the AD/HD end of the spectrum," N. Katherine Hayles argues that hyper-attentiveness is a mode whereby "normal stimulation is felt as boredom and relatively high levels of stimulation are necessary for [young people] to feel engaged and interested."[4] Despite the speed and hyper-lively quality of digital media—its mode of presentification—living with digital media is a condition of perceptual boredom. Distraction is a way to account for the pull to be stimulated, which is not only embodied in the human subject, but is an aspect of the socio-machinic assemblage of everyday life, which runs on boredom.[5] According to the logic of the digital banal, boredom itself is a kind of reification, appearing throughout culture as distraction, effacing the material conditions of digital media, which programmatically makes users in its own rote image. Of course, such boredom manifests most explicitly as a culture of banality: the taken for granted, barely noticeable presence of digital media in everyday life; the light touch of reciprocity that so often defines online social interactions; the lingua franca of GIF-able affect, and hallelujah emojis.

Distraction and boredom are related aspects of the digital banal. Taking these modes seriously as everyday experiences enables us to see not just the always-on-ness, but also the everywhere-ness of digital media. In this chapter I will be discussing the representation of boredom and distraction in Jonathan Lethem's 2010 novel *Chronic City* and Danica Novgorodoff's 2009 graphic novel *Refresh Refresh*.[6] In both these texts the characters' encounters with digital media are simultaneously delineated by screens and complexly *everywhere*. I am particularly interested in the way that everywhere-ness is drawn in these novels partly as a kind of malaise. In other words, in these novels we know that the digital is not a distinct realm, a cyberspace, because the anticipation of digital encounters is apprehended as atmosphere rather than location.[7] In different ways both texts are interested in the idea of cyberspace, but it is not a tenable concept in either text. So far, this book has discussed texts in which the mediational condition is a given. But in *Chronic City* and *Refresh Refresh* the blurring of online/offline, real/virtual lives is a visible concern in scenes of characters sitting in front of screens, watching and waiting for something to happen. Throughout I argue that, although this act of waiting posits a differential mode between the everyday and digital media, neither novel can hold on to that difference; the online activity being anticipated is also the everyday reality at stake.

Both texts are set in a roughly contemporary moment—*Refresh Refresh* in the early years of the 2003 invasion of Iraq by US and UK forces and *Chronic City* sometime shortly after the financial crash of 2008. Both novels imagine outmoded media: in *Refresh Refresh*, rural American, lower-income families have old-fashioned box-set TVs and chunky laptops (no light-as-air tech here); in *Chronic City*, despite the relative wealth and connectivity of the main characters in New York City, a dial-up modem and cathode ray tube monitor are the primary modes of Internet access. The image of slower, more visible digital media means that the characters' boredom and distraction resonates with readers' potential boredom and distraction as they are pulled away from the presentification of contemporary digital media toward scenes of becoming socio-machinic assemblage in a long-form narrative. For Jonathan Lethem this is an explicit tactic: "I gave my characters a dial-up modem, and burdened them with explicit retro-stupidity on the whole matter of the Internet. Once they were firmly 'dated,' I could advance them heedlessly into the 'future' that's already everyone's taken-for-granted past."[8] In *Chronic City* and *Refresh Refresh* we read the digital banal as a kind of slowed-down present moment; the mode of waiting becomes a way of attending to the digital machinations of everyday life.

WAITING

Waiting is an affectively significant aspect of contemporary culture. Digital media provides us with the appearance of seamless immediacy, and in many respects life is getting faster.[9] Waiting doesn't disappear, but instead takes on new sociocultural freight. In the always-on culture of today, we can send messages across the globe immediately, but we are still going to have to wait for a response if the person at the other end is otherwise occupied. The possibility of immediacy reframes the act of waiting as a kind of inefficiency, and so we are all drawn into the cycle of being always available. At a more micro level, what is often effaced from discussions of speed in the digital age is that computation itself takes time. As with Berta's airport wait, or with Lisbeth Salander waiting for her search to turn up results, computation itself is a durational process: however much faster the machine is this year from last year, it still takes time. The expectation of immediacy produces new kinds of impatience so that any wait at all for computation feels like an unnecessary hassle. This affective mode of anticipation is a novel feeling of becoming-with digital media. In chapter 1 "refreshing" was discussed as an aspect of time under the conditions of the digital banal: the production of an unresolving mediational present defined by the function of code as source after the fact—perpetually an event that is becoming. *Chronic City* and *Refresh Refresh* return us to this scene and to the subject clicking on "Refresh," to specific agents embodied in particular places, apprehending distinct atmospheres, anticipating mediational experience.

Chronic City tells the story of a parallel contemporary New York City. It follows a groups of characters who are variously connected to the cultural and governing elite of the city as they negotiate new conditions of precarity: a "gray fog" in downtown Manhattan is both a financial and social catastrophe; farther north, rapid gentrification threatens the stability of the characters' neighborhoods, working lives, and ability to make sense of the world around them via any narrative other than conspiracy. The novel is sprawling in a literal kind of sense; there are lots of loose threads, connections, and plot points that are scattered across a post-9/11 Manhattan cityscape. As Susan Kollin has described it, *Chronic City* highlights "the challenges posed by globalization, hyper-capitalism, digital labor, and widespread ecological decline," and it explores "the obstacles preventing the characters from developing deep connections with each other and with what David Abram calls 'the more-than-human world.'"[10] *Chronic City* is also a novel about a group of friends, mostly men, who are "chronically under-employed" (some by choice, others not) and who sit around, get stoned, chat about film, art, and conspiracy theories, and look up stuff on the Internet.[11] The novel imbibes the banal as narrative method.

Refresh Refresh is a graphic novel adaptation of a short story by Benjamin Percy.[12] Percy's story is set in the small desert town of Tumalo, Oregon, where three teenage boys, Josh, Cody, and Gordon, anxiously await news of their fathers, soldiers lately posted to Iraq. The boys fight and drink and act out roles of masculinity in a space suddenly bereft of men. The "refresh, refresh" of the title is the song of the boys at their computers, clicking "Refresh" on the web pages of their e-mail accounts, hoping the next reload will bring new messages, e-mails from their missing dads: "Sometimes, on the computer, I would hit refresh, refresh, *refresh*, hoping. In October I received an email that read: 'Hi Josh. I'm OK. Don't worry. Do your homework. Love, Dad.' I printed it up and hung it on my door with a piece of Scotch tape."[13] The scene of the boys at their screens is not a central part of the story, occurring only twice and mostly dwarfed by the physical, often-violent encounters that are the main subject of the narrative. And yet, the phrase "Refresh Refresh" is the title. The image of the boys clicking "Refresh"—"We could only cross our fingers and wish on stars and hit refresh, *refresh*, hoping they would return to us"—is drawn out for the reader through the title.[14] It is de facto emblematic, made to mean something in a story that might otherwise privilege its representation of the physical social encounter over the more prosaic figure of the household computer and the body who sits with it.

In *Chronic City*, embodiedness and embeddedness mean that the mundane is the narrative drive: characters are embedded in "the facts of their physical selves: eating and sleeping and shitting."[15] Former child star Chase Insteadman ambles through a celebrity Manhattan life until he meets Perkus Tooth. Perkus was once a music and film critic who had a sideline in pasting up countercultural broadsides, which are described in the novel as a cross between 1970s punk collages and 1990s adbusters. Chase and Perkus form a bond, get stoned, and unravel various power conspiracies at the heart of Manhattan governance. These conspiracies are simultaneously offline, online, and in outer space, and all of these locales are understood to be interconnected and overly mediated. In the novel there is a version of a platform—a bit like *Second Life*, but more explicitly gamed—called *Yet Another World*. Although this is an online game, the phrase "another world" could just as easily describe the ways that the rapidly changing Manhattan exists in a parallel dimension to the friends' activities in front of the computer monitor. Chase narrates:

> If anything epitomized Perkus's curious disadvantages, his failure to find traction in the effective world, it was the state of his computing. ... His lumpy Dell looked ten years old, Cro-Magnon in computer years. He connected by his phone line, which he transferred by hand from his living-room Slimline. ... Watching that Dell painstakingly assemble a page view, images smoothed pixel by pixel, was agony.[16]

Perkus lives in a world of smartphones and Wi-Fi; waiting is an anachronism. The slowness of life online—of getting online—in Perkus's apartment is something the other characters not only come to terms with but begin to value.

In Novgorodoff's graphic novel the phrase "refresh, refresh" turns into panels depicting laptops: Josh, Cody, and Gordon are depicted in front of laptop screens, lit by the backlight of their machines. These panels are always in dialogue with those around them. As in the story, the encounter with e-mail is framed by its everyday-ness, but in the graphic novel the strength of the visual relationships between panels more emphatically articulates this—we observe digital media coming into view. The structure of the graphic novel is broken into small chapters. The book begins by introducing the setting and depicting the families sending their fathers off to war. The next three chapters describe the home lives of the three boys as they are left. The first sequence depicts Josh, who is left to live with his grandfather: they eat a TV dinner and watch the news; streams of speech emanate from the TV describing the situation in Iraq. Josh gets up to get some ice cream; on his way back, he passes his laptop. His web page is open to a Yahoo! e-mail account, and he has no messages. Novgorodoff shows the phrase, "refresh, refresh," not through those words but by drawing a pointer arrow hovering over the "Refresh" button, with two sound bubbles breaking the image: "click," "click." The sequence of panels shows Josh giving his grandfather the ice cream then returning to the laptop (see figure 5.1). He clicks again, and he has "1 unread message" from his dad (see figure 5.2). The scene places the laptop as fully immersed in the context of a domestic tableau; it is a visual, touchable, audible object. The casing of the laptop is drawn ambiguously; it is identifiable as a lap-

FIGURE 5.1 Clicking on "Refresh." *Refresh Refresh*, written by Danica Novgorodoff and colored by Hilary Sycamore, with Benjamin Percy and James Ponsoldt (New York: First Second, 2009), 10. Reprinted by permission of Roaring Brook Press, a division of Holtzbrinck Publishing Holdings LP, all rights reserved.

top, but there are no particular details. The monitor is drawn displaying windows, and it is possible to discern the layout as that of an Apple operating system; the e-mail provider is Yahoo! Novgorodoff includes such logos and windows to introduce the various corporate and named frames that mediate our encounters with digital media.

In moments of waiting for pixels to load and e-mails to arrive, there is time to notice the material medium. Anticipation—which also registers as impatience, boredom at having to wait—is a mode of distraction whereby the narrative perspective turns its attention to something less pressing. In scenes that flip the digital banal, the computer is brought to our attention rather than effaced from it. Paradoxically, this attention is

FIGURE 5.2 One new message. *Refresh Refresh*, written by Danica Novgorodoff and colored by Hilary Sycamore, with Benjamin Percy and James Ponsoldt (New York: First Second, 2009), 10. Reprinted by permission of Roaring Brook Press, a division of Holtzbrinck Publishing Holdings LP, all rights reserved.

bestowed as a banal kind of observation rather than an urgent intervention. The details, which Novgorodoff draws and Chase narrates, are in tension with the thing-ness of the machines: they look just like any laptop or desktop, but always also visible are the kinds of platforms they are, the corporate and technical frames of this everyday experience of being in mediation. The digital banal is a way to apprehend the processes of effacement that obscure and block the mediational conditions of contemporary life from view. Waiting for the computer in *Chronic City* and *Refresh Refresh* affords us the opportunity to consider the digital with reference to a temporarily discrete object: to bring into view computation as an everyday thing.[17]

BIDING AND BIDDING

When Josh receives an e-mail from his dad, the object of the computer recedes; the interface is foregrounded. Here the interface is a temporary instance of mediation, a gathering of concerns, a witnessing of an everyday computational thing that connects with a reader's witnessing of the narrative. The figure of the laptop moves in and out of the panel frames in a way that keeps it in the corner of the reader's eye—it is always in the room, persistently present. The details of the screen are shown to a greater or lesser degree, depending on how present the laptop is in the narrative. There are various panels depicting laptops throughout the novel, and these seem connected with those depicting TVs, camcorders, jukeboxes, and arcade video games: they all necessitate the artist's consideration of what details are relevant. The reader is faced with the artistic decision: what is the matter of these technological objects, and is it enough to suggest the figure of their shapes, or is it important to also name them and show their processes, their interfaces?

In *Chronic City*, as with much of Jonathan Lethem's work, the fiction compulsively names real-world things, people, events, histories. The novel cites "Chet Baker, Myrna Loy, the Rolling Stones, *The Twilight Zone*, Molly Ringwald, and the 1980s teen sit-com *Square Pegs* alongside Gilles Deleuze and Félix Guattari, Mike Davis, Donna Haraway, J. G. Ballard, and Jean Baudrillard, and in the process enable[s] it all to make sense."[18] Importantly for thinking through the digital banal, one of the more prominent real-world artifacts that makes it in to the novel is eBay. In interview, Lethem has described eBay as a real-world reference that works to estrange the fiction from the reader. The characters are totally floored by their experiences with eBay, and something so often associated with the mundane in everyday life becomes an affective novelty in the text. In the words of Lethem, for Chase and Perkus, eBay "constitutes a mind-blowing excursion into cyberpunkery."[19] For hundreds of millions of users since its launch in 1995, eBay has, or does, constitute a daily online activity. More than a garage sale or auction house, eBay is a site in which the terms of value accorded to things and experiences are negotiated. It is a platform that has led the way in shaping the discourse of authenticated individual user identities, even as it asserts the corporate identity of the platform brand in everyday life.[20] While an unimaginable range of things is bought and sold on eBay, the common dynamic of interaction is trust: "Establishing a claim to authenticity is central; as a peer-to-peer value system, eBay relies on establishing trust through item descriptions and feedback options."[21] In *Chronic City* the object sought on eBay is a chaldron, a type of ceramic. Later in the novel the chaldron is revealed to be a virtual object—currency for the massive online role-playing game *Yet Another World*. When the reader first encounters a chaldron, it is a poster in an acupuncturist's office. The chaldron appears in various states, but as an eBay item, it conforms to the mode of the site, traversing the cult and the mundane, the rare and the common, the sublime and the banal.[22]

The scene in which Perkus introduces the other main characters to the chaldron can be read as an extended meditation on the digital banal; the elliptical state induced by the slow dial-up modem and weed is a narrative prop that enables the reader to witness mediation in process. The chapter opens with the arrival of Richard Abneg (a former leftist squatter and old friend of Perkus's, now aide to New York City mayor Arnheim) and Georgina Hawkmanaji (Richard's girlfriend, a Turkish heiress) at Perkus's apartment. The meeting is really an intervention, organized by Chase, who is concerned about Perkus's increasing obsession with chaldrons; the others have yet to encounter one. After smoking cannabis and listening to drone music, Perkus decides the group is ready to see the chaldron. The characters are described as if negotiating some kind of threshold, one that marks the border between consciousness and other (drug-induced) heightened state: "The four of us seemed to throb there where we'd gathered in Perkus's dim lair, . . . the four of us like the chambers of a collective beating heart, pulsing with expectancy."[23] Perkus opens the eBay page featuring the chaldron, and eventually it materializes: "the finished image of a chaldron, all the pixels now smoothed around the edges."[24] Chase narrates: "The glowing peach-colored chaldron smashed all available frames or contexts, gently burning itself through our retinas to hover in our collective mind's eye, a beholding that transcended optics."[25] Thresholds are traversed as the group does not simply see the screen, but collectively beholds the object; the image is not burned *onto* their retinas but *through* them. In this description, the representation of a digital object is also a description of the deceptive luminosity of the screen and the altered state of the group.

It suggests that the figure of the chaldron can be held in real space, as a thing that has "transcended optics." This description of the first moment when the group collectively sees the chaldron articulates both the potential immateriality and the insistent materiality of viewing life on a screen, and it effectively effaces the distinction.[26] The effect of the chaldron is all-encompassing, and yet, "there were words bordering the screen, I suppose— text with a seller's description, the latest bids on the item in question, . . . a margin of Perkus's computer-desktop bordering those."[27] Although these contexts are "smashed" by the luminescence of the chaldron, their presence is asserted in the text. The chaldron produces a suspension of time, a collective pause, or at least the appearance of it, but the narrative resolves that emerging event: the bid fails, the page completes. Here, then, the potentially affective novelty that is becoming the event (the experience of "watching" the chaldron) is almost effaced by the future that will have been (the closure of the bidding process).

In this scene the unresolving mode of refreshing that exemplifies online protocol is in tension with the preformatted means of social production and the interaction instantiated by the program. The fact that Perkus has little income—and a cultural inclination toward active resistance—dictates his access to digital technology. His dial-up connection is slow, and his computer is cased in "dun-colored" plastic.[28] These elements in the novel help slow down the narrative blending of alternative worlds and surreal plotlines. They are material deficits that have an emphatic impact on the form of the characters' encounters with digital culture: "We never held on the item's main page long enough for Perkus's rotten dial-up connection to complete the chaldron's image, so it now remained elusive, jittery."[29] The motif of slowness is literal. The material contingencies of digital communication are situated visibly in the narrative: the description of the slow dial-up connection articulates something slow about the characters' (and perhaps the readers') awareness of the material Internet. According to the Pew Research Center, in 2010 (the year *Chronic City* was published) 5 percent of US adults still had a dial-up connection.[30] While members of this 5 percent are statistically unlikely to be of the same demographic as Lethem's characters—creative practitioners, politicians, financiers, media personalities, all living in Manhattan—Lethem's anti-cyberpunkery stance is not a totally fictional conceit.

Later in the text it is revealed that Biller, a homeless man (formerly a creative economy worker) who lives outside Perkus's apartment, is the maker of many chaldrons; he is a gold farmer for *Yet Another World*.[31] Whether digital environments are drawn as virtual worlds populated with avatars or social media networks documenting subjects' lives, the economies of these worlds are both distinct from a predigital moment and entirely symptomatic of historical systems of capital. *Chronic City*'s interest in what Edward Castronova calls "virtual economies" is a way to make visible the conditions of social life under the conditions of social media as a new iteration of labor. "Virtual economies" are economic models found in games or virtual world platforms. In addition to games and MMORPGs (massively multiplayer online roleplaying games), today we have witnessed other kinds of virtual economies become common: from Bitcoin (often associated with the virtual economies of darknet marketplaces) to in-app purchasing. In virtual worlds, "the entire physical universe is open to direct and costless manipulation by the owners of the game. The human beings behind the avatars are real, and physical, and subject to the laws of Earth, but the avatars themselves do not inherently face any physical constraints at all."[32] While it is important to recognize the discourses of power and sovereignty that are distinct to virtual economies, virtual economies in *Chronic City* also afford us the opportunity to witness the digital media infrastructures of finance in general—for example, the infrastructure needed for high-frequency trading or server capacity for MMORPGs. In addition, digital economies often conform precisely to offline market modes (to neoliberal market policy) but in distinct forms, and in ever more embodied ways. As has been discussed throughout this book, being online is, in and of itself, to be capitalized on: "Social life on the Internet has become the 'standing reserve,' the site for the creation of value through ever more inscrutable channels of commercial surveillance."[33]

Biller steals his Internet access from Perkus. Perkus's dial-up connection is precarious, which adds to the precarity of its main user, not Perkus but Biller. Lethem's Biller is a working homeless person: he is paid for his specific skill set. The professional digital worker, despite seeming to be part of cutting-edge, future-proof labor markets, operates precariously. In today's economy of precarious labor practices, whether exploitative, cooperative, collaborative, we witness "the formation of a new socio-technical and politico-ethical multitude."³⁴ The precarity of the dial-up in *Chronic City* might stand in for the precarity of the whole digital culture: the chaldrons and their makers. This is also a precarity of the multitude always emerging; the precarious subjects of Lethem's novel are conscripted in these emerging labor practices as user-agents. Following Judith Butler, "Precarity is to a large extent dependent upon the organization of economic and social relationships, the presence or absence of sustaining infrastructures and social and political institutions."³⁵ Precarity is felt as and through the destabilizing effects of neoliberal antagonisms between capital and the state and public and private spheres as well as the commodification of empathy as an answer to a shrinking of the social state. Precarity is often felt as a personal affliction rather than the potential common state of interdependency, and this is engendered by the individuating processes of networked digital culture. *Chronic City* imagines this precarity as interdependence—in it, we are all the precarious user-subject, whose personal online practices are also always labor practices, producing data/content.

In *Chronic City* the precarious dial-up gives way to a precarious subject, who gives way to a precarious city. As Perkus describes it, "There was some rupture in this city. Since then, time's been fragmented. Might have to do with the gray fog. . . . We've been living in a place that's a replica of itself, a fragile simulacrum, full of gaps and glitches." The indeterminacy of the landscape of the novel is rendered most acutely when the group fails to get a winning bid on the chaldron; they blame the networks of power that run Manhattan. Through eBay the novel mediates new ways of being and having value in contemporary culture. Today, "under the new postfordist economies, desire and identity are part of the core economic base and thus woven into the value chain more than ever before"; material production is outsourced, and our affective subjectivity is the capital base.³⁶ In *Chronic City* the characters are all players—playing, being played, and reaping diminished returns for their entertainment-come-labour. The novel affords an opportunity to witness the banal ways we are absorbed in the new economies of digital labour, but also to highlight the critique that gets lost when we recognize this: that not everyone is absorbed alike. Online and off, difference manifests as commodified categories that are used to define and position us as cultural, social, consumer subjects.

DISTRIBUTED NETWORKS

In *Chronic City* the representation of a city where everyone is suffering the effects of climate change is offset by the representation of a city where everyone feels precarity differently. Chase's status as celebrity "*unperson*" is not the same as Biller's homelessness, but both subject markers are considered as part of a shared contemporary condition of the novel. *Chronic City* is interested in the ways that "new forms of subjectivity and connection" manifest through new "networks of communication, cognition, and affect."[37] This is similar to the concerns of *Refresh Refresh*. The digital objects and networks of that narrative could appear as a de facto neutral medium, bringing word from abroad, collapsing geopolitical distances into the abstraction of virtuality. Instead, *Refresh Refresh* represents the scene of e-mail as a coming together (not a collapsing) of temporalities and territories. The act of anticipation, clicking "Refresh," disrupts the folding of time that the Internet might otherwise connote. The boys' present presses on their dads' present in the Middle East; it calls this present into time, demands a response. The difference is the gap. The e-mail rarely comes. The narrative bears witness to a temporal state that could be latency or anticipation, or both, with the unresolving present effaced by the reification of power to control time implied in the act of clicking "Refresh."

About two-thirds of the way through *Refresh Refresh* is a short sequence of panels that begins with drawings of a bleak snowy landscape. A plane trails overhead and a fawn is shown rummaging through the snow and leaves. The next panel is a cut—the light screen of Josh's empty in-box is a panel on its own without the outer box of a laptop, and then it zooms out to show Josh sitting in front of the glow of the screen, which Novgorodoff draws as a dark-bordered rectangle of white-blue.[38] The colors of the snowy landscape are closely connected to the colors of the screen: cold and wintery and vacant. The fawn is a strip of warm browns and reds in the panels depicting the landscape; these warm colors are echoed in the panel of Josh in front of the screen—the room is bathed in a yellow light. In this sequence of panels Novgorodoff seems to draw connections between the vastness of the landscape and the vastness of the laptop monitor—the interface to another kind of dispersed landscape. This is a slow time, a duration that passes in the drawing of vast, imagined spaces. The fawn, Josh himself, the electric light of the living room, these things are warm in contrast to the wilderness and the representation of digital distance (Josh's empty in-box). Digital media (the laptop) is intricately framed in relation to bodies, environment, and narrative and is rhythmically positioned in among panels of natural, analogue, and human agents. The laptop in this story is a point of ambiguous, faulty connection (vague and white like the wintery forest), but it is also a specific, articulated presence, an object in the room, with correspondence designed by global companies and cables and plastic and other physical matter always attached.

Refresh Refresh is structured seasonally; it begins in summer (the town waves off the soldiers in shorts and T-shirts) and ends in winter (with snow). Despite this movement, the organization of narrative in *Refresh Refresh* emphasizes repetition and roteness as a challenge to any sense of time progressing. Scenes of fighting are repeatedly juxtaposed with scenes of the boys' laptops. Dialogue is sparse, adding to the sense that nothing happens. Novgorodoff's pages are divided into six panels (two by three), of varying configurations. The exceptions are pages that are split in half, marking the beginning of a new chapter: a single object denoting something about the chapter is in a white space in the top half; narrative panels are in the bottom half. In October (marked by a jack-o'-lantern) the final page of the chapter depicts Josh, Cody, and Gordon fighting.[39] Two panels in the top row show close-ups of Gordon: he punches Josh, and then a punch lands on Gordon's face. They all wear boxing gloves. The scene is in the woods at the edge of the town. Blood and dirt are everywhere. Speech-bubble vapors escape from the boys' mouths, either empty or grunting, "hn." In the middle row of the page, a single panel depicts a panorama of the boys in situ: piles of wood, trees, birds, telegraph poles. The narrative makes more sense the further out we get; now we can hear the boys, "Bam," "Bam." In the bottom row the perspective shifts to the sky; this could be anywhere. In this panel a solitary bird flies and the sound bubbles of the fight, "Bam," get smaller, quieter, the higher they travel. On the opposite page is a new chapter, but the colors are so similar to the fight scene that it reads as a continuation. A pair of tactical military boots is strewn about in the top half of the page. In the bottom half, three mini-panels on top of one another on the left of the page zoom in on a Yahoo! page—Josh has no e-mails. Reading across to a single panel on the right of the page, we zoom out to see Josh sitting at his desk, tweaking a webcam. Describing this two-page sequence as I have done here affords the opportunity of reading the digital banally and of reading the human subjects of the story mediationally. Across these pages we are reminded of the contemporary condition of becoming-with media that Kember and Zylinska describe: mediation is a constellation of "acts and processes of producing and temporarily stabilizing the world into media, agents, relations, and networks."[40] When reading comics, we reread in ways not likely with prose. Here, the final images of the laptop remain present as you glance back over the fight scene before turning the page. The two scenes press on each other, temporarily stabilizing the narrative world into a particular mediational configuration.

Throughout *Refresh Refresh* Josh, Gordon, and Cody struggle to understand why their fathers are fighting. Josh describes the local community as hoping "that this shitty mess will end" so that the men can come home "and eat dinner with us again." The text boxes with these words overlay a series of panels depicting everyday locales: the supermarket, the gas station, the liquor store.[41] Each space is populated by "the people that are left." These words appear to belong to Josh because the series of panels begins and ends with Josh in his room, recording a video of himself for his dad. In this sequence the text goes from speech bubble to text box to speech bubble. The speech bubbles are voiced by Josh; the text boxes function as voiceover. The voiceover has the added effect of representing Josh's thoughts as general, connoting the mood of the town rather than the individual. Throughout *Refresh Refresh* the homepages depicted on laptop monitors often include snippets of news headings about what is happening in Iraq. The local military recruitment officer, Corey Lightener, is a constant presence in the boys' lives—he is at the local bar, in the local arcade, visiting their moms to check up on them (he is also described as a sexual predator, taking advantage of women who are suddenly lonely or bereaved). The war in Iraq is therefore visible in the town, but as a mood; the townspeople don't want to properly see the "shitty mess." The connection offered by the virtual is both desired and effaced; the boys want to hear from their dads, but they are not able to address the violence wrought by global networks implicated in digital communications or the globalized culture that makes such networks thinkable.

In *Refresh Refresh* the reader is able to mediate through networks that the characters can't always see. In *Chronic City* such networks are revealed through the characters. When Perkus does finally discover a chaldron, he is disappointed. The chaldron Perkus sees (which turns out to be a hologram) is technically owned by the mayor, but not because he bought it; rather, it was a gift from Claire Carter, the mayor's aide, who received it from her brother, who is revealed to be the creator of *Yet Another World*—and as such is technically the owner of all virtual chaldrons. The one real chaldron Perkus sees is not, in fact, the commodity hunted down on eBay, but a gift. Given Lethem's documented interest in gift economies, the reader might assume that the chaldron-as-gift indexes some of the more radical ways in which digital cultural production reconfigures economies of exchange. But the chaldron-as-gift is (yet another) marker of power *imbalance* and of the way new media networks reproduce the status quo. The holographic chaldron is unique; the common chaldrons are the virtual objects produced by Biller using Perkus's dial-up connection. The chaldron Perkus encounters in the flesh has no more spiritual value than the digital objects that Perkus did not realize he was first chasing, and its material value is bound up entirely in the kind of power structure that Perkus stands against.

> Perkus saw immediately that what stood at his feet wasn't anything as definite as a ceramic, let alone . . . the pixel-dense lures he'd ogled on eBay. This chaldron was a hologram, and when Claire Carter switched off the tiny laser at the bottom of the vitrine it blinked out completely.[42]

In this particular section of *Chronic City*, the networks that define various spaces in the novel—the power-circle symbolized by the mayor's office, the space of Perkus's apartment as a node (networked to the web), and the cyberspace of *Yet Another World*—are all shown to be intricately linked. "Chaldron" is portmanteau for chalice and cauldron—both commonplace and rare. The chaldron's evasive materiality is manifest on the page as the word "chaldron," as well as its presence in the narrative as a hologram.[43] The mysticism of the chaldron is a gesture that effaces the process that the object enables in the text. The figure of the chaldron functions as a reification of digital media: it gestures toward the sovereignty of the program as it divests the magic of that program (the reveal of the holographic mode). The novel depicts the chaldron in terms that reiterate the inevitability of its incomprehensibility and unattainability.

And yet the narrative itself provides the reader with an opportunity to think critically about what a network is and how it operates.

Chronic City makes a metaphor out of one of the key tenets of the digital banal: connectedness is reified as a particular kind of social program and as an inevitable aspect of human progress, but this blocks affective comprehension of our new mediational interconnectedness with nonhuman agents—computational and biological. What I term "blocking" is read by Susan Kollin as *Chronic City*'s description of characters relating to their environment by means of "distraction, denial, and discourses of crisis."[44] Evoking Lauren Berlant, Kollin suggests, "Yearnings for spectral objects in 'Yet Another World' reveal the cruel optimism shaping efforts to retain a class position and reclaim attachments to a material existence that appears beyond reach."[45] The virtual economies of *Yet Another World* are stored in servers that cause pollution, which confounds seasonal expectations for Manhattan weather: "Despite all global rumors, the city was suffering a ferocious November."[46] The computational culture of high-speed trading is a root of a crash, which throws the characters into precarity and manifests as the gray fog that cloaks downtown in the novel. The fog may also be the ash of the Twin Towers, symbolized in the novel by the *Fjord*, a work of public art, a chasm "hewn out of the earth by unnatural force," a substitute ground zero, a legacy of an attack rooted in the conditions of violence specific to remote warfare and globalized neoliberal orthodoxy distributed efficiently as social media.[47] While none of these effects and incidents are in and of themselves banal, the way we overlook the digital interconnectedness of their taking place is an effect of the impression of the digital as something banal.

A NON-TURNING-POINT ARTICULATION OF HISTORY

Both *Refresh Refresh* and *Chronic City* are post-9/11 novels. That event and its aftermath determine the environmental and political landscape of each. When discussing contemporary American literature, it is hard not to consider the ways in which the event of 9/11 has shaped the national historical narrative. The novels discussed in the next chapter are more definitely *about* 9/11; they feature quite explicit ruptures and cataclysms and apocalypses that scar the landscape of Manhattan. In *Refresh Refresh* and *Chronic City* such scarring is presented as a kind of ennui, a frustration with the physical environment and its precarity that begets a turn to the "virtual" as an environment that might still hold some frontier potential. These two concerns—9/11 and new virtual worlds—are historically entwined. Retrospectively 9/11 has been claimed as the end of the "American century" but also as the end of the long 1990s, an American decade. Between the fall of the Berlin Wall in 1989, and the attack on the World Trade Center in 2001, the United States appeared to enjoy a period of peace. Despite the continuation of violence, for example military operations and occupations in the Gulf, and the Los Angeles riots of 1992 sparked by the police's beating of Rodney King, the United States was able to understand itself as enjoying a period of calm.[48] The attitude was summed up by President Clinton's final State of the Union address in January 2000: "Never before has our nation enjoyed, at once, so much prosperity and social progress with so little crisis and so few external threats."[49] September 11, 2001, retrospectively becomes a turning point: from then on there is a discernible shift in American cultural, political, and social rhetoric in response to the sudden appearance of "crisis" (the Enron crash and subsequent market downturn) and "external threat" (9/11). In cultural analyses the events of 9/11 have come to stand in as a marker of the new millennium more generally, a kind of deferral of catastrophe and apocalyptic momentum that did not happen when the clocks struck midnight on December 31, 1999.

The centrality of 9/11 to discourses of recent American studies is in part due to its status as spectacle. There are shifts in culture that are far less visible than 9/11, but which have had, and continue to have, far-reaching consequences: the development of the World Wide Web and ubiquitous computing. As is discussed in chapter 4 with regard the Californian ideology, the increasing ubiquity of digital media in everyday life produces a particular effect of the digital banal: newness is reified as new devices, which are sold to us increasingly quickly, while the affective novelty of new kinds of mediation is effaced—reiterated as the progress that was always going to come. When nothing came crashing down in the wake of Y2K, users and markets carried on with the new normal: increasing the efficiency of life by way of digital media.[50] It is difficult to see these slower histories in contemporary literary fiction, particularly when the emergent historical situation they signify is merging with more visible and often more urgent happenings. *Refresh Refresh* and *Chronic City* invite us to pay attention to some incredibly banal scenes: waiting for an e-mail, bidding on an eBay item, making digital objects in great numbers. These scenes have been considered here in place of some significant others: environmental damage and the effects of climate change, the underemployment of young people and older people across the sociopolitical spectrum, the ramifications of the perception that American masculinity is under threat, the absence of social cohesion across the geography of the United States, the effect of 9/11 on the national cultural imaginary. The digital banal is to be witnessed alongside these happenings; it can draw our attention to these conditions as being interconnected and relational to one another. The digital banal may appear less timely than narratives that focus on 9/11 and climate change, but it, too, is intimately related to the post-postmodern millennialism of the contemporary literary imagination.

The digital banal offers a way to critique event-based narratives of recent history, which often preclude any sense of the historical subject as a mediational figure. Reading 9/11 as a turning point in American history reduces "complex historical forces to a mechanistic theory of cause and effect, or privileges catastrophic events at the expense of more subterranean political, social and cultural currents that might turn out to have more profound effects on shaping the future."[51] In the spectacle of 9/11 a far longer history of US foreign policy was witnessed. But beyond this, we can perhaps now perceive that throughout the twentieth century more prosaic categories of change emerged, nonetheless remarkable and nonetheless tied up in US defense and military strategy. The subterranean currents emerging as visible tides are *digital media*: objects and systems that are not wholly new but are shaping anew social and cultural paradigms. The digital banal functions as, among other things, a critical framework from which to counter the dominance of work in the field of American literary and cultural studies that hinges on 9/11 as a catalyst for change. Instead, an increasingly pervasive digital culture may most mark the way we understand contemporary America. I will go on to explore a postmillennial, retrospective orientation of the digital banal at length in the next chapter.

An alternative story to the 9/11 turning point is that after the Y2K bug failed to appear, technology took on a dark side in the cultural imaginary through narratives of cyberterrorism and surveillance culture. The digital banal is rendered in the final pages of *Refresh Refresh* as a condition in which the exceptional and the everyday comingle, coproducing an emerging historical situation.⁵² The army recruiter, Corey Lightener, turns up at Josh's door. Josh's dad has been killed. Josh, Cody, and Gordon fight Lightener; they beat him and then drag him into the woods. They tie him to a log on the precipice of a cliff and abandon him. Instead of returning home, Josh goes to the military recruitment office and huddles on the pavement for the night. Josh's story is then suspended: a series of black-and-white watercolors of desert terrain and billowing smoke fill the following eight pages. In this alternative landscape are silhouettes of tanks and guns. Then comes what is perhaps the most arresting image of the novel: centered in a white page is a small black-and-white painting of a hooded figure sitting cross-legged, wearing the full-body suit made infamous by the images of Iraqi detainees being tortured by American soldiers at Abu Ghraib.

The figure here is in no way identifiable, but it recalls a very specific group of bodies and a very particular image of violence. The regular narrative then resumes with Josh, in a hoodie, curled into himself on the pavement outside the recruitment center. When the center opens in the morning, Gordon and Cody pick him up and take him inside. The sequence is startling for the way it makes the two spaces—Iraq and Oregon—proximate, but not continuous. Josh's tragedy is not *the same as* that of the figure sitting cross-legged in the Iraq sequence, but it is not discrete either. There is no option for the reader but to understand these terrains and bodies as interconnected, as relational.

The final panel of *Refresh Refresh* is a single half-page panel; in keeping with the sparse textual nature of the novel, there is no dialogue. The panel depicts the foyer of the Army recruitment center, emptied after the boys have been led into the adjoining office to enlist. In the room are standard waiting-room armchairs, a world map, the to-be-expected Uncle Sam "I Want You" poster, and other notices. The room is waiting-room green. Behind the reception counter is a just-visible blank computer monitor. It matters that this screen is shown within the innocuous office environment. Falling off the right edge of the panel, the computer monitor is barely present. *Refresh Refresh* and *Chronic City* are texts of the digital banal, but there are other ways to read them. In many ways, each underperforms its digital investments; they are ambivalent about their own digital makeup. And yet, on the last page of *Refresh Refresh*, as we read from left to right, the computer is the final thing we see. The blank monitor is the medium of the mood that has been and the site of a situation emerging.

6

SPECULATING ON THE REAL ESTATE OF THE DIGITAL BANAL

MEDIATION CITY

Digital media is often described as facilitating a collapse of geographical distance and the instantiation of non-place-based communities. These aspects of living with digital media do not, however, preclude their converse reality: large urban centers are more digitally connected than rural areas, and across the globe, Internet access is not equal. Community and habitat are more resistant to geographical borders and, at the same time, just as governed by geopolitics as ever before. Today, "against the widespread assumption between the 1960s and late 1990s that electronic communications would necessarily work to *undermine* the large metropolitan region, all the evidence suggests that the two are actually supporting each other."[1] The connectivity of the Internet has not led to a geographically wider spread of people: populations continue to amass in urban areas; rural areas continue to be less well connected.[2] The very physical space of the Internet—the locations and material presence of server farms and underwater cables—contributes to the continuation of a divide between urban and rural landscapes. The representations of new media and New York City discussed in this chapter are not arbitrary; the urban scene shapes and is shaped by everyday mediation. This mediation incorporates both urban media infrastructures and the urban culture as it has accreted through time. Lisa Parks and Nicole Starosielski note that an "emergent system" may be built on top of an existing one, "expos[ing] the path dependencies of infrastructural formations," revealing "how an established node can be used to generate new markets and economic potentials."[3] Cities are better connected in part because they have always been media infrastructures.

Media infrastructures are "situated sociotechnical systems that are designed and configured to support the distribution of audiovisual signal traffic."[4] In urban centers media infrastructures are layered; cities themselves are historically shaped by the demands of communication, of mediation.[5] The production of space in a city is always already mediated. "Built environments have been transformed into wireless footprints," but those footprints are possible because the city has long been becoming-with media.[6] In our urban environments we are always in a multiplex media mode: from underground networks to traffic light systems, from Wi-Fi in cafés to augmented-reality gaming. We increasingly move through "the automatic production of space, ... new landscapes of code that are now beginning to make their own emergent ways."[7] The media infrastructures of a contemporary city are both its coded materiality and its built environment.[8] Regarding New York City, Ingrid Burrington writes, "New York's network infrastructure is ... messy, sprawling, and at times near-incomprehensible. However, the city's tendency toward flux is a strange blessing for the infrastructure sightseer: markings and remnants of the network are almost everywhere, once you know how to look for them."[9]

Gary Shteyngart's *Super Sad True Love Story*, Jennifer Egan's *A Visit from the Goon Squad*, and Colson Whitehead's *Zone One* are all post-9/11 novels that allude to a city that has fractured. The various environmental, temporal, and geopolitical ruptures in these novels represent a break with normal service. In each case, the temporary disruption of everyday life affords an opportunity to witness and apprehend what was always already complex about that life. In what follows, the digital banal is considered with regard to our urban built environments and common communication networks. The infrastructures that support daily life are media infrastructures. The infrastructural conditions of mediation are built things—a reiteration of how the urban landscape has always been. The digital banal describes a condition whereby an already-embeddedness of digital media in everyday life is in tension with the blocked affective novelty of becoming-with digital media. Digital media is always already embedded in urban life—a precondition of the New York City of all three novels.

The affective novelty of this condition, which is effaced as the invisibility of media infrastructures, is displaced onto the personal and cultural expression of the characters. In these texts characters think and speak digitally. The novels discussed below are perhaps the least banal of all the texts addressed in this book. They are postapocalyptic, rapturous, and occasionally a little in awe of a techno-sublime, but in each the spectacle is narrated as a kind of temporal glitch taking place while whatever is normal is refreshed. The present is disturbed, but fleetingly. The transience of exceptionality is just another way of saying that all the rest is banal.

As with many of the texts discussed in this book, all three novels are completely invested in the mundanity of everyday life lived with digital media: they reflect and speculate on all the ways the things that we do every day—consume, work, talk—are also ways of becoming-with digital media. All three novels are set in a New York City of alternative worlds and times. They are all, along with *Chronic City*, satires of gentrification, new media, and the financialization of everything. The most explicit acknowledgement that these might be broadly millennial, and sometimes specifically post-9/11, is Egan's *A Visit from the Goon Squad*. In this novel the "Footprint" is an empty space downtown, where "the weight of what happened ... more than twenty years ago was still faintly present"; standing at the site characters feel "a sound just out of earshot, the vibration of an old disturbance."[10] Colson Whitehead's *Zone One* is a postapocalyptic zombie novel: in the aftermath of the zombie event, Manhattan has been quarantined, and survivors are put to work preparing for a new governing order. In Shteyngart's *Super Sad True Love Story*, the "Rupture" is a militarized digital blackout inflicted on US citizens after America has defaulted on paying back its loans to China; riots break out as the Wi-Fi goes down, stock markets crash, and transportation systems fail. All three novels can be thought of as writing a postmillennial retrospective of the digital banal, a reckoning with an emerging situation of digital mediation as it might have been.

RUPTURING MEDIA INFRASTRUCTURES

Gary Shteyngart's *Super Sad True Love Story* is set in a near-future America, where fiscal collapse is both immanent and underway. US citizens are being categorized along ethnic and class lines by the "ARA (the American Recovery Authority)," the governing body, to mark out those who will survive the Rupture—the total devolution of the United States. Wealthy white Americans are most likely to survive the cull. The book comprises a chronology of long-form diary entries and retrieved electronic communications from its two main protagonists and narrators: Lenny Abramov (a second-generation Russian immigrant) and Eunice Park (a second-generation Korean immigrant). In the novel Lenny is thirty-nine and the sole representative of the old guard. The culture Shteyngart presents is one that has rejected any "bound, printed, nonstreaming Media artifact" (books) and "verballing" (talking) in favor of electronic communication and instant messaging.[11] Lenny's nostalgic affection for literature and conversation is incongruous. Onboard a plane returning him to the United States from Italy, where the novel opens, Lenny takes out a "battered volume of Chekhov's stories" and begins reading. Eventually Lenny realizes he is being watched: "I noticed that some of the first-class people were staring me down for having an open book. 'Duder, that thing smells like wet socks,' said the young jock next to me, a senior Credit ape at LandO'LakesGMFord."[12] Lenny's anachronistic attachment to old-world artifacts and modes of communication is contrasted sharply, and continually, with the abbreviated speech of the much younger Eunice Park, the object of Lenny's romantic affection. Eunice's voice is represented in the book through transcripts of her GlobalTeens account—a social media site loosely akin to Facebook. Details of the format ("Long-Form Standard English Text") and a GlobalTeens Super Hint ("Switch to Images today! Less words = more fun!!") prelude each of Eunice's entries. The first entry from Eunice, username Euni-Tard, is to a friend: "Hi, Precious Pony! What's up, twat? Missing your 'tard? Wanna dump a little sugar on me? JBF."[13] The entries become increasingly literary as Eunice negotiates her relationship with Lenny and the shifting post-Rupture landscape. Throughout the book the difference between Lenny and Eunice remains marked. At no point does Eunice communicate through the diary form, but Lenny is represented writing GlobalTeens entries. Shteyngart shores up the distinction through font: GlobalTeens communication has its own distinct font, as do Lenny's diary entries, and updates from CRISISNET—a newsfeed directly broadcast to networked devices—are always shown in all caps.

In *Super Sad True Love Story* the characters navigate an intense urban-digital environment. Credit Poles, formerly lampposts and telegraph poles, stand at every street corner broadcasting the data streams of passersby—bank statements, Social Security numbers, health records; privacy is an unmentionable privilege. Today, public anxiety about hacking is in part produced by the tacit assumption—constituted formerly somewhere deep in eight-point-font terms and conditions—that although we give away our data, we have designated where and to whom it goes; it is not for public broadcast, but is a commodity to be treated with reverence. *Super Sad True Love Story* satirizes these presumptions. Lenny sees a woman "cross herself in front of the church and kiss her fist, her Credit ranking flashing at an abysmal 670 on a nearby Credit Pole."[14] Data is broadcast by the smartphone-type device that is compulsory for the citizens of New York, the äppärät ("Let me see your äppärät. Good fucking Christ. What is this, an iPhone?").[15]

Shteyngart was born in Leningrad in 1972, and in his other novels he has repeatedly written his characters as displaced and in transit across Russian and American continents. In *Super Sad* Lenny Abramov is the son of Russian immigrants, but throughout the novel defines himself as American, or more specifically, as a New Yorker. The relation Lenny has to Russia echoes Shteyngart's own and serves a particular function in the novel. In interview Shteyngart states, "When I was growing up in the Soviet Union, it collapsed.... I have an uncanny feeling we're not doing very well here, too. I think I have a sixth sense when it comes to failing empires."[16] The parallel that Shteyngart draws in this interview is one between unstable states and failing political systems. The naming of the central device of the novel, the äppärät, is undoubtedly a reference meant to underscore his broader position: the Apparat is literally the "party machine" of the Communist party in Russia. In *Super Sad* the äppärät reflects the way personal digital devices are socio-technical media, or apparatuses, mobilizing and producing social, media, and political infrastructure.

Significantly, the äppärät is worn as a pendant, and it is compulsory to have it on at all times. On the one hand, the device as adornment, as accessory, belies the way it is empirically embedded in the built and social environment of the city. On the other, the appearance of the äppärät as simply adornment emphasizes the automation of social practice as it may have been becoming: you *could* take it off, but you won't; it appears to be a tool deployed by the body, but it is the thing that verifies the body. The äppärät as a pendant gives the false impression that the äppärät is a choice, that it is worn by citizens as a fashion item, worn on your person but not as part of your person. The object banally reifies the illusion of choice as novelty itself, a luxury accessory; the network of the äppärät, however, is far more embedded and indiscrete.

In situ, the äppärät brings about seamful, rather than seamless, mediational affects. Wordplay abounds as characters use their devices to FAC (form a community). When someone says "Let's FAC," Lenny hears "Let's *fuck*"; his friends correct him, saying that FACing is when you use your äppärät to rate another user: "It's, like, a way to judge people. And let them judge you."[17] In the novel FACing transposes a digital network over an embodied social space. The characters FAC in a bar, rating all strangers in their vicinity. Once Lenny enables the FAC settings on his äppärät, the process becomes quickly autonomous: "Streams of data were now fighting for time and space around us."[18] Lenny's own profile reveals that all of his recent purchases have been "bound, printed, nonstreaming Media artifacts." To this revelation, his friend cries, "Lenny Abramov, last reader on earth!" And then, "staring directly into his äppärät's camera nozzle: 'We're FACing pretty hard now, people. We're getting Lenny's RateMe *on*.'"[19]

Shteyngart presents the immediacy with which Lenny receives digital data, re-presented as ratings on his personal device, as a moment of slippage between digital and embodied spaces—the streaming takes place around them. Äppäräts and Credit Poles are nodal points in the network of Shteyngart's novel, both for the digital network represented within the novel and for the reader—as warped reconfigurations of our contemporary digital environments. The projection of data as ratings is both further abstraction—a visualization of data—and a substitution for the invisible media infrastructure that supports it. In the bar sequence Lenny is able to improve his rating live by posting appealing things about himself and elicits sympathy by appearing on his friend's live video channel talking about his love for Eunice. The presentification of life further underscores the anachronism of Lenny's affective attachment to, if not critical apprehension of, history. We might also read the presentification of these sequences as making visible what is otherwise effaced: the automatic production of space and the city as media infrastructure.

After the Rupture, Lenny writes in his diary: "My äppärät isn't connecting. I can't connect."[20] He then informs the reader of a suicide note found in his building. A young person had written that "'he reached out to life,' but found there only 'walls and thoughts and faces,' which weren't enough."[21] In the same diary entry, Lenny describes his reaction to seeing a child on the street looking lost and hungry: "Out of instinct, I took out my äppärät and pointed it at the kid, as if that would make things right."[22] When Lenny's äppärät fails, so too does his ability to connect. Connection is a significant marker of the digital banal: the presumed novel progression of being better connected digitally is a reification and effacement of the social, material, and political infrastructures that modulate connection as a condition of being on earth. Being connected is rarely disclosed for the mediational condition that it is: that we are connected as humans by the precarity of climate change, wrought at least in part by the infrastructure of digital modernity, or that our digital connections are produced along with our subjectivity, as subjects and citizens of the algorithmic social sphere of automated governance. Lenny can connect with those around him—and does, helping Eunice take care of the elderly in his building—but he cannot *connect* in the sense that he is locked out of the media infrastructure. The novel's ironic play is that in the absence of a digital network, characters do turn to each other and form a physical community right where the reader would expect one to be, in an apartment building. But Lenny sees only the failure of this kind of community to provide solace. His embodied experience, once isolated, is somehow lacking. He rejects the unaugmented reality that remains in the shadow of the failed äppäräti. Writing about the suicide note of the young person in his building, Lenny notes in his diary: "He needed to be ranked, to know his place in this world. And that may sound ridiculous, but I can understand him. We were all bored out of our fucking minds. My hands are itching for connection."[23] Itchy hands are the bodily affect of immaterial connection, which materializes as the absence of connectivity.

In the interstices of the everyday, the vanished code has left a shadow, or even produced a gap, not easily replaced by embodied interaction. Shteyngart's representation of the digital in these encounters, in many respects, echoes our own ambiguity of digitally coded space. It is also an affective encounter with the complexity of digitally mediated existence through its absence. The affective quality here is the failure to imagine a postdigital mode that is fully *after* the digital. Writing about the automatic production of space in contemporary urban environments, Nigel Thrift and Sean French suggest that software is "able to be negatively assimilated into the domain of thought as a figure or metaphor representing some social else, thus allowing it to be captured within a linguistic or semiotically contrived field, rather than disclosed as an agent of 'material complexification.'"[24] The indistinct textuality of code enables its effacement, even exclusion, from analyses of networked environments. In the absence of the äppärät network, Shteyngart's characters highlight the digital "as a figure or metaphor representing some social else" through their mournful negotiation of its absence. They do not understand, or even discuss, its material relations, the socioeconomic systems it enacts, or its elusive architecture. Rather, in words, on the pages of Lenny's diary, in a suicide note, and in place of dialogue on the streets of New York, the digital is grieved as a kind of person, and it is appreciated as both a mode and a mood.

LEAVING FOOTPRINTS FOR WHATEVER COMES NEXT

Jennifer Egan's *A Visit from the Goon Squad* has been described as a "network" of stories.[25] The novel is nearly a collection of short stories; it is organized along the lines of an LP, with an A-side and a B-side, and so it is also a bit like a concept album. Chapters work as discrete entities, but characters dip in and out of each other's stories; particular attention is paid to a handful of reoccurring characters. The novel is about a group of people involved in the music and media industries in the United States (mainly, but not exclusively, in California and New York) from the 1970s to the 2020s. *A Visit from the Goon Squad* follows Egan's earlier work in exploring technology as an explicitly social concern, imagining uncanny identities and relationships that arise from different mediated environments.[26] Egan's work is always about media, and mediation, but is consummately aware that aspects of living with digital media remain invisible, incomprehensible.[27]

The novel is organized polychronically, with chapters jumping around in time and space. *A Visit from the Goon Squad* deploys polychronicity to capture the sense of urban space as "a cacophony of different and competing temporalities all impacting on the city at the same time."[28] Although the period of time encompassed by the novel is relatively brief—less than fifty years—the polychronic structure gestures at deeper histories of media, culture, and ecology that surface throughout the narrative. The later (which is to say, future) chapters of the novel are the primary concern here, but it is important to keep hold of the novel's future-oriented anticipation as intimately related, and materially proximate, to other times. On safari in Mombasa, in 1973, Charlie, daughter of Lou (a reoccurring character), dances with a warrior who is performing at the hotel.

> Thirty-five years from now, in 2008, this warrior will be caught in the tribal violence between the Kikuyu and the Luo and will die in a fire. He'll have had four wives and sixty-three grandchildren by then, one of whom, a boy named Joe, will inherit the *lamella*: the iron hunting dagger . . . now hanging at his side. Joe will go to college at Columbia and study engineering, becoming an expert in visual robotic technology that detects the slightest hint of irregular movement (the legacy of a childhood spent scanning the grass for lions). He'll marry an American named Lulu and remain in New York, where he'll invent a scanning device that becomes standard issue for crowd security.[29]

Joe appears in the final chapter of the novel, at a large concert partially organized by Lulu. Both appear in a world beyond the novel in Egan's Twitter story "Black Box."[30] The way the future disturbs the present in *Goon Squad* is strange. Although the programmed future of the novel attests to the present as a temporal mode that will be done with, moved on from, the overlaying of discrete periods blocks the narrative from actually moving on; instead, what will have been collapses into what is becoming. In this sequence the future that is becoming-with digital media is affectively addressed through the emerging presence of Joe—still many years away from existence.

Toward the end of the book the future that the warrior begets begins to actualize, but it does so in a way that further prevents the appearance of a fully resolved media subject, inhabiting a discrete moment in time and space. The penultimate chapter is set in the 2020s and is narrated by Alison, the twelve-year-old daughter of Sasha (the closet the novel has to a main character). This chapter of the book is presented entirely in the form of PowerPoint slides. The PowerPoint slides are Alison's journal entries describing her life at home with her parents, Sasha and Drew, and her brother, Lincoln. They live on the edge of a desert, where there used to be lawns, but now "you need a lot of credits for a lawn or else a turbine, which is expensive."[31] The PowerPoint chapter mobilizes the reified novelty of digital media as a shiny new thing, distinct from everyday life—the everyday of a realist novel—to potentially efface the affective novelty of the mediational subject for whom PowerPoint actually makes more sense as a form to think with. In other words, the PowerPoint journal is a reification of the mediational subject, which deflects rather than disturbs the novel's interest in mediational subjectivity. Reviews of *Goon Squad* all mention the PowerPoint chapter, often describing it as a surprisingly effective gimmick or novelty.[32] The condition of the digital banal is one in which the novelty of digital media is always already commodified and empty. The observation that PowerPoint is a nice gimmick is a nonengagement with PowerPoint as used in life writing. In interview, Egan has described the difficulty of writing fiction through PowerPoint: it is a "totally static," "pixelated/pointillist" form.[33] But, through the tension between the anticipation of narrative fiction and the affordances of the PowerPoint mode, we witness what is at stake in living digitally: a genre of becoming medial subjects.

In the series of banal slides, several describe what it is like to live on the edge of the desert in the future. Alison and her dad go for a late-night walk. In a slide titled, "After a Long Time, We Reach the Solar Panels," three rows of three arrows, pointing from left to right, are filled with text describing the solar panels. The panels "go on for miles; . . . [it's] like finding another city or planet. . . . They look evil, . . . like angled oily black things, . . . but they're actually mending the Earth."[34] The solar panels link the hyperconnectivity of the final chapter—set in a New York City where people prefer to text rather than talk—to the rest of the environment. The banality of the digital condition is punctured by the strangeness of the new media infrastructures, the new nodes of energy, panels "like a black ocean I've never seen close-up."[35] Alison Carruth suggests that in these slides depicting the panels, we encounter "a material trace of, and effort to visualize, the escalating energy requirements of this culture in which nearly every experience, exchange, and thought finds its way onto IT networks."[36] Among the slides about the solar panels is a slide of "Facts About Dad": "His hair is thick and wavy, unlike a lot of dads.... When he can't sleep he walks into the desert.... It's a mystery why he loves mum so much."[37] The statements are presented in a series of six opaque text boxes, which look like upright solar panels. These rhomboids might also represent rows of server cabinets, storage for the vast, digitally distributed networks that comprise the urban community of the final chapter. The ties across the chapter are loose, but they are nonetheless present. Alison's journal is a record of her life, her family—as journals have always been. The journal is also a digital file; the server cabinets/solar panels are the stored record of Alison's journal and the energy keeping it going. The solar panels or servers are totems of a post-digital culture; the new banal of environmental capacity in the time after digital technology is ubiquitous. The digital journal appears as a distraction, a gimmick, but it is the intraface through which the novel can register the affective novelty of becoming-with media.

The final chapter of the novel is set in New York City at the same time as Alison's journal. The connection between this urban setting and the desert of the previous chapter is medial. As Carruth notes, "The final two chapters draw a line from a North American desert and its renewable energy resources to the digital lives of elite, highly connected Americans."[38] In New York City the hours of daylight are artificially altered, casting the city in odd lights, odd moods. The city has built a wall to manage the hours of sunlight. The Anthropocene period is in its dying days, and so sunlight itself must be rationed. Crowds congregate around the wall, called the Waterwalk, to experience sunset:

> When they climbed the steps to the *WATERWALK!* as the wall's boarded rampart was exuberantly branded, they found the sun still poised, ruby-orange and yolklike.... She ran toward the iron fence along the wall's outer edge, always jammed at this hour with people who probably (like Alex) had barely noticed sunset before the wall went up.[39]

The Waterwalk scene positions technology, climate change, and urban development—as well as technological solutions to mediating the more dramatic effects of climate change and urban development—in close proximity.

Many of the characters' lives hinge on the music industry. In the 2020s the music industry is devoted to the "pointers" market. Pointers are children who have buying power through their smartphone toys, "kiddie handsets." Children simply point in the direction of a sound they like and click, and the track is downloaded, "the youngest buyer on record being a three-month-old in Atlanta, who'd purchased a song by Nine Inch Nails called 'Ga-ga.'"[40] Tangential to this, the music industry targets its adult audience through "parrots": people who are paid by various organizations to spread promotional excitement about a product via digital social networks. "Bennie had never used the word 'parrot'; since the Bloggescandals, the term had become an obscenity.... 'Who's paying you?' was a retort that might follow any bout of enthusiasm."[41] The commodified social culture of postdigital life finds voice in the nostalgic turns of Bennie Salazar, a music producer who began working with punk musicians in the 1970s and has never settled into the corporate record industry. According to Bennie, "The problem was precision, perfection; the problem was *digitization*, which sucked the life out of everything that got smeared through its microscopic mesh."[42] Bennie speaks the fetishization of the analogue, which is often associated with postdigital life: a nostalgia for what was, coupled with the convenience of what has become.

The final chapter mainly follows Alex, who is working for Bennie to promote a massive concert at the Footprint. Alex finds his technological present familiar, but not natural, just as the reader recognizes Egan's near-future but is made to attend to its differences. Alex is a music promoter who is embedded in the parrot system while feeling deeply uneasy about technology and its effects. For most of the time that the novel spends with Alex, he is working with Lulu. Alex and Lulu's communication takes place almost entirely through the instant messaging mode of "Ts." In the world of *Goon Squad*, the prevalence of shorthand typed communication renders verbal interaction awkward, oddly conspicuous:

>Lulu T'd: *Nvr met my Dad. Dyd b4 I ws brn.* Alex read this one in silence.
>"Wow. I'm sorry," he said, looking up at Lulu, but his voice seemed too loud—a coarse intrusion.... He managed to T: *Sad.*[43]

Egan's *"Sad"* foreshadows our contemporary "feels."[44] Throughout the novel T-ing is represented in italics; it is visually distracting on the page, drawing the eyes away from the main body of text toward its graphic difference. The presentation of T-ing as italicized dialogue, rather than as a distinct typeset or format (as in *Super Sad True Love Story* and *How Should a Person Be?*), introduces a shift in tone to something more personal. The Ts are asides serving to undermine the flow between the modes of communication represented on the page: T-ing, dialogue, and narration. Characters misunderstand and miscommunicate in ways that enable a reader to attend to the material-social contingencies of that communication.

T-ing has retrospectively become a form of premediation. Lulu is also the narrator of Jennifer Egan's Twitter story "Black Box." The future Lulu of "Black Box" is a spy who tells her story through a series of mental dispatches, lessons that she learns on her mission, conveyed seemingly in real-time, which Egan published as discrete tweets—Ts, perhaps. In *Goon Squad*, when Alex and Lulu are T-ing one another about the view from Alex's apartment, soon to be blocked entirely by a skyscraper, there is a slippage in the shorthand communication: "*nyc*, Lulu wrote, which confused Alex at first; the sarcasm seemed unlike her. Then he realized that she wasn't saying 'nice.' She was saying New York City."[45] This easy slip is familiar, symptomatic of a language that can only be condensed in so many ways. Alex's wife, Rebecca, is an academic whose current research project is investigating this new mode of expression. Rebecca's "new book was on the phenomenon of word casings, a term she'd invented for words that no longer had meaning outside quotation marks, . . . words that had been shucked of their meanings and reduced to husks."[46] There is a tension between Lulu's sincere use of T-ing and Rebecca's interest in the mechanisms by which sincerity is acknowledged. As is discussed in chapter 3, such investments mark the point at which the digital banal describes the condition of post-postmodern discourse. This tension in *Goon Squad*, picked up again after the novel's publication, as in Egan's own experimentation with Twitter, links the novel's concerns to the world of its circulation. New affective discourses are the displaced affective novelty of life embedded in media infrastructure and of sociality and presence as always already mediational.

Online speech has always been unstable in ways delineated by the immediacy of the network and the operations of code. In the early days of the web, chat room users uttered "speech momentarily frozen into artifact," a "curiously ephemeral artifact."[47] Today, the small screens of our daily digital encounters demand a new verbal vernacular, a constantly refreshing textual shorthand. Across digital communications history, the vernacular is consistently performative, a kind of "speaking-writing," or "seeing-saying."[48] Such a vernacular makes certain lexical permutations more common, where for immediacy's sake we might LOL or ROTFL rather than say anything more idiosyncratic. In *Goon Squad* the quick communication of T-ing conversely produces its own point of slowness. The reality effect of the sequence is itself disrupted by the consciously clunky movement between ways of seeing-saying and speaking-writing. T-ing is disruptive on the page; Alex has to think through and parse what he reads. And yet, such a representation of instant messaging is also an attempt at verisimilitude, a representation of a real everyday language of digital media. Perhaps this is a stress point of the novel's depiction of digital everyday life: the reality effect of the digital everyday might make visible the construction of the representational mode.

At the end of *A Visit from the Goon Squad*, the reader encounters a different kind of reanimated media: the concert in the Footprint. The concert brings together hundreds of thousands of people at a site that is architecturally bereft. The humanity that Egan ascribes to the gathering is only enabled by the lack of architectural structure, the lack of steel and concrete. The poignancy of the gathering is enabled by the connection that the audience holds with the distinctly human form onstage, undigitized, only amplified. When Scotty Hausman (Bennie's old friend, who has been "rescued" from obscurity) begins to play an acoustic set, "a swell of approval palpable as rain lift[s] from the center of the crowd."[49] For the characters in the novel, "it may be that two generations of war and surveillance had left people craving the embodiment of their own unease in the form of a lone, unsteady man on a slide guitar."[50] The last major spectacle of the novel is one that is consciously untechnological. The unplugged performance and the rapt attention of the crowd is an engagement with liveness in a nonmediational sense. That said, the crowd is only present because Alex worked the distributed digital network of parrots. The scene of Scotty's performance may at first appear to be a rejection of digital media, but this is just a temporary suspense of the narrative investment in a wholly mediational urban subject.

Digital media is always already embedded in urban life; the affective novelty of this condition, which is effaced as the invisibility of media infrastructures, is displaced into the personal and cultural expression of the characters. At the height of his experience of the concert, Alex, physically close to the stage and to the music, wants to reach out to his wife, who is far away in the crowd:

> He panned the rapt, sometimes tearstained faces of adults, the elated, scant-toothed grins of toddlers.... At last he found Rebecca.... They were too far away for Alex to reach them, and the distance felt irrevocable.... Without the zoom, he couldn't even see them. In desperation he T'd Rebecca, *pls wAt 4 me, my bUtiful wyf,* then kept his zoom trained on her face until he saw her register the vibration, pause in her dancing, and reach for it.[51]

The media infrastructure of the concert does not disappear because Scotty reappears. It is most acutely drawn in this moment, when the norm of the digital banal is disturbed by nostalgia for the imaginary of a predigital moment. Alex's embodied media response to his emerging situation undermines the nondigital moment as it is imagined and reveals the everyday habit of the reader as itself a kind of affective novelty. Alex is able to reflect on the contingencies of his own presence: "Alex felt what was happening around him as if it had already happened and he were looking back."[52] The experience of the show is polychronic: technologies and stories of the past, present, and future coexist and render the show nostalgic for what never was, or for what might have been. Nostalgia is mediated by future-oriented technologies of memory making—the show is archive material before it is over, displayed on social media timelines. The crowd that amasses to watch Scotty play his slide guitar is Alex's online network made flesh; the city begins with the digital, and the embodied community is only visible through a digital lens. While the show is exceptional, the experience of mediation—"our being in, and becoming with, the technological world, ... of intra-acting with it,"—is the present, ongoing, unresolving condition.[53]

THE UNMEDIATIONAL CONDITION OF THE UNDEAD

Colson Whitehead's *Zone One* is a postapocalyptic zombie narrative. It follows protagonist Mark Spitz and a crew of survivors in their new occupation as "sweepers." The novel is set in Manhattan, though Spitz frequently experiences flashbacks to the times during and before the outbreak. A makeshift government (called American Phoenix) has established itself in Buffalo and set about the work of building the *postapocalypse*. Teams of sweepers are sent to clear out the skels (fully gone zombies) and stragglers (infected zombies who haunt their previous workplaces and domestic residences) from Zone One, an area of Manhattan where (wealthy) survivors will start life again. When the novel opens, some time has passed since the Last Night (the zombie event), and survivors have been diagnosed with PASD (Post Apocalypse Stress Disorder). The work of the sweepers is to make sure Zone One is ready for life to resume, which is to say, for a postapocalypse everyday to begin. The novel is mundane and slow; it narrates new kinds of rote labor. Although the Zone One project is about making way for a new everyday life, the novel offers up this intermediary activity as its own new everyday life: "You never heard Mark Spitz say 'When this is all over' or 'Once things get back to normal.' ... If you weren't concentrating on how to survive the next five minutes you wouldn't survive them."[54] The perpetually present alertness is the new normal, the new everyday: you sleep, you wake up, you go kill the undead; you do so in a state of hyperanticipation.

Throughout the novel the banality of zombie life is asserted. The character of Mark Spitz is mediocre, an everyman, suited to the task of sweeping because he is as unexceptional as the zombies he sweeps. As Mark Spitz's team of sweepers works the blocks of Manhattan, they encounter the detritus of former lives. These scenes produce an alternative narrative to the zombie tale. *Zone One* is "a story of lost love, at first glance contemporary America's [love] for its own cultural protocols—from sidewalk etiquette to sitcom vectors—but beyond that, humanity's love for ritual, its dependence on ways of imposing meaning on the void."[55] Ritual is embodied by sweepers, but also by the objects they find. Touring abandoned buildings, Spitz and his team encounter recalcitrant electronic things. These are turned off and silent or, stranger, appear animate long after their determined functions have ceased to exist. In old office buildings the sweepers find scenes of suspended media action:

> A beat-up telephone trailed its umbilicus, caught mid-crawl from the premises. The copy machine dominated the back room, buttons grubbed by fingerprints, paper tray sticking out like a fat green tongue. The straggler's right hand held up the cover and he bent slightly.[56]

Such devices are "the sad machines that had shut off in the middle of their humble duties, waiting for orders."[57] If these remainders still happen to work, they serve to witness grim tales of exhausting survival: "Her mind was gone, sure, but she made it through, and her followers took care of her, wiping spittle from her lips as she murmured her prophesies into her digital recorder."[58] The "shiny new digital recorder" of Sheila Heti's present is what will have been a remainder of the mediational subject in postapocalyptic life.

The digital subject is reproduced in *Zone One* as yet another data subject. The sweepers are tasked with producing data on the area of Zone One, with capturing new information that will inform the decisions of life to come. As Mark Bresnan argues, "Despite (or perhaps because of) the loss of many forms of digital technology and global information networks due to the zombie outbreak, data collection and analysis remains a powerful compulsion in *Zone One*."[59] The ground zero of *Zone One*'s Manhattan is—similar to *Super Sad* after the Rupture—a life *after* new media. The characters in both *Zone One* and *Super Sad* are haunted by the digital; they live postdigital lives, not like the postdigital now, but like the postdigital as it might signal the complete end to discrete digital devices. Rather than mediation as Kember and Zylinska suggest, we might think of the particular, total life after new media that these novels witness as *un*mediation. The individual subject is unmediated, just as the zombies are undead. In *Super Sad*, unmediation is Lenny's techno-tic; he is always reaching for his device. In *Zone One*, Spitz, in all his banal nonglory, is a subject that comes together—he is *becoming* as he is narrated in the postapocalyptic, after-media landscape—in quite explicit terms of unmediation. The novel remembers the time before as an experience of mediation. In next-generation New York, slogans for the new government pop into Spitz's head, "insistent as malware," and as far as the stragglers go, "cognition was out . . . once it overwrote the data of self."[60] Here mediation is simile, is metaphor; it is the concrete referent that used to be, enabling Spitz to narrate the future as a recognizable entity. The present is, then, an emerging situation delineated by processes of mediation undone.

Before the Last Night, Spitz worked in the "Customer Relationship Management, New Media Department," of a multinational coffee company:

> It was his job to monitor the web in search of opportunities to sow product mindshare and nurture feelings of brand intimacy. As his supervisor put it. . . . He dispatched bots into the electronic ether, where they mingled among the various global sites and individual feeds, and when the bots returned with a hit or blip, he sent a message: "Thanks for coming, glad you liked the joe!"[61]

Spitz was a digital economy worker, a knowledge worker. As Bresnan observes, this work is described in terms "overwhelmingly banal, no less mechanistic than the sort of assembly-line work that has increasingly moved to developing nations."[62] Soren Forsberg suggests that Whitehead's description of this labor is pointedly leveled at contemporary entrepreneurial culture, which is "often glamorized in the press and in popular culture." Instead, "Mark Spitz might as well be a greeter at Wal-Mart, a job that also requires little in the way of skill. What such jobs require instead is a particular mood or attitude—a *commitment to service*, say— which holds such importance in the political fiction of personal responsibility."[63] Spitz is then doubly unmediated: his life before was conditioned by the industry of new media, and his current condition is being produced through the unmediation of everyday life, when former workstations populated with blank monitors strike him as "dioramas of productivity."[64] In a narrative about a group of survivors, the rhetoric of "personal responsibility" reverberates in a generic sense. But Spitz is not the lone renegade, and what is valorized in both his pre- and postapocalyptic vocations is his ability to be part of a system: Spitz the bot, Spitz the sweeper.

The novel's interest in Spitz's distinction is always through this lens; his precarious individual agency, his survival, is sustained by his commitment to service.

The novel is keenly aware of the kinds of inequality and subjectivity that mark the new precarious careers of knowledge work and technical labor. Spitz's race goes unmarked until the end of the novel, when a joke about his namesake (an Olympian swimmer) interpolates Spitz as black: "'Plus the black-people-can't-swim thing.' 'They can't? You can't?' 'I can. A lot of us can. Could. It's a stereotype.'"[65] The reveal of Spitz as black is also a reveal of "racism [as] a zombie presence."[66] The novel has presented the reader with something like a postracial society, only to reveal the fallacy as such. Moreover, "Whitehead sutures the promise of rebirth to the reanimation of racism, with the implication that the two are intrinsically linked, that the pre- and post-apocalyptic worlds are both haunted by, in Mark Spitz's terms, 'the monstrous we overlook every day.'"[67] In the context of the digital banal and the agency of becoming unmediationally, Spitz's race is another remainder of the reader's present, wherein networked capitalism, reliant on the affective labor of everyone, disproportionately exploits people of color.[68] Spitz's status as a black former knowledge worker is also an allusion to popular generic depictions of digital labor, which, as Martin Kevorkian has argued, are shown "time and time again" to represent a "computer-fearing strain in American whiteness" as "an aspect of white identity that defines itself against information technology and the racial other imagined to love it and excel at it."[69] Spitz's "good work" is recognized by his bosses, but he is not personally invested in the work—at best, it "wasn't the worst job he'd ever had."[70] The refusal to present in a particular mode is a condition of Spitz as a figure of flat affect. His reveries are a means of blocking affective engagement with the present; in this way, Spitz's banality is also a refusal to perform normative investments in systems that are the means of his exploitation.

In its focus on remaking a city, *Zone One* is "a narrative of becoming, in which humanity must adapt to a hostile, potentially post-human world."[71] The novel's investment in thinking digitally points to this "narrative of becoming" as a representation of the unresolving presentification of digital time. Through flashback, the future that the novel represents is anticipated as the past that is becoming. In *Zone One* attention is drawn "to the omnipresence of digital information networks almost every time

[Spitz] flashes back to the time before the outbreak."⁷² The novel opens with a passage that describes everyday media from before and alludes to a future of unmediation.

> His parents were holdouts in an age of digital multiplicity, raking the soil in lonesome areas of resistance: a coffee machine that didn't tell the time, dictionaries made out of paper, a camera that only took pictures. The family camera did not transmit their coordinates to an orbiting satellite.⁷³

Spitz's parents are described as being unmediated: they are becoming through the condition of mediation they have chosen not to be. This passage is part of a reverie that carries the narrative into the present moment, where Spitz is clearing an apartment building much like the one his uncle used to live in. Counter to his parents, Uncle Lloyd always had new technological things: "wireless speakers, . . . a squat blinking box that served as some species of multi-media brainstem."⁷⁴ On visiting Lloyd, the boy Spitz "searched for the fresh arrival first thing."⁷⁵ This flashback mediates the present. The stragglers are "snared in bygone moments" full of media, but the straggler-mode is distinct from the condition of unmediation that defines the survivors.⁷⁶ When encountering redundant media, survivors are agents of what is no longer: "He knew he had to visit Uncle Lloyd's apartment, to sit on the sectional one last time and stare at the final, empty screen in the series."⁷⁷

Unmediation is a condition of being haunted. The survivors are not only in a condition of unmediation but are also experiencing the unburying of media phenomena. The media infrastructures of Manhattan are reanimated in the thoughts of Spitz, which—in an inversion of the digital banal—reify the affective novelty of mediation in order to efface the perceived deadness of now. In the aftermath of the Last Night, Spitz ends up stranded in Connecticut, waiting out a blizzard in the storeroom of a toy store. In the flashback to Connecticut, Spitz flashes back further, to the time before the snowy last days, when "the pipes poured and electrons filled the multifarious cables" so that the "ambient heat of the ground prevented such quick accumulations."⁷⁸ In Connecticut, Spitz is only aware of the absence of live networks: "the snow piled swiftly on the deadened earth."⁷⁹ Media infrastructure is registered in its environmental mode as an ambient condition of presence. The banal intrusions of memory are occasionally met in the text with a noisy equivalent. In the office (a reappropriated Chinese restaurant) Spitz and his sweeper colleagues are listening to old pop songs on a "digital player": "Mark Spitz was startled by the DJ's sudden bluster: 'Hey! All you out there. Hope you're getting a chance to enjoy this sunshine today!'"[80] The interruption is a recording, but in the moment Spitz is confused and wonders if some radio stations are up and running. There is no live media, and the DJ is just a voice from "some random afternoon before the disaster, a ghost transmission."[81] The ghost transmission is not a ghost in the machine, it just sounds like one as it hails Spitz from elsewhere. It is a recording of a once-live thing, now another track on someone's playlist. The voice is deemed undead—the encounter a condition of unmediation—in the instance when Spitz does not understand that he is hearing a reanimated media event. The uncanny effect of the DJ is the unmediational affect, which itself points to everyday encounters of animated—that is to say, lively—media.

In *Zone One* the novel's estranging mode of the digital banal is a commitment to the daily ritual of unburying the unremarkable digital life that once was. The reader is given a condition of unmediation in its everyday mode, moving through Friday and Saturday, and ending at Sunday. The days are long because the narration tracks Spitz's reveries and flashbacks to situate the present day within a longer duration—a slow time. When Spitz is fighting off a group of skels that caught him unawares, he gets distracted, thinking of old TV shows, old teachers, things that the skels remind him of. Drawing attention to its own novelistic construction, Whitehead's prose here acknowledges the license it is taking: "How long did it take for [the skel's] wig to fall off? (Time slowed down in situations like this, to grant dread a bigger stage)"; . . . "(Yes, time slowed down to give those competing factions in him room to rumble, the dark and the light)."[82] The repetition of an elliptical "slowed down" in what are not quite action scenes points to the banal drive of the text. The novel slowly traverses the presentification of the urban media infrastructure as an uncanny everyday, a remainder of the prezombie moment, when such infrastructure went mostly unseen.

Zone One underperforms its own investments in digital media while nonetheless having them present, "as insistent as malware."[83] If the digital banal is a mechanism of obfuscation, by which the computational and related environmental and economic networks that define us as subjects are often made invisible to us, then *Zone One* is a narrative effectively aware of its own digital banality. As with *Super Sad True Love Story* and *A Visit from the Goon Squad*, *Zone One* offers us New York City as a thick media infrastructure, expressed and embodied by characters as becoming-with technology in multiplex ways. By staging various ruptures and temporary breaks in historic moments, the novels upend narratives of progress that so commonly attach themselves to popular depictions of digital media. In all three novels time is spent attending to the deeply embedded affective novelty of becoming-with digital media. Writing about *Super Sad True Love Story*, Brendan Byrne notes that the relationships in that novel are most intimate when online. Eunice and her sister are often silenced in oppressive real-world family scenarios, but "when they are on chat, they cut at one another, plead for forgiveness, profess their love.... It's a real, fundamentally wet and screaming relationship—but only online."[84] The same description could apply to Alison or Lulu, and such feeling seeps through Spitz's accounts of life before. Across the three novels the characters experience the reification of digital media as future devices (in *Goon Squad* and *Super Sad*) or as mediational pasts (in *Zone One*), coupled with a reiteration of digital life as inevitable and just there. The texts themselves attend to the operation of this banal and to the affective novelty it elides.

CONCLUSION

After the Digital Banal

In 2013 the artist Hito Steyerl announced, "The Internet is Dead."[1] In other words, there is no discrete experience of being online; everything is online. This sentiment encapsulates the sense of contemporary postdigital life as one in which we are always digitally mediated—as data, statistics, profiles, nodes, traces—regardless of our discrete encounters with devices. In the words of David M. Berry, digital mediation is the condition by which a "computer requires that everything is transformed from the continuous flow of our everyday reality into a grid of numbers that can be stored as a representation of reality which can then be manipulated using algorithms."[2] It is the digital inflection of Kember and Zylinska's becoming-with media. This process is ongoing, unresolving, perpetually present. It is also a process that effaces itself in action: we cannot see all the ways that transformation takes place. Digital mediation is a method for understanding contemporary reality as determined by "new knowledges and methods for the control of reality."[3] The emerging historical situation of the contemporary moment can be witnessed as the digital banal. The digital banal is the condition by which the embeddedness of digital media in everyday life is visible only as an expectedness of technological progress, effectively blocking the affective novelty of new media. The work of this book has been to attend to scenes that reproduce the digital banal, and in so doing to allow the digitally mediated conditions of the present to disturb the surface of that present. The scenes discussed throughout *The Digital Banal*, from Nev's door-stopping long-distance lovers in *Catfish* to Berta Walton's pause at the airport check-in desk, evoke a power to estrange and make visible their own digital banality.

This book began where the software culture of today begins, with code. In the digital films of David Fincher we find code represented as a medial problematic: the more screen time given over to the characters of code, the more the computational processes of code resist interpretation. What these films are able to substantiate is less a visual grammar of code than a temporal one. The films offer up what I refer to as a digital time, an unresolving present that is always in a state of retrospective anticipation, and so never fully becomes history. In Fincher's work we find digital culture more broadly: the anticipation of retrospective moments (Fincher's digital history films) and the unceasing drive of commands for recollections (a literal recalling of data in everyday life that appears here as the recall of history) are brought to screen by a reification of the ineluctable difference of the medium—the strangeness of code—which is reiterated as a banal program of writing the future. Screens and code are the primary interfaces of digital mediation. The rest of the book is particularly concerned with the way that these interfaces are instantiated as social practices in ever more diffuse ways. In chapter 2 the remix writing of Jonathan Lethem and Mark Amerika is read as a gesture toward the ways that social and artistic commons are delineated by the affordances of the digital banal, which are described in chapter 1. In Lethem's and Amerika's work, the reiteration of a literary commons—literary history—is a command to be expected; processes of digitization make reiteration the default mode of utterance in the contemporary moment.

The formulation of the digital banal accounts for the machinations of code as potentially blocking ways to connect otherwise; in Lethem's and Amerika's work this formulation appears as the argument that remix is the *only* way to write now. Additionally, Lethem's and Amerika's essays are generative ways to negotiate the agency of writing itself in the emerging historical present, which in turn reveals the common agency of all users-come-authors in the era of ubiquitous digital media. In chapter 3 the relation between writing and social life is more fully explored. The digital banal is mobilized as a way to understand social media as a reification of new social conditions of becoming-with media and of being subject to media. Attending to scenes of social mediation in the film and

TV show *Catfish* and in Sheila Heti's novel *How Should a Person Be?*, this chapter shows that the commodification of social life in reality discourses—novels drawn from life, documentary film, reality TV—is also an opportunity to witness the contemporary subject becoming-with media. Paying attention to the ways these stories authenticate the social activities of a person by their online presence (*Catfish*) or digital recording devices (*How Should a Person Be?*) is a rethinking of what post-postmodern literary criticism has tended to see as a new sincerity. Instead, the banal tones of the reality genre—the reification of everyday life—is read as an explicitly digital mode wherein the affective novelty of becoming a digital social subject is reified and reiterated as the validation of being seen and authenticated by digital interfaces.

In the second half of this book, the machinations of digital mediation are explored as habits and habitats. The fourth chapter reads two different fictional representations of Silicon Valley—Ellen Ullman's take on 1980s software development in *The Bug* and Dave Eggers's rendering of a post-Facebook corporation in *The Circle*—in order to apprehend the lag between them. Together these novels tell the story of the stretched-out now of software as ideology. In the earlier fiction, code is elevated to the status of a sovereign language; in the latter code is unseen, and the affective labour of the customer experience employee is privileged. This chapter considers the historical shift in Silicon Valley from the asphalt and retail-park landscape of gray cubicles and open-plan boxes in Mike Judge's *Office Space* (1999) to the playtime campus of scooters and foam chairs and private buses in Mike Judge's *Silicon Valley* (2014). In the space between the two times is the effect of the digital banal. The effacing operation of an increasing distance from the material history of software is a block on knowing software better, which simultaneously enables the reiteration of novelty as this very lack—we are sold "invisible" tools to know *each other* better.

Chapter 5 considers a set of scenes tangential to the campuses of Silicon Valley: computers in living rooms, users waiting for e-mails and waiting for their online shopping, banal sites of everyday digital life. The fifth chapter positions the digital banal as a concept more fully in the world by looking at texts that may be more likely thought of as post-9/11 novels or novels about contemporary environmental concerns. Jonathan Lethem's *Chronic City* and Danica Novgorodoff's *Refresh Refresh* are texts that underperform their digital investments. To read these texts for the digital banal may appear counterintuitive, but the approach offers a rich way to understand the texts' more general engagements with the rhetoric of global connectivity that emerged in the wake of 9/11, as well as the precarity endemic to neoliberalism and climate change, as inextricably also engagements with being a digital subject.

The indelibility of the digital banal is most fully attended to in the sixth and final chapter. Here, various spectacular future narratives—from raptures and ruptures to a zombie apocalypse—attempt to imagine a postdigital life, only to find the digital condition banally recurring, reiterating the mediational condition of becoming-with technology despite the end of digital technology, or the end of the world brought about by digital technology. In Colson Whitehead's *Zone One*, Jennifer Egan's *A Visit from the Goon Squad*, and Gary Shteyngart's *Super Sad True Love Story*, New York City appears as a deep media infrastructure; the citizens who navigate its streets are equally embedded media subjects. In keeping with the mode of the digital banal, these novels narrate a condition whereby digital media is always already embedded in urban life—a precondition of the New York City of all three novels. The affective novelty of this condition, which is effaced as the invisibility of media infrastructure, is displaced onto the personal and cultural expression of the characters.

Glancing at the contents of currently available monographs and edited collections published on contemporary literature will tell you that literature today is barely interested in its digital conditions. Other than works explicitly interested in the potential antagonisms of old and new media, novels today are, by scholarly accounts, not interested in the technological devices, informational logic, and networked sociality of contemporary digital culture. Turning to mainstream and popular press reviews and essays suggests that contemporary fiction actually has a problem with its new media conditions. As author David Gates puts it, if his characters were to spend as much time online as he does, "would their lives be eventful enough to write about?"[4] In other words, is everyday digital life too boring for literature? And what about its contemporaneity? For Gates, the issue at stake is how to "deal with the problem of writing something that may be dated by the time the book comes out." In Gates's novel *Preston Falls*, published in 1998, he has "a now-hilarious account of an e-mail exchange—'He hit Send,' and so forth."[5] Is "he hit send" an anachronism in the 2010s? I could update the description with a WhatsApp or Twitter button, but would one term or another block the affective resonance of the act? Laura Miller locates the nowness of digital time as being itself a problem; authors "have mostly shied away from writing about this, perhaps hoping that, like TV, it could be safely ignored."[6]

Such commentary belies an anxiety that, when digital media remains absent from contemporary fiction about contemporary living, we lose an opportunity as readers to better understand our presence in the world. As Allison K. Gibson has suggested, regardless of "the trouble technology might cause, when it's absent from contemporary novels, a big white elephant appears on the page and starts ambling around."[7] The big white elephant may be a device, the quality of being online, or the postinternet environs of the Internet of Things; its absence may be an effacement or a refusal, or perhaps a fear of the unknown. For Jacob Silverman, a "novelist's task is not to expect something from the Internet, nor to simply invoke it as a potent technological symbol of a character's pathology. . . . It has to, in some sense, be taken for granted . . . just as a writer would with a telephone."[8] The concerns listed here can all be considered in terms of the digital banal. These authors and critics are aware that there is no way to elide the digital conditions of everyday life; the issue at hand is the quality of attention and the affective resonance of the work. A novel that attempts to represent the contemporary condition is itself conditioned by the dominant logic, but it might also make tangible something of this logic. A novel might make visible, or reveal, some of those codes—mediation, computation—of the contemporary moment that otherwise remain hidden.

This book is committed to saying that now, in this present, we must critically apprehend digital media, and see the work that goes into making objects, systems, networks, and ways of organizing life so invisible and seemingly inevitable. This book will also be published after its moment of thinking, and into a world in which the effacing conditions of digital media have been undone a little. The digital conditions of the 2016 US elections were very visible—as tweets and memes and hacks and e-mails and servers, and as the new extrajudicial formations and shifting international relations of distributed digital networks. The shocks of the election process were soon normalized because they were being registered through the medium of their initial disturbance. Such is the process of the digital banal, through which novelty is always being incorporated as the to-be-expected, and the banal is always surfacing as the lived political reality of becoming-with digital media. In response, *The Digital Banal* takes digital media as a given, but it attends to the composition of this given, and in so doing, recovers its immanent novelty.

NOTES

INTRODUCTION: THINKING WITH THE DIGITAL BANAL

1. Apple, "iPhone 4 Tour," accessed April 23, 2016, www.apple.com/ca/channel/iphone/iphone-4/tour/.
2. As the Internet becomes increasingly ubiquitous, our online practices are now "funnelled through platforms." Joss Hands, "Introduction: Politics, Power and 'Platformativity,'" *Culture Machine* 14 (2013): 1, accessed February 14, 2015, https://www.culturemachine.net/index.php/cm/article/viewArticle/504.
3. Mary Holland, "A Lamb in Wolf's Clothing: Postmodern Realism in A. M. Homes's *Music for Torching* and *This Book Will Save Your Life*," *Critique: Studies in Contemporary Fiction* 53, no. 3 (2012): 214, doi:10.1080/00111611003767621.
4. His research topic is Richard Nixon.
5. Holland, "A Lamb in Wolf's Clothing," 217.
6. A. M. Homes, *May We Be Forgiven* (London: Granta, 2013), 93, 324, 389.
7. Ibid., 95, 136, 391.
8. Ibid., 475.
9. See, in particular, the message exchange with Harry's cancelled lunch date, ibid., 95.
10. Roland Barthes, "The Reality Effect," in *The Rustle of Language*, trans. Richard Howard (Berkley: University of California Press, 1989), 142.
11. Holland, "A Lamb in Wolf's Clothing," 234n13.
12. Homes, *May We Be Forgiven*, 297.
13. See Marshall McLuhan, *Understanding Media: The Extensions of Man* (1964; New York: Routledge, 1997); Jay David Bolter and Richard Grusin, *Remediation: Understanding New Media* (Cambridge, MA: MIT Press, 1999); Lev Manovich, *The Language of New Media* (Cambridge, MA: MIT Press, 2001); N. Katherine Hayles, *Writing Machines* (Cambridge, MA: MIT Press, 2002); Matthew G. Kirschenbaum, *Mechanisms: New*

Media and the Forensic Imagination (Cambridge, MA: MIT Press, 2008); Alexander R. Galloway, *The Interface Effect* (Cambridge: Polity, 2012).

14. Bolter and Grusin, *Remediation*, 15.
15. Sarah Kember and Joanna Zylinska, *Life After New Media: Mediation as a Vital Process* (Cambridge, MA: MIT Press, 2012), 77 (the original passage is italicized). Kember and Zylinska's evocation of "mediation" is informed by the philosophies of being and technology of Martin Heidegger, and to a lesser extent Bruno Latour. Following Heidegger and Latour, we can understand mediational ontology as a hybrid, multiplex condition: "Allowing the world to come to presence today entails taking into account more than singular relationalities, for a singular perspective is not enough to understand even the simplest of technological appearances." See Arianne Conty, "Techno-Phenomenology: Martin Heidegger and Bruno Latour on How Phenomena Come to Presence," *South African Journal of Philosophy* 32, no. 4 (2013): 315, doi:10.1080/02580136.2013.865099. Kember and Zylinska refer to this condition as our "humachinic world, with its hybrid ontologies and uncertain ethics" (*Life After New Media*, 14). For Kember and Zylinska, "media need to be perceived as particular enactments of *tekhnē*, or as temporary 'fixings' of technological and other forms of becoming. This is why it is impossible to speak about media in isolation without considering the process of mediation that enables such 'fixings'" (*Life After New Media*, 21).
16. Kember and Zylinska, *Life After New Media*, xviii, 164 (original is italicized).
17. Holland, "A Lamb in Wolf's Clothing," 230. Here Holland is paraphrasing Jonathan Culler's discussion of realism in "Convention and Naturalization," in *Structuralist Poetics: Structuralism, Linguistics, and the Study of Literature* (Ithaca, NY: Cornell University Press, 1975), 131–60.
18. These are statistics recorded in March 2017. See the Statistics section of the *Facebook Newsroom*, accessed May 22, 2017, http://newsroom.fb.com/company-info/.
19. Ibid.
20. Kember and Zylinska, *Life After New Media*, 158 (italics in original).
21. For example, on Facebook and "mood manipulation," see Adam D. I. Kramer et al., "Experimental Evidence of Massive-Scale Emotional Contagion through Social Networks," *PNAS* 111, no. 24 (June 2014): 8788–90, doi:10.1073/pnas.1320040111; Robinson Meyer, "Everything We Know about Facebook's Secret Mood Manipulation Experiment," *Atlantic*, June 28, 2014, accessed December 16, 2016, http://www.theatlantic.com/technology/archive/2014/06/everything-we-know-about-facebooks-secret-mood-manipulation-experiment/373648/.
22. On Internet users as profiled neoliberal data subjects, see Clare Birchall, "'Data.gov-in-a-Box': Delimiting Transparency," *European Journal of Social Theory* 18, no. 2 (2015): 185–202, doi:10.1177/1368431014555259; Clare Birchall et al., "Openness and Opacity: An Interview with Clare Birchall," *Networking Knowledge: Journal of the MeCCSA Postgraduate Network* 9, no. 1 (2016), accessed December 15, 2016, http://ojs.meccsa.org.uk/index.php/netknow/article/view/419. My description of the subject as a profiled software litany refers to how a user becomes a profile through predetermined selective criteria. In other words, the commercial web produces profiles delineated by what Lisa

Nakamura has called "menu-driven identities." Such profile options often block or limit the ways mixed, intersectional, and multiplex identities can be owned, enacted, and mobilized on social networking sites. An individual emerges on social media as a result of a range of preset menu options. I make this point here to also recognize that the profile identities that form the banal affect of social media also banally reiterate offline assumptions and privileges of race and gender. Writing in a pre–Web 2.0 moment, Nakamura articulates what is at stake in the menu-driven future: "As portals [social media platforms] come to overlay the web and become hegemonic and dominant means for navigating it, it is all the more important we become sensitive to the ways that these mediations categorize racial and gender identity." Lisa Nakamura, *Cybertypes: Race, Ethnicity, and Identity on the Internet* (New York: Routledge, 2002), 113.

23. Lauren Berlant, "Faceless Book," *Supervalent Thought* (blog), December 25, 2007, accessed April 23, 2016, https://supervalentthought.com/2007/12/25/faceless-book/.

24. Katherine Losse, *The Boy Kings: A Journey into the Heart of the Social Network* (New York: Free Press, 2012), 72.

25. Press reports indicate that Facebook has hit capacity in the United States and that young people prefer dedicated messaging apps such as Snapchat and WhatsApp (owned by Facebook) over Facebook. See Parmy Olson, "Facebook Was the One Network People Used Less in 2014," *Forbes*, January 27, 2015, accessed July 25, 2016, http://www.forbes.com/sites/parmyolson/2015/01/27/facebook-active-users-decline/#6fad4b3a411b; Deepa Seetharaman, "Survey Finds Teens Prefer Instagram, Twitter, Snapchat for Social Networks," *Wall Street Journal*, October 16, 2015, accessed July 25, 2016, http://blogs.wsj.com/digits/2015/10/16/survey-finds-teens-prefer-instagram-snapchat-among-social-networks/. I use the example of Facebook here because it, along with YouTube, inculcated the particular kind of pact users make with social media platforms that is likely to remain long beyond the Web 2.0 platform era: for free or cheap services that are perceived to make life simpler, users are content to be the product. See Rob Horning, "Know Your Product," *New Inquiry*, July 29, 2015, accessed July 25, 2016, https://thenewinquiry.com/blog/know-your-product/.

26. See Ann Pellegrini and Jasbir Puar, "Affect," *Social Text* 27, no. 3, 100 (2009): 36, doi:10.1215/01642472-2009-004.

27. Ngai places Berlant's *Cruel Optimism* alongside her own work in an archive of recent critical writing on the "minor." See Sianne Ngai, "On Cruel Optimism," *Social TextOnline* (January 2013), accessed April 23, 2016, http://socialtextjournal.org/periscope_article/on-cruel-optimism/. Ngai and Berlant have also coedited a special issue of *Critical Inquiry* (December 2016), entitled "Comedy Has Issues," following their shared interest in flat affects and comedy. The works of both, which address minor aesthetic and affective cultural forms, include Sianne Ngai, *Our Aesthetic Categories: Zany, Cute, Interesting* (Cambridge, MA: Harvard University Press, 2012); Sianne Ngai, *Ugly Feelings* (Cambridge, MA: Harvard University Press, 2005); Lauren Berlant, "Structures of Unfeeling: Mysterious Skin," *International Journal of Politics, Culture, and Society* 28, no. 3 (September 2015): 191–213, doi:10.1007/s10767-014-9190-y; Lauren Berlant, *Cruel Optimism* (Durham, NC: Duke University Press, 2011).

28. The aesthetic qualities listed here are more explicitly of interest in Ngai's work on "interesting" culture, but they also describe Berlant's work on William Gibson's *Pattern Recognition* and Colson Whitehead's *The Intuitionist* in Lauren Berlant, "Intuitionists: History and the Affective Event," *American Literary History* (August 2008), doi:10.1093/alh/ajn039. In her review of *Cruel Optimism*, Ngai draws out the way Berlant's work "transforms a 'merely' affective stance into an intellectual lever or tool"; I would suggest that Ngai relatedly uncovers the political potential of "merely" aesthetic forms; see Ngai, "On Cruel Optimism." In the work of Kathleen Stewart (who acknowledges a close relation between her own thinking and Berlant's work) a similar description of low engagement is found: "From the perspective of ordinary affects, things like narrative and identity become tentative though forceful compositions of disparate and moving elements: the watching and waiting for an event to unfold, the details of scenes, the strange or predictable progression in which one thing leads to another, the still life that gives pause, the resonance that lingers, the lines along which signs rush and form relays, the layering of immanent experience, the dreams of rest or redemption or revenge. Forms of power and meaning become circuits lodged in singularities." Kathleen Stewart, *Ordinary Affects* (Durham, NC: Duke University Press, 2007), 5–6.

29. Sianne Ngai, "Merely Interesting," *Critical Inquiry* 34, no. 4 (Summer 2008): 788, doi:10.1086/592544.

30. Ngai, *Our Aesthetic Categories*, 146.

31. Ngai, "Merely Interesting," 793–94.

32. Berlant, "Structures of Unfeeling, 193.

33. Lauren Berlant, "Thinking about Feeling Historical," *Emotion, Space and Society* 1 (2008): 4–9, doi:10.1016/j.emospa.2008.08.006.

34. Ibid.

35. Susanna Paasonen, "Bit on Networked Affect," *Susanna Paasonen* (blog), March 3, 2016, accessed April 23, 2016, https://susannapaasonen.org/2016/03/03/bit-on-networked-affect/. Recent scholarship on new media and affect includes work on new media image culture and studies of the sociological conditions of "networked affect." See Mark B. N. Hansen, *New Philosophies for New Media* (Cambridge, MA: MIT Press, 2004); Steven Shaviro *Post-Cinematic Affect* (Winchester: Zero Books, 2010); Jodi Dean, *Blog Theory: Feedback and Capture in the Circuits of Drive* (Cambridge: Polity, 2010); Ken Hillis, Susanna Paasonen, and Michael Petit, eds., *Networked Affect* (Cambridge, MA: MIT Press, 2015).

36. This wording is taken from a description for an event on Internet culture, titled "Bland Boring Banal: A Symposium on Lackluster Feeling and Digital Media in Extreme Times," held in Amsterdam in 2015, at which Lauren Berlant was a keynote speaker. Website accessed December 15, 2016, https://blandboringbanal.wordpress.com/about/.

37. In making this claim, Wendy Chun is responding to Alexander R. Galloway's work on code, which, Chun argues, anthropomorphizes code in order to claim human sovereignty over the system. For Chun, while there is a danger in granting programming code an agency *other than* human, there is equally a problem in assuming that complex computational systems are entirely in the control of their programmers. See

Alexander R. Galloway "Language Wants to Be Overlooked: On Software and Ideology," *Journal of Visual Culture* 5 (2006): 315–31, accessed February 16, 2011, doi:10.1177/1470412906070519; Wendy Hui Kyong Chun, "On 'Sourcery,' or Code as Fetish," *Configurations* 16, no. 3 (Fall 2008): 299–324, accessed February 16, 2011, doi:10.1353/con.0.0064.

38. Chun, "On 'Sourcery,'" 307 (italics in original).
39. Wendy Chun, *Programmed Visions: Software and Memory* (Cambridge, MA: MIT Press, 2011), 25.
40. Berlant, "Thinking about Feeling Historical," 5n8
41. Erkki Huhtamo, "Web Stalker Seek Aaron: Reflections on Digital Arts, Codes, and Coders," in *Code: The Language of Our Time, Ars Electronica 2003*, ed. Gerfried Stocker and Christiane Schöpf (Ostfildern-Ruit, Ger.: Hatje-Cantz, 2003), 115.
42. Caroline Bassett, *The Arc and the Machine: Narrative and New Media* (Manchester: Manchester University Press, 2007), 2 (emphasis in original).
43. Matthew MacLellan and Margrit Talpalaru, "Editors' Introduction: Remaking the Commons," *Reviews in Cultural Theory* 2, no. 3 (2011–12): 1, accessed August 22, 2012, http://mediamargins.net/wp-content/uploads/2012/09/RCT-SP-On-the-Commons.pdf. By "the commons" I mean the commons as cultural works that are available for public use, the web as common "space," and the commons as a political and social formation counter to privatization.
44. Galloway, *The Interface Effect*.
45. I am thinking here of Lauren Berlant's "non-sovereign love" as a way of figuring out how we might think of everyday affective relations, presents, and so on, as political in ways that are neither resistance nor subjectivation because these interpretations are already normative and limiting. Nonsovereignty is about "violating your own attachment to your intentionality, without being anti-intentional." Lauren Berlant, Michael Hardt, Heather Davis, and Paige Sarlin, "'On the Risk of a New Relationality': An Interview with Lauren Berlant and Michael Hardt," *Reviews in Cultural Theory* 2, no. 3 (2011–12), accessed August 22, 2012, http://reviewsinculture.com/2012/10/15/on-the-risk-of-a-new-relationality-an-interview-with-lauren-berlant-and-michael-hardt/. This position directs us to thinking about ways of abiding-with and becoming-with as violating an anticipated attachment to intentionality. In Wendy Chun's *Updating to Remain the Same*, Chun references Berlant's thinking in *Cruel Optimism*, and I read something of Berlant's nonsovereignty in Chun's call to loiter in networks. Although such a call is rhetorically willing a sovereign subject to step forward, the end effect described by Chun is precisely one of "violating your own attachment to intentionality." For Chun, "To loiter online, we would have to create technologies that acknowledge, rather than make invisible, the multitude of exchanges that take place around us—technologies that refuse the illusory boundary between audience and spectacle, author and character." If creating technologies here is not simply understood as the making of objects or systems, but also as the techniques for abiding-with while using them, as is more the case in Chun's conceptualization of technology in *Updating*, then intentionality is clearly at stake in the thinking about loitering. And so, "loitering is ephemeral" in the sense that

it is a way to violate attachment to intentionality that is anticipated in our interpolations as networked subjects. Wendy Chun, *Updating to Remain the Same: Habitual New Media*. Cambridge, MA: MIT Press, 2016, 160.

1. DAVID FINCHER'S GRAMMAR OF CODE

1. I use the future anterior formulation of "what will have been," or "what will have become," as a way to frame the kinds of presentness and historical subjects that occupy the films under discussion. The future anterior is here used as an estranging phrase, something that makes visible the temporal function of the films. This is less to evoke Derrida's sense in which the future anterior signifies the radical coming of the future and more to cite his description of the "fabulous retroactivity" of the American declaration of Independence, the "they will have become a people." See Jacques Derrida, "Declarations of Independence," in *Negotiations: Interventions and Interviews, 1971-2001*, ed. and trans. Elizabeth Rottenberg (Stanford, CA: Stanford University Press, 2002), 46–54. Fincher's films are caught up in telling histories that will have been, but this is, I argue, a production of the present, rather than a commitment to the impossibility of a present. I will elaborate on this discussion by way of Mark Currie's and Wendy Hui Kyong Chun's writing on "presentification" later in this chapter.
2. See "Technical Workflows," *CEITON Technologies*, accessed May 22, 2017, http://www.ceiton.de/CMS/EN/workflow/system-centric-bpms.html.
3. I am specifically interested in the visual imagery of computation and programming and the editorial processes by which programming and code appear to drive the narrative. To this end, I approach the films in this chapter as Fincher's films, each with techniques in common (as opposed to, say, thinking of *The Social Network* as an Aaron Sorkin film).
4. Michael Goldman, "Going Tapeless," *Millimeter* 34, no. 6 (2006): 8–16, accessed February 17, 2015, accessed May 22, 2017, http://www.creativeplanetnetwork.com/news/news-articles/going-tapeless/386899; David E. Williams, "Cold Case File," *American Cinematographer* 88, no. 4 (April 2007): 32–51, accessed May 22, 2017, https://www.theasc.com/ac_magazine/April2007/Zodiac/page1.php.
5. Although the subject of Salander's detective work in the archives of the Vanger Corporation is not digital (she is looking through print archives), her systems for cross-referencing and building the timeline are (she is using a database she has constructed with details of all the murders). This is one of the ways in which the logic of the hacker subject is fully attended to: everything Salander does might be seen as her thinking with the computational.
6. In this analysis I have chosen to work closely with Currie's and Chun's disparate but (I am arguing) related writing on experiences of "presentification." The effect that I am ascribing to presentification might alternatively be ascribed to the continuum of digital cinema time: film is no longer a sequence of cuts but rather a continuous flow of data. See William Brown, *Supercinema: Film-Philosophy for the Digital Age* (New York:

Berghahn, 2013); Garrett Stewart, *Framed Time: Toward a Postfilmic Cinema* (Chicago: University of Chicago Press, 2007). In this chapter "presentification" and "workflow" are terms I am using to link concerns of programming and time in film to more generalized experiences of programming and time in everyday life. Digital time as discussed here is not only a cinematic conceit; it is an effect of the digital banal as a condition of everyday life lived with digital media.

7. Matthew G. Kirschenbaum, *Mechanisms: New Media and the Forensic Imagination* (Cambridge, MA: MIT Press, 2008).

8. See Lisa Parks and Nicole Starosielski, eds., *Signal Traffic: Critical Studies of Media Infrastructures* (Urbana: University of Illinois Press, 2015).

9. Johanna Drucker, Review of *Mechanisms: New Media and the Forensic Imagination*, by Matthew Kirschenbaum, *Digital Humanities Quarterly* 3, no. 2 (2009), accessed April 29, 2016, http://digitalhumanities.org/dhq/vol/3/2/000048/000048.html.

10. Zadie Smith, "Generation Why?," *New York Review of Books*, November 25, 2010, accessed April 15, 2011, http://www.nybooks.com/articles/2010/11/25/generation-why/.

11. Throughout this chapter I refer to film edits as "cuts." As William Brown notes, this word is a remainder from the filmic medium. See Brown, *Supercinema*, 2. Given that my concern is digital cinema, "cut" is not referring to literal cuts (in film) but rather a break or a cutaway between shots, scenes, and sequences.

12. For details of Facemash, see S. F. Brickman, "Face Off," *Harvard Crimson*, November 6, 2003, accessed January 27, 2017, http://www.thecrimson.com/article/2003/11/6/face-off-computer-guru-mark-e/; B. M. Schwarz, "Hot or Not? Website Briefly Judges Looks," *Harvard Crimson*, November 4, 2003, accessed January 27, 2017, http://www.thecrimson.com/article/2003/11/4/hot-or-not-website-briefly-judges/.

13. Melissa Gira Grant, "Girl Geeks and Boy Kings," *Dissent* (Winter 2013), accessed July 22, 2015, https://www.dissentmagazine.org/article/girl-geeks-and-boy-kings. See also Katherine Losse, *The Boy Kings: A Journey into the Heart of the Social Network* (New York: Free Press, 2012), discussed further in chapter 4.

14. Lisa Nakamura, "The Comfort Women of the Digital Industries: Asian Women in David Fincher's *The Social Network*," *In Media Res*, January 17, 2011, accessed July 14, 2016. http://mediacommons.futureofthebook.org/imr/2011/01/17/comfort-women-digital-industries-asian-women-david-finchers-social-network. For critique of the representation of race and labor in popular fiction narratives about computer expertise, see Martin Kevorkian, *Color Monitors: The Black Face of Technology in America* (Ithaca, NY: Cornell University Press, 2006).

15. Writer of *The Social Network* Aaron Sorkin makes this point in an interview with Charlie Rose. See Aaron Sorkin and David Fincher with Charlie Rose, "The Social Network," video, *Charlie Rose*, September 28, 2010, accessed January 27, 2017, https://charlierose.com/videos/14347.

16. Wendy Chun, "Crisis, Crisis, Crisis, or Sovereignty and Networks," *Theory Culture Society* 28, no.6 (2011): 101, accessed December 2, 2011, doi:10.1177/0263276411418490.

17. Reviewing *The Social Network* for *The Guardian*, Peter Bradshaw describes the programming in the early scenes as "an evil-genius frenzy." See Peter Bradshaw, Review

of *The Social Network*, *Guardian*, October 14, 2010, accessed May 1, 2016, http://www.theguardian.com/film/2010/oct/14/the-social-network-review.

18. David Fincher, "Commercials/Music Videos," in *The Director's Cut: Picturing Hollywood in the 21st Century*, ed. Stephan Littger (New York: Continuum, 2006), 169.

19. Wendy Chun, "The Enduring Ephemeral, or The Future Is a Memory," *Critical Inquiry* 35 (Autumn 2008): 153, doi:10.1086/595632.

20. Mark Currie, *About Time: Narrative Fiction and the Philosophy of Time* (Edinburgh: Edinburgh University Press, 2007), 22.

21. Mark Currie, "The Expansion of Tense," *Narrative* 17, no. 3 (October 2009): 355, doi: 10.1353/nar.0.0027.

22. Ibid., 366n5.

23. Wendy Chun, *Programmed Visions: Software and Memory* (Cambridge, MA: MIT Press, 2011), 49.

24. Currie, "The Expansion of Tense," 356. Currie's work on time moves from consideration of narrative to consideration of verbs and how these linguistic substitutes for action encode certain temporal propensities in language.

25. Currie, *About Time*, 18.

26. The Facebook timeline was launched in September 2011. The feature presents user's posts and personal dates as a timeline—ostensibly from birth to the present. The feature replaced the previous default homepage setting, the wall, which organized a user's post as a list. See "How Do I Post to My Timeline," Facebook, accessed May 8, 2016, https://www.facebook.com/help/1462219934017791. The focus here is on thinking of Facebook timelines as producing an enduring ephemeral, refracted through *The Social Network* as a depresentification of narrative time, digital time, and the time of the film's production. More generally, we may think of Facebook profiles as "a narrative act," a "meaning-making mode" for members. See Laurie McNeill, "Social Networking Sites and Posthuman Auto/Biography," *Biography* 35, no. 1 (Winter 2012): 71.

27. Chun, "The Enduring Ephemeral," 148.

28. Ibid., 148.

29. Ibid., 166-67 (emphasis in original).

30. I am using the pronoun "his" throughout because the primary suspects of the case as depicted in the film are all male.

31. Amy Taubin makes a similar point in a review of the film. See Amy Taubin, "Nerds on a Wire," *Sight and Sound* 17, no. 5 (May 2007).

32. *Zodiac*, directed by David Fincher, 2007, Warner Home Video, 2007, DVD.

33. Jacques Derrida, *Paper Machine*, trans. Rachel Bowlby (Stanford, CA: Stanford University Press, 2005), 20.

34. Friedrich Kittler, "Gramophone, Film, Typewriter," trans. Dorothea Von Mücke and Philippe L. Similon, *October* 41 (Summer 1987): 101–18, doi:10.2307/778332.

35. Todd Kushigemachi, "Nostalgia Goes Digital: Turning Back Time in the Films of David Fincher," *PopMatters*, October 10, 2011, accessed December 3, 2013, http://www.popmatters.com/feature/144591-nostalgia-goes-digital-turning-back-time-in-the-films-of-david-finch/.

36. Sean Cubitt, *The Cinema Effect* (Cambridge, MA: MIT Press, 2004), 246.
37. Fincher's *The Girl with the Dragon Tattoo* is, however, inextricable from questions of authenticity in terms of its status as adaptation. See Anna Westerståhl Stenport and Garrett Traylor, "The Eradication of Memory: Film Adaptations and Algorithms of the Digital," *Cinema Journal* 55, no. 1 (Fall 2015): 74–94, doi:10.1353/cj.2015.0058.
38. Jennifer S. Light, "When Computers Were Women," *Technology and Culture* 40, no. 3 (1999): 455–83, accessed December 3, 2013, https://muse.jhu.edu/article/33396.
39. See Chun, *Programmed Visions*; Wendy Chun, "On Software, or the Persistence of Visual Knowledge," *Grey Room* 18 (2004): 26–51, doi:10.1162/1526381043320741; David Allen Grier, *When Computers Were Human* (Princeton, NJ: Princeton University Press, 2005); David Allen Grier, "The ENIAC, the Verb 'To Program' and the Emergence of Digital Computers," *IEEE Annals of the History of Computing* 18, no. 1 (1996): 51–55, doi:10.1109/85.476561.
40. In describing this scene as one in which Blomkvist "seeks" Salander's help, I recognize that I am glossing over the malignant threat in Blomkvist's request. The audience is to understand that he will not turn Salander in for invasion of privacy during her investigation of him because he is a "good guy"; that said, the threat remains and influences the power dynamic of their relationship in its early stages.
41. The audio track for this scene is full of beeps and processing noises typically used in films; this heightens the sense in which the machine is "working," but also substantiates a fictive inauthenticity—it being unlikely that those undertaking covert work would leave the volume of their device on loud.
42. The Unix window displays green text on a black background. Although it is possible to customize the color palette for Unix, the green-on-black is a reference to monochrome computer monitors mostly used in the 1960s and 1970s, and in the film it is a visual signifier of Salander's hacker credentials and computing knowledge.
43. Chun, *Programmed Visions*, xii.
44. Ibid., 129.
45. For an analysis of *The Girl with the Dragon Tattoo* as a Swedish franchise revealing the already-embeddedness of neoliberalism in Swedish government, see Anna Westerståhl Stenport and Cecilia Ovesdotter Alm, "Corporations, Crime, and Gender Construction in Stieg Larsson's *The Girl with the Dragon Tattoo*," *Scandinavian Studies* 81, no. 2 (Summer 2009): 157–78, accessed January 27, 2017, http://www.jstor.org/stable/40920850.
46. David Fincher, Director's Commentary, *The Girl with the Dragon Tattoo*, Directed by David Fincher, 2011, Sony Pictures Home Entertainment, 2012, DVD.
47. This recuperative gesture is made by Niles Schwartz in the blog post, "'Fuck You You Fucking Fuck': David Fincher's Cyber Fairy Tale of (Mis)Communication, *The Girl With the Dragon Tattoo*," *Niles Files* (blog), December 27, 2011, accessed February 17, 2014, http://nilesfilmfiles.blogspot.co.uk/2011/12/fuck-you-you-fucking-fuck-david.html.
48. Donna Haraway, "A Cyborg Manifesto," in *The Cybercultures Reader*, ed. Daniel Bell and Barbara M. Kennedy (New York: Routledge, 2000), 311.

49. This is not to suggest that the female computers were more or less empowered than the female students in *The Social Network*; rather, this is intended to draw attention to the shifting position of women in the science and technology industries and the cultural turn to programming as (male) wizardry, which is discussed by Chun.
50. There is work to be done to consider the misogyny, or not, of Fincher's films. Given debate around Fincher's more recent adaptation of Gillian Flynn's novel *Gone Girl*, such an analysis would be timely. However, I have yet to think this through or to situate these films as adaptations of books in which the political unconscious appears troubled by misogyny, and so I don't want to rush further analysis here.

2. JONATHAN LETHEM'S AND MARK AMERIKA'S COMMON WRITING

1. Michael Hardt, "Reclaim the Common in Communism," *Guardian*, February 3, 2012, accessed February 19, 2015, http://www.theguardian.com/commentisfree/2011/feb/03/communism-capitalism-socialism-property. I quote Hardt here to evoke a way in which "the common" has materialized as a literal and metaphoric term for collectivity, sociality, and collective action in the contemporary moment. I do not mean to cite Hardt's, or Hardt and Negri's work as *the* critical claim for the common. For critique of Hardt and Negri's work on the commons, see Amy J. Elias, "The Commons . . . and Digital Planetarity," in *The Planetary Turn: Relationality and Geoaesthetics in the Twenty-First Century*, ed. Amy J. Elias and Christian Moraru (Evanston, IL: Northwestern University Press, 2015), 37–69; and Joss Hands, @ *Is For Activism: Dissent, Resistance and Rebellion in a Digital Culture* (London: Pluto Press, 2011). The argument offered here is less an interrogation of the commons as a political ideology than it is an investigation into how a digital commons is used and cited and how contentions of the commons are elided within narratives of its de facto accessibility and progressive orientation.
2. Matthew MacLellan and Margrit Talpalaru, "Editors' Introduction: Remaking the Commons," *Reviews in Cultural Theory* 2, no. 3 (2011–12): 1, accessed August 22, 2012, http://mediamargins.net/wp-content/uploads/2012/09/RCT-SP-On-the-Commons.pdf.
3. Jonathan Lethem, "The Ecstasy of Influence: A Plagiarism Mosaic," in *Sound Unbound: Sampling Digital Music and Culture*, ed. Paul D. Miller aka DJ Spooky that Subliminal Kid (Cambridge, MA: MIT Press, 2008), 39–40.
4. Nick Dyer-Witheford, "The Circulation of the Common," paper presented at Immaterial Labour, Multitudes and New Social Subjects: Class Composition in Cognitive Capitalism, King's College, University of Cambridge, April 2006, accessed May 14, 2016, http://www.fims.uwo.ca/people/faculty/dyerwitheford/commons2006.pdf.
5. Here I mean to suggest that Lethem's and Amerika's work is thinking with a left-wing politics of the communal and is anxious about owning an individual authorship, but it is (as I argue at the end of this chapter) ultimately ambivalent in its commitment to and participation in the commons. Also, perhaps, what we see in this work is a "professional critique" in the sense that Stefano Harney and Fred Moten outline in *Under-*

commons—whereby the works' (that is, the authors') attachment to the literary institution (which is represented by Lethem and Amerika as particularly white and patriarchal) means it is always already negligible in its commitment to a commons. In other words, the commons that Lethem and Amerika call forth exists within political discourse and does not conjure a radical, as in foundational, outside (the undercommons of Harney and Moten's writing). In keeping with the rest of this book, my turn to the banal is with the intent of looking to recover novelty as disturbance, if not as an actual radicality as refusal, or breaking, or destroying, from institutionalized texts (mainstream films, literary fiction, and so on). See Stefano Harvey and Fred Moten, *The Undercommons: Fugitive Planning and Black Study* (Wivenhoe, UK: Minor Compositions, 2013).

6. Jesse Darling, "Arcades, Mall Rats, and Tumblr Thugs," *New Inquiry*, February 12, 2012, accessed January 6, 2015, http://thenewinquiry.com/essays/arcades-mallrats-tumblr-thugs/; see also Jennifer Chan, "Notes on Post-Internet," in *You Are Here: Art After the Internet*, ed. Omar Kholeif (Manchester: Cornerhouse Publications, 2014): 106–23.
7. Dyer-Witheford, "The Circulation of the Common"; see also "What We Do," Creative Commons, accessed May 20, 2016, https://creativecommons.org/about/.
8. David M. Berry, *Copy, Rip, Burn: The Politics of Copyleft and Open Source* (London: Pluto Press, 2008), 90.
9. Joss Hands, "Platform Communism," *Culture Machine* 14 (2013): 15, accessed February 14, 2015, http://www.culturemachine.net/index.php/cm/article/view/510/525.
10. In chapter 3 I discuss Sheila Heti's interest in Andy Warhol as similarly linking banal technics through time.
11. Hillel Schwartz, *The Culture of the Copy: Striking Likeness, Unreasonable Facsimiles* (New York: Zone Books, 1998), 314.
12. Friedrich Kittler, "Gramophone, Film, Typewriter," trans. Dorothea Von Mücke and Philippe L. Similon, *October* 41 (Summer 1987): 104–5, doi:10.2307/778332.
13. Mark Amerika, *remixthebook* (Minneapolis: University of Minnesota Press, 2011), 137.
14. Ibid., 161, 117. Across the book as a whole, there are around a dozen uses of the phrase "enduring aesthetic fact," or related phrases such as "enduring aesthetic experiences" (18, 19, 33, 34, 40, 57, 61, 65, 66, 161, 218, 229, 242)—these were found by cross checking my notes with a search of the text on Google Books. According to another search, there are seventeen references to the term "inhabiting" throughout Amerika's book. Conceptually there are dozens more, as this phrase becomes linked to various tropes of new writers emerging and merging through older writers.
15. Ibid., 18 (emphasis in original).
16. Ibid., 34.
17. Ibid., 33.
18. Kittler uses the term "discrete" to reference the way each letter of the keyboard corresponds to one specific command prompt. As N. Katherine Hayles describes it, "One keystroke yields one letter, . . . the signifier itself is spatially discrete, durably inscribed, and flat." N. Katherine Hayles, "Virtual Bodies and Flickering Fingers," in *The Visual Culture Reader*, 2nd edition, ed. Nicholas Mirzoeff (New York: Routledge, 2002), 153.

19. Lucas D. Introna, "The Enframing of Code: Agency, Originality and the Plagiarist," *Theory Culture Society* 28, no. 6 (2011): 133, doi:10.1177/0263276411418131.
20. Kittler has written explicitly on code in an entry titled "Code." See Friedrich Kittler, "Code (or, How You Can Write Something Differently)," in *Software Studies / A Lexicon*, ed. Matthew Fuller (Cambridge, MA: MIT Press, 2008), 40–47.
21. Gary Hall, "Introduction: Pirate Philosophy," *Culture Machine* 10 (2009): 2, accessed February 14, 2015, http://www.culturemachine.net/index.php/cm/article/view/367/374.
22. Amerika, *remixthebook*, 117.
23. All references to the essay in this chapter refer to the version published in *Sound Unbound*. Looking at the collections in which Lethem's essay has appeared, it is arguable that it has been well established as part of the canon of work around remix and reappropriation culture in the digital age. I focus here on what the systems of representation within the essay are, how they operate, and how this might produce a digital-literary reading/study.
24. Jonathan Lethem, interview with David E. Gates, "A Kind of Vast Fiction," *PEN America*, 12 (2010): 26.
25. Lewis Hyde, *The Gift: Imagination and the Erotic Life of Property* (1983; Edinburgh: Canongate, 2007), 155.
26. Lethem, "The Ecstasy of Influence," 39.
27. Amerika, *remixthebook*, 138.
28. Mary Douglas, foreword to *The Gift: Form and Reason for Exchange in Archaic Societies*, by Marcel Mauss (New York: Routledge, 2002), x.
29. Jonathan Lethem, interview with Zara Dinnen, *Dandelion Journal* 2, no. 1 (2011), accessed December 3, 2013, http://dandelionjournal.org/index.php/dandelion/article/view/48/57.
30. Berry, *Copy, Rip, Burn*, 28.
31. Roland Barthes, *S/Z*, trans. Richard Miller (Oxford: Blackwell, 1992), 10.
32. Lethem, "The Ecstasy of Influence," 26. The lines, "All mankind is of one author, and is one volume; when one man dies, one chapter is not torn out of the book, but translated into a better language; and every chapter must be so translated," are from John Donne, "Meditation 17," and they appear as the epigraph to Lethem's essay.
33. Lethem, "The Ecstasy of Influence," 27.
34. Bernard Stiegler, "The Carnival of the New Screen: From Hegemony to Isonomy," in *The YouTube Reader*, ed. Pelle Snickars and Patrick Vonderau (Stockholm: National Library of Sweden, 2009), 53.
35. As Irit Rogoff explains in the preface to an interview with Stiegler, "terms such as 'short-circuit' indicate a break or a departure in thought and 'long circuit' that intimate a range of connectivities that allows for the passage of thought across time." Bernard Stiegler, interview with Irit Rogoff, "Transindividuation," *e-flux Journal* 14 (March 2010), accessed February 26, 2015, http://www.e-flux.com/journal/transindividuation/.
36. See Bernard Stiegler, *Technics and Time, 1: The Fault of Epimetheus*, trans. Richard Beardsworth and George Collins (Stanford, CA: Stanford University Press, 1998).
37. Ian James, "Bernard Stiegler and the Time of Technics," *Cultural Politics* 6, no. 2 (2010): 211, doi:10.2752/175174310X12672016548360.

38. Stiegler, "Transindividuation."
39. Ibid.
40. Ibid.
41. Ibid.
42. Introna, "The Enframing of Code," 131 (emphasis in original).
43. For a discussion of Barthes's enduring text, see N. Katherine Hayles, "Print Is Flat, Code Is Deep: The Importance of Media-Specific Analysis," *Poetics Today* 25, no. 1 (2004): 67–90, doi:10.1215/03335372-25-1-67. An alternative framework for thinking of the author in digital culture is Mark Poster's figure of the "digital author," later taken up by Kathleen Fitzpatrick as a networked constellation through which the writer and text are constituted *with* others. See Mark Poster, "The Digital Subject and Cultural Theory," in *The Book History Reader*, 2nd edition, ed. David Finkelstein and Alistair McCleery (New York: Routledge, 2006), 486–93; Kathleen Fitzpatrick, *Planned Obsolescence: Publishing, Technology, and the Future of the Academy* (New York: New York University Press, 2011).
44. Hands, "Platform Communism," 17.
45. Jodi Dean, "Communicative Capitalism: Circulation and the Foreclosure of Politics," *Cultural Politics* 1, no. 1 (2005): 53, doi:10.2752/174321905778054845.
46. Hands, "Platform Communism," 15.
47. Ibid., 15.
48. Ibid., 15.
49. The Promiscuous Materials Project is now no longer running. The Internet Archive's Wayback Machine has the most recent snapshot, from March 3, 2016. See http://web.archive.org/web/20160303202555/http://www.jonathanlethem.com/promiscuous_materials.html, last accessed May 28, 2016.
50. Lethem, "The Ecstasy of Influence," 42.
51. Ibid., 40 (original was italicized).
52. Aaron Wexler, "Notes from the Artist," James Hotels, accessed May 24, 2017, http://www.jameshotels.com/new-york/soho/explore-hotel/artatthejames/aaron-wexler.
53. Aaron Wexler explained his artistic process of "sampling and transforming" in e-mail correspondence with the author, January 6, 2010.
54. Wexler, e-mail to the author, January 6, 2010.
55. W. J. T. Mitchell, "The Work of Art in the Age of Biocybernetic Reproduction," *Modernism/modernity* 10, no. 3 (September 2003): 498, doi:10.1353/mod.2003.0067.
56. Lethem, interview with Zara Dinnen.
57. Elias, "The Commons . . . and Digital Planetarity," 61.

3. BEING SOCIAL IN A POSTDIGITAL WORLD IN *CATFISH* AND *HOW SHOULD A PERSON BE?*

1. Umberto Eco, *The Name of the Rose* (Boston: Mariner Books, 2014), 571.
2. Lee Konstantinou, "Periodizing the Present," *Contemporary Literature* 54, no. 2 (Summer 2013): 411, doi:10.1353/cli.2013.0013 (original was italicized).

3. Warren Buckland, "Wes Anderson: A 'Smart' Director of the New Sincerity?," *New Review of Film and Television Studies* 10, no. 1 (2012): 2, doi:10.1080/17400309.2011.640888 (emphasis in original).
4. Jennifer Chan, "Notes on Post-Internet," in *You Are Here: Art After the Internet*, ed. Omar Kholeif (Manchester: Cornerhouse Publications, 2014), 110.
5. "What Names Are Allowed on Facebook?" accessed June 10, 2016, https://en-gb.facebook.com/help/112146705538576; the wording on the site has since been updated.
6. Alexander R. Galloway, *The Interface Effect* (Cambridge: Polity, 2012), 40 (emphasis in original).
7. Ibid., 39.
8. "Let's Enhance" is a meme mocking the way that forensic investigators in crime films and TV shows are always zooming in on and enhancing images to extract more data, but the data of an image is finite—you can't make more. I highly recommend pausing your reading and checking out Duncan Robson, "Let's Enhance," YouTube video, December 13, 2009, accessed July 25, 2016, https://www.youtube.com/watch?v=Vxq9yj2pVWk.
9. Sarah Kember and Joanna Zylinska, *Life After New Media: Mediation as a Vital Process* (Cambridge, MA: MIT Press, 2012), 153.
10. Max took a hiatus from the third season of *Catfish* to work on a feature film *We Are Your Friends* (the reference is not to Facebook but to a song by Simian Mobile Disco). See Susannah Alexander, "Catfish Host Max Joseph Takes Hiatus, Replaced by Five Guests," *Digital Spy*, January 11, 2015, accessed July 7, 2015, http://www.digitalspy.com/tv/ustv/news/a620697/catfish-host-max-joseph-takes-hiatus-replaced-by-five-guests/.
11. In particular, *Catfish* has been likened to *The Blair Witch Project* (1999). See Mary E. Williams, "Horror's First Viral Hit: How 'The Blair Witch Project' Revolutionized Movies," *Salon*, June 13, 2014, accessed July 7, 2015, http://www.salon.com/2014/06/13/horrors_first_viral_hit_how_the_blair_witch_project_revolutionized_movies/.
12. Mary Pols, "Fish Tale," *Time*, September 27, 2010, accessed April 15, 2011, http://content.time.com/time/magazine/article/0,9171,2019606,00.html.
13. "Kya and Alyx," season 1 episode 6, *Catfish: The TV Show*, created by Max Joseph, Ariel Schulman, and Yaniv Schulman, MTV, December 17, 2012.
14. Sheila Heti and Claire Cameron, "How Should a Writer Be? An Interview with Sheila Heti," *Millions*, June 12, 2012, accessed June 12, 2016, http://www.themillions.com/2012/06/how-should-a-writer-be-an-interview-with-sheila-heti.html.
15. "BAFTA Introduces New 'Constructed Reality' Award," BBC News, November 9, 2011, accessed June 10, 2016, http://www.bbc.com/news/entertainment-arts-15652404.
16. Claire Faragher et al., "Is Structured Reality Corrupting Documentary?," *BAFTA*, Soundcloud podcast, accessed June 11, 2016, https://soundcloud.com/bafta/structured-reality-documentary-debate.
17. Sheila Heti, *How Should a Person Be?* (London: Harvill Secker, 2013), 2.
18. Ibid., 2–3.
19. Mark Andrejevic, *Reality TV: The Work of Being Watched* (Lanham, MD: Rowman and Littlefield, 2004), 8.

20. Rachel E. Dubrofsky and Megan M. Wood, "Posting Racism and Sexism: Authenticity, Agency and Self-Reflexivity in Social Media," *Communication and Critical/Cultural Studies* 11, no. 3 (2014): 284, doi:10.1080/14791420.2014.926247.
21. Heti, *How Should a Person Be?*, 22–23.
22. Ibid., 23.
23. Ibid., 18, 96, 105; on p. 105 Sheila and Margaux lie in bed in the hotel room they are sharing and watch as, "on my computer, an heiress gave her boyfriend a hand job."
24. Ibid., 89.
25. James Wood, "True Lives: Sheila Heti's *How Should a Person Be?*," *New Yorker*, June 25, 2012, accessed May 30, 2017, http://www.newyorker.com/magazine/2012/06/25/true-lives-2.
26. Heti, *How Should a Person Be?*, 107–8.
27. Ibid., 108.
28. Pat Hackett, introduction to *The Andy Warhol Diaries*, ed. Pat Hackett (New York: Warner Books, 1989), xvi.
29. Sianne Ngai, "Merely Interesting," *Critical Inquiry* 34, no. 4 (Summer 2008): 790, doi: 10.1086/592544.
30. Sianne Ngai, *Our Aesthetic Categories: Zany, Cute, Interesting* (Cambridge, MA: Harvard University Press, 2012), 146.
31. Ibid., 146.
32. Ibid., 271n105.
33. Pansy Duncan also makes this connection in her discussion of postmodern film and the emotion of boredom. Duncan connects Foster's and Ngai's explorations of shock and tediousness in avant-garde aesthetic culture. Pansy Duncan, *The Emotional Life of Postmodern Film: Affect Theory's Other* (New York: Routledge, 2016), 167.
34. See chapter 5 of Hal Foster *The Return of the Real: The Avant-Garde at the End of the Century* (Cambridge, MA: MIT Press, 1996), 127–70.
35. For discussion of Warhol's work as sound art, see Gustavus Stadler, "'My Wife': The Tape Recorder and Warhol's Queer Ways of Listening," *Criticism* 56, no. 3 (Summer 2014): 425–56, doi:10.1353/crt.2014.0025.
36. Stadler, "'My Wife,'" 441.
37. Lee Konstantinou, "We Had to Get Beyond Irony: How David Foster Wallace, Dave Eggers and a New Generation of Believers Changed Fiction," *Salon*, March 27, 2016, accessed June 10, 2016, http://www.salon.com/2016/03/27/we_had_to_get_beyond_irony_how_david_foster_wallace_dave_eggers_and_a_new_generation_of_believers_changed_fiction/.
38. Heti, *How Should a Person Be?*, 56.
39. Stadler, "'My Wife,'" 428.
40. Heti, *How Should a Person Be?*, 57.
41. Ibid., 59.
42. Ibid., 103.
43. Ibid., 35 (italics in original).
44. Galloway, *The Interface Effect*, 42 (emphasis in original).

45. Ibid., 44.
46. Ibid., 44–45.
47. Ibid., 39.
48. Heti, *How Should a Person Be?*, 81.
49. Ibid., 82 (emphasis in original).
50. Chan, "Notes on Post-Internet," 115, 108.
51. Ibid., 116.
52. Jodi Dean, *Blog Theory: Feedback and Capture in the Circuits of Drive* (Cambridge: Polity, 2010); Jodi Dean, "Communicative Capitalism: Circulation and the Foreclosure of Politics," *Cultural Politics* 1, no. 1 (2005): 51–74, doi:10.2752/174321905778054845; Tiziana Terranova, "Free Labor," in *Digital Labor: The Internet as Playground and Factory*, ed. Trebor Scholz (New York: Routledge, 2013), 33–77.
53. Wood, "True Lives."
54. Konstantinou, "Periodizing the Present"; Nicoline Timmer, *Do You Feel It Too? The Post-Postmodern Syndrome in American Fiction at the Turn of the Millennium* (Amsterdam: Rodopi, 2010); Stephen J. Burn, *Jonathan Franzen at the End of Postmodernism* (London: Bloomsbury, 2008); Adam Kelly, "Beginning with Postmodernism," *Twentieth Century Literature* 57, nos. 3–4 (Fall/Winter 2011): 391–422, doi:10.1215/0041462X-2011-4009.
55. Timmer, *Do You Feel It Too?*, 22.
56. In Jameson's formulation, "A seemingly realistic novel like [E. L Doctorow's] *Ragtime* is in reality a nonrepresentational work that combines fantasy signifiers from a variety of ideologemes in a kind of hologram." Fredric Jameson, *Postmodernism, or, The Cultural Logic of Late Capitalism* (Durham, NC: Duke University Press, 1991), 23.
57. Konstantinou, "Periodizing the Present," 419.
58. Kelly, "Beginning with Postmodernism," 393.
59. See Richard Grusin, ed., *The Nonhuman Turn* (Minneapolis: University of Minnesota Press, 2015); Rosi Braidotti, *The Posthuman* (Cambridge: Polity Press, 2013).
60. Timmer, *Do You Feel It Too?*, 359.
61. Ibid., 359.
62. Oliver L. Haimson and Anna Lauren Hoffmann, "Constructing and Enforcing 'Authentic' Identity Online: Facebook, Real Names, and Non-Normative Identities," *First Monday* 21, no. 6 (June 2016), doi:10.5210/fm.v21i6.6791.

4. TWENTY YEARS OF CALIFORNIAN IDEOLOGY IN *THE BUG* AND *THE CIRCLE*

1. Ellen Ullman, *The Bug* (New York: Telese/Doubleday, 2003), 171.
2. Ibid., 174.
3. Ibid.
4. Wendy Hui Kyong Chun, "On Software, or the Persistence of Visual Knowledge," *Grey Room* 18 (2004): 30, doi:10.1162/1526381043320741.

4. CALIFORNIAN IDEOLOGY IN *THE BUG* AND *THE CIRCLE* 185

5. Ellen Ullman, *Close to the Machine* (San Francisco: City Lights Books, 1997).
6. (Ro)Bert(a) Walton is a pun on Mary Shelley's "Robert Walton." See Benjamin Anastas, "The Soul of a New Machine," *New York Times*, June 15, 2003, accessed June 13, 2016, http://www.nytimes.com/2003/06/15/books/review/15ANASTAT.html.
7. Ullman, *The Bug*, 323.
8. Ibid., 4.
9. Ibid., 4–5.
10. Ibid., 5. Berta is not explicitly identified as white—I determine her to be white based on the proximity of her character to the author, as presented in Ullman's memoir *Close to the Machine*. I discuss 9/11 as a turning point in American literary history in chapter 5.
11. Ibid.
12. Ibid., 6.
13. Ibid., 7–8.
14. Ibid., 5.
15. Lauren Berlant describes the unresolving present as a "stretched-out now," which "merges an intensified present with senses of the recent past and near future." See Lauren Berlant, "Thinking about Feeling Historical," *Emotion, Space and Society* 1 (2008), 5n8, doi:10.1016/j.emospa.2008.08.006.
16. Ullman, *The Bug*, 347.
17. Ibid., 348.
18. Ibid.
19. Ibid., 336.
20. Wendy Chun, "On 'Sourcery,' or Code as Fetish," *Configurations* 16, no. 3 (Fall 2008): 303, doi:10.1353/con.0.0064.
21. Alexander R. Galloway, "Language Wants to Be Overlooked: On Software and Ideology," *Journal of Visual Culture* 5 (2006): 315–31, doi:10.1177/1470412906070519 (emphasis in original).
22. Gabriella Coleman, *Hacker, Hoaxer, Whistleblower, Spy: The Many Faces of Anonymous* (New York: Verso Books, 2014), 34. Given that the Jester is a figure of the programmer—it is made by Ethan and then given the power of affective agency by Ethan—I think we can consider the bug as akin to Coleman's hacker-trickster figure, a "provocateur and saboteur." Working through Lewis Hyde's writing about the trickster, Coleman suggests that various hacker actions and collectives might be productively thought of as tricksters. In *The Bug* the Jester is the hacker, and it is Ethan and Berta who are trolled by their own creation. The characterization of the jester as a cultural figure who "speaks truth to power" is discussed in David Carlyon, "The Trickster as Academic Comfort Food," *Journal of American & Comparative Cultures* 25, nos. 1–2 (March 2002): 14, doi:10.1111/1542-734X.00003.
23. Ullman, *The Bug*, 180 (emphasis in original).
24. Ibid., 179 (emphasis in original).
25. Ibid., 12.
26. Dave Eggers, *The Circle* (London: Hamish Hamilton, 2013), 1.

27. Ibid., 5.
28. Ibid., 9.
29. Ibid., 5.
30. Ibid., 7.
31. Ibid., 12.
32. See Fred Turner, *From Counterculture to Cyberculture: Stewart Brand, the Whole Earth Network, and the Rise of Digital Utopianism* (Chicago: University of Chicago Press, 2006).
33. David Silver, "Looking Backward, Looking Forward: Cyberculture Studies 1990–2000," in *Web.studies: Rewiring Media Studies for the Digital Age*, ed. David Gauntlett (Oxford: Oxford University Press, 2000), 19–30, available online as David Silver, "Introducing Cyberculture," *Resource Centre for Cyberculture Studies*, accessed June 13, 2016, http://mysite.du.edu/~lavita/edpx_3770_13s/_docs/Intro%20Cyberculture%20 copy.pdf. See also David Bell and Barbara M. Kennedy, eds., *The Cybercultures Reader* (New York: Routledge, 2000); Michael Benedikt, *Cyberspace: First Steps* (Cambridge, MA: MIT Press, 1992).
34. "Boosterish" is in Caroline Bassett, "New Maps for Old?: The Cultural Stakes of '2.0,'" *Fibreculture Journal* 13 (2008), accessed April 5, 2012, http://thirteen.fibr eculturejournal.org/fcj-088-new-maps-for-old-the-cultural-stakes-of-2-0/; the quote from *Wired* is cited in Caroline Bassett and Chris Wilbert, "Where You Want to Go Today (Like It or Not): Leisure Practices in Cyberspace," in *Leisure/Tourism Geographies: Practices and Geographical Knowledge*, ed. David Crouch (New York: Routledge, 1999), 192n2.
35. Richard Barbrook and Andy Cameron, "The Californian Ideology," *Science as Culture* 26, no. 6 (1996): 44–72, published online at *Hypermedia Research Centre*, accessed June 13, 2016, http://www.hrc.wmin.ac.uk/theory-californianideology-main.html.
36. Ibid.
37. Ibid.
38. Richard Barbrook, "The Owl of Minerva Flies at Dusk," in *The Internet Revolution: From Dot-Com Capitalism to Cybernetic Communism*, Network Notebook 10 (Amsterdam: Institute of Network Cultures, 2015), 11.
39. Turner, *From Counterculture to Cyberculture*, 260. For histories of the particular blend of new left and new right politics that characterized developments in software and the World Wide Web in the postwar period, see also Thomas Streeter, *The Net Effect: Romanticism, Capitalism, and the Internet* (New York: New York University Press, 2010); Nathan Ensmenger, *The Computer Boys Take Over: Computers, Programmers, and the Politics of Technical Expertise* (Cambridge, MA: MIT Press, 2010).
40. Turner, *From Counterculture to Cyberculture*, 261.
41. Ibid., 261.
42. Frank Pasquale, *The Black Box Society: The Secret Algorithms that Control Money and Information* (Cambridge, MA: Harvard University Press, 2015), 8.
43. Barbrook and Cameron, "The Californian Ideology."

44. Products and practices developed in some of the biggest proprietary technology companies of today—Apple, Microsoft, Facebook—are built on either open or hacked source code. Chris Kelty has written extensively about open-source and free software from the particular perspective of what it means to those engaged in producing the technical and social protocols of digital media. He writes that geeks are "a public constituted around the technical and moral ideas of order that allow them to associate with one another." Chris Kelty, *Two Bits: The Cultural Significance of Free Software* (Durham, NC: Duke University Press, 2008), 27. For Kelty, geeks constitute a recursive public that holds a particular social imaginary about what new digital media is and should be: "Techniques and design principles that are used to create software or to implement networking protocols cannot be distinguished from ideas or principles of social and moral order for these informants. Openness . . . is a practice and a concept on which recursiveness depends: If one cannot access and see the software and protocols, if they are not open, this particular public cannot exist. . . . The right to create software is seen in a similar light as the right to state an opinion." Chris Kelty, "Geeks, Social Imaginaries, and Recursive Publics," *Cultural Anthropology* 20, no. 2 (May 2005): 186–87, accessed June 22, 2016, http://www.jstor.org/stable/3651533. This culture is an unspoken common sense in *The Bug*, appearing as everyday working practices at Telligentsia, but in *The Circle*, only the character of Kalden/Ty seems aware of the cultural lineages and social norms of software production.
45. Ullman, *The Bug*, 148.
46. Eggers, *The Circle*, 19–24. Margaret Atwood argues that *The Circle* is a Menippean satire, "distinct from social satire in viewing moral defects less as flaws of character than as intellectual perversions," and discusses the names of the characters and the various literary and historical plays Eggers makes. See Margaret Atwood, "When Privacy Is Theft," *New York Review of Books*, November 21, 2013, accessed June 22, 2016, http://www.nybooks.com/articles/2013/11/21/eggers-circle-when-privacy-is-theft/.
47. TruYou is barely an exaggeration of Facebook's "real name policy," which is the technical point at which the user encounters Facebook's view of itself as an "online identity registrar." Oliver L. Haimson and Anna Lauren Hoffman, "Constructing and Enforcing 'Authentic' Identity Online: Facebook, Real Names, and Non-Normative Identities," *First Monday* 6, no. 21 (June 2016), doi:10.5210/fm.v21i6.6791. See also D. E. Wittkower, "Facebook and Dramauthentic Identity: A Post-Goffmanian Theory of Identity Performance on SNS," *First Monday* 4, no. 19 (April 2014), doi:10.5210/fm.v19i4.4858.
48. Eggers, *The Circle*, 20.
49. *Daily Mail* review, quoted on the front cover of Penguin 2013 edition of *The Circle*, available on Google Books, accessed June 22, 2016, https://books.google.co.uk/books?id=5VZ5AAAAQBAJ&lpg=PP1&dq=the%20circle%20eggers&pg=PT6#v=onepage&q&f=false.
50. Alexander R. Galloway, *The Interface Effect* (Cambridge: Polity, 2012), 137.
51. Ibid.
52. Eggers, *The Circle*, 110.

53. Ibid., 371.
54. Ibid., 29.
55. Ibid., 178–79.
56. Ibid., 459.
57. Ibid., 5–6, 216.
58. Ibid., 218–19.
59. Matthew G. Kirschenbaum describes storage as the material thing that "enabled reliable real-time, nonsequential access to large reserves of information"; but it is also a kind of "imaginary, . . . a focalized expression of the collecting impulse underpinning everything from the Web's myriad niche cultures . . . to the global garage sale of eBay." Matthew G. Kirschenbaum, *Mechanisms: New Media and the Forensic Imagination* (Cambridge, MA: MIT Press, 2008), 5.
60. Eggers, *The Circle*, 222, 224.
61. Ibid., 230.
62. Ibid., 232.
63. Christine T. Wolf, "DIY Videos on YouTube: Identity and Possibility in the Age of Algorithms," *First Monday* 21, no. 6 (June 2016), doi:10.5210/fm.v21i6.6787.
64. See Caroline D. Hamilton, *One Man Zeitgeist: Dave Eggers, Publishing and Publicity* (New York: Continuum, 2010); Elizabeth Twitchell, "Dave Eggers's *What is the What*: Fictionalizing Trauma in the Era of Misery Lit," *American Literature* 83, no. 3 (2011): 621–48, doi:10.1215/00029831–1339890; James Clements, "Trust Your Makers of Things! The Metafictional Pact in Dave Eggers' *You Shall Know Our Velocity*," *Critique* 56, no. 2 (March 2015): 121–37, doi:10.1080/00111619.2013.866541.
65. Nitasha Tiku, "*Circle* Jerks: Why Do Editors Love Dave Eggers?," *Gawker*, October 2, 2013, accessed July 22, 2015, http://gawker.com/circle-jerks-why-do-editors-love-dave-eggers-1440226375.
66. Most notably, the cover of the *New Times Magazine* for September 29, 2013, is devoted to an extract of *The Circle* published in the issue. The headline is, "We Like You So Much and Want to Know You Better."
67. Dave Eggers, interview with Gaby Wood, "Dave Eggers Interview," *Telegraph*, October 5, 2013, accessed July 3, 2016, http://www.telegraph.co.uk/culture/books/authorinterviews/10356543/Dave-Eggers-interview.html.
68. Katherine Losse, quoted in Tiku, "*Circle* Jerks."
69. Ibid.
70. Rebecca Solnit, "Resisting Monoculture," *Guernica*, January 7, 2014, accessed August 17, 2015, https://www.guernicamag.com/daily/rebecca-solnit-resisting-monoculture/.
71. Tiku, "*Circle* Jerks."
72. Melissa Gira Grant, "Girl Geeks and Boy Kings," *Dissent* (Winter 2013), accessed July 22, 2015, https://www.dissentmagazine.org/article/girl-geeks-and-boy-kings.
73. Wolf, "DIY Videos on YouTube."
74. Eggers, *The Circle*, 108.

5. REFRESH, UPDATE, WAIT, OR, LIVING WITH THE DIGITAL BANAL IN *CHRONIC CITY* AND *REFRESH REFRESH*

1. Personal and ubiquitous computing and wireless connectivity engender an explosion of thinking about distraction as it was conceived in relation to mass media. See William Bogard, "Distraction and Digital Culture," *CTheory* a088 (October 2000), accessed July 4, 2016, www.ctheory.net/articles.aspx?id=131; Nicholas Carr, *The Shallows: How the Internet is Changing the Way We Think, Read and Remember* (London: Atlantic Books, 2010); Jonathan Crary, *24/7: Late Capitalism and the End of Sleep* (London: Verso, 2013); N. Katherine Hayles, "Hyper and Deep Attention: The Generational Divide in Cognitive Modes," *Profession* (2007): 187–99, doi:10.1632/prof.2007 .2007.1.187; Alan Jacobs, *The Pleasures of Reading in an Age of Distraction* (Oxford: Oxford University Press, 2011).
2. Bogard, "Distraction and Digital Culture."
3. Ibid.
4. Hayles "Hyper and Deep Attention," 190.
5. Bogard, "Distraction and Digital Culture."
6. Jonathan Lethem, *Chronic City* (London: Faber and Faber, 2010); Danica Novgorodoff, *Refresh Refresh*, with Benjamin Percy and James Ponsoldt (New York: First Second, 2009). Benjamin Percy is the author of the short story, "Refresh Refresh," on which Novgorodoff's comic is based. James Ponsoldt adapted Percy's story for a screenplay, which subsequently became the basis for Novgorodoff's graphic novel. Ponsoldt is also the director of *Smashed* (2012) and *The Spectacular Now* (2013), both films about the everyday lives of lower-income, disaffected young people, as well as *The End of the Tour* (2015), a reconstruction of David Lipsky's *Rolling Stones* interview with David Foster Wallace, and *The Circle* (2017), the film adaptation of Eggers's novel. It is worth noting this, as Ponsoldt's own creative investments are evident in his adaptation, which expands on Percy's interest in the mundane, slow violence of life in contemporary America, substance abuse among young people, and life lived with new personal technologies. I privilege Novgorodoff here as author and artist because I am interested in the ways digital media are drawn and placed in the narrative.
7. "Cyberspace" is a term broadly associated with Internet use and virtual reality from the late 1980s onward, made popular by its use in William Gibson's 1984 novel, *Neuromancer*. At the time of *Neuromancer*'s publication, the World Wide Web did not exist and the Internet was not commonly accessible. Gibson describes his imaginary cyberspace as a "consensual hallucination experienced daily by billions of legitimate operators," a "graphic representation of data abstracted from the banks of every computer in the human system." William Gibson, *Neuromancer* (1984; London: Harper-Voyager, 1995), 51. As is hopefully clear, the argument in *The Digital Banal* is premised on a post-cyberspace conception of what digital media is and of what digital communication (life online, so to speak) materially and culturally comprises. The present chapter posits the move forward from cyberspace as a particular concern of Lethem's *Chronic City*. Instead of cyberspace, here I discuss a complex understanding of being online all the

time and of digital media as extending and operating beyond a distinct digital realm. In doing so I consider the ways social norms, such as passing time, shopping, and working, are shaped through the habitual use of digital media. In pursuing this concern, I follow the argument of many Internet studies and social media theorists who view digital media and the Internet as embedded, inextricable dimensions of everyday life. See Maria Bakardjieva, *Internet Society: The Internet in Everyday Life* (London: Sage, 2005); Nancy K. Baym, *Personal Connections in the Digital Age* (Cambridge: Polity Press, 2011); Caroline Haythornwaite and Barry Wellman, eds., *The Internet in Everyday Life* (Oxford: Blackwell Publishing, 2002). See also Julie E. Cohen's work on cyberspace as (or as not) a legally bound/binding space in Julie E. Cohen, "Cyberspace as/ and Space," *Columbia Law Review* 107, no. 1 (January 2007): 210–56; Julie E. Cohen, *Configuring the Networked Self: Law, Code and the Play of Everyday Practice* (New Haven, CT: Yale University Press, 2012). Working through histories of critical discourses about race in cyberspace, Lisa Nakamura's essay "Cyberrace" offers a comprehensive account of the attitudes and methodologies associated with discourses of "cyber" since the 1990s. See Lisa Nakamura, "Cyberrace," *PMLA* 123, no. 5 (2008): 1673–82. Perhaps most apposite for the discussion in this chapter (as it accounts for online/offline experience) is Ken Hillis's formation of the web as a "dynamic" of ritual, fetish and sign, "anywhere, everywhere, and nowhere but always on the move." Ken Hillis, *Online a Lot of the Time: Ritual, Fetish, Sign* (Durham, NC: Duke University Press, 2009), 2.

8. Jonathan Lethem, interview with David E. Gates, "A Kind of Vast Fiction," *PEN America* 12 (2010), 26.

9. In Rob Nixon's *Slow Violence* he argues that today, "fast is faster than it used to be, and story units have become concomitantly shorter. In this cultural milieu of digitally speeded up time, and foreshortened narrative, the intergenerational aftermath becomes a harder sell." Rob Nixon, *Slow Violence and the Environmentalism of the Poor* (Cambridge, MA: Harvard University Press, 2011), 13. Critiquing the allure of a procession of apocalypses, booms, and busts, *Slow Violence* is a call to address recent history as part of a longer duration, to situate the spectacle of the contemporary within the long view. Nixon's specific concerns are environmental. He is drawing attention to narratives of environmental and climate violence that are lost in the noise of the media spectacle, which—even as it reports environmental disaster—brackets all events within discrete news cycles. Technology is a concern to Nixon, but only insofar as it is part of the problem: our culture of speed is all one way, getting faster. *Refresh Refresh* and *Chronic City* elicit an interest in slowness in the sense that both texts are quite slow—they have long stretches of no action—and both texts use slowness as a way to narrate the everyday. Discussing digital media in relation to Nixon's work would be to misread his investments in slowness, but I reference it here because Nixon's approach to slowness is one that I think can be borrowed and reworked. If the digital banal is a condition that is always receding from view, creative interventions of slowness offer a way to apprehend it.

10. Susan Kollin, "Not Yet Another World: Ecopolitics and Urban Natures in Jonathan Lethem's *Chronic City*," *LIT: Literature Interpretation Theory* 26, no. 4 (2015): 255, doi: 10.1080/10436928.2015.1092346.

11. Ibid., 255.
12. Benjamin Percy, "Refresh, Refresh," in *Refresh, Refresh* by Benjamin Percy (London: Jonathan Cape, 2008), 3–20.
13. Ibid., 8 (emphasis in original).
14. Ibid., 10.
15. Jonathan Lethem, "Q&A with Jonathan Lethem," Occasional Music: A Symposium on the Work of Jonathan Lethem, Birkbeck College, London, July 10, 2010.
16. Lethem, *Chronic City*, 94.
17. For a more in-depth analysis of the computer as "thing" in *Refresh Refresh*, see Zara Dinnen, "Things that Matter: Representing Everyday Technological Things in Comics," *Studies in Comics* 3, no. 2 (Winter 2013), doi:10.1386/stic.3.2.313_1.
18. Kollin, "Not Yet Another World," 256.
19. Lethem, "A Kind of Vast Fiction," 26. In lots of ways, *Chronic City* is a corrective and homage to William Gibson's cyberpunk writing. As well as *Chronic City*'s shifting presentation of online activity as a distinct territory, a cyberspace, there is the hallucinatory aspect of meditation (see note 25 below) and the interest in eBay as a new frontier. In 1999 William Gibson published a meditation on his obsession with eBay in the essay "My Obsession" in *Wired*. Gibson describes sitting down to work in the morning and immediately opening eBay in a "dream state"; he gets "deep into eBay," driven by the desire to "import a unique object, physically, out of cyberspace." Gibson, "My Obsession," reprinted in *Everyday eBay: Culture, Collecting, and Desire*, ed. Ken Hillis, Michael Petit, and Nathan Scott Epley (New York: Routledge, 2006), 19–30.
20. See Ken Hillis, Michael Petit, and Nathan Scott Epley, introduction to *Everyday eBay*, 1–17.
21. Susanna Paasonen, "'Virgin Mary in Grilled Cheese Not a Hoax! Look & See!': Sublime Kitsch on eBay," in *Everyday eBay*, 203.
22. Ibid., 203.
23. Lethem, *Chronic City*, 140–41.
24. Ibid., 141.
25. Ibid.
26. The hazy tone of the characters' online expeditions mocks cyberpunk aesthetics—the "consensual hallucination" of William Gibson's cyberspace. Perkus Tooth is perhaps an anti-Case (the jacked-in protagonist of *Neuromancer*). Perkus's heightened consciousness may reveal the conspiracy around him—like Case, he is singled out for his perceptive intellectual faculty. His headaches, his ellipses, and his smoking offer up moments in which he goes off into some other place to return enlightened. But he does not enter the grid; Perkus's heightened consciousness is precisely what keeps him off-grid and unable to master the cybernetic systems of power, which he perceives as forms of control.
27. Lethem, *Chronic City*, 141.
28. Ibid.
29. Ibid., 148.
30. See "3% of Americans Use Dial-Up at Home," *Pew Research Center*, accessed May 24, 2017, http://www.pewresearch.org/fact-tank/2013/08/21/3-of-americans-use-dial-up-at

-home/; Dave Beede and Anne Neville, "Breaking Down the Urban-Rural Broadband Divide," *National Telecommunications and Information Administration*, June 5, 2013, accessed September 9, 2014, https://www.ntia.doc.gov/blog/2013/breaking-down-urban-rural-broadband-divide.

31. "Chinese gold farmer" is the name given to video game players who play nonstop to accrue virtual currency, which is then exchanged for money offline. This work is a new kind of industrial labor and is hugely exploitative; gamers receive very little in return for what they extract. See Julian Dibbell, "The Life of the Chinese Gold Farmer," *New York Times Magazine*, June 17, 2007, accessed July 12, 2016, http://www.nytimes.com/2007/06/17/magazine/17lootfarmers-t.html?_r=0. The final chapter of Galloway's *The Interface Effect* argues that we may see the Chinese gold farmers as an intensified version of all our digital labors in post-Fordist economies. The "gold farmer is an allegorical portrait for how identity exists online, a portrait not so much of the orientalized other, but of ourselves" in a post-Fordist economy, "a mode of production that makes life itself the site of valorization, that is to say, it turns seemingly normal human behavior into monetizable labor." Alexander R. Galloway, *The Interface Effect* (Cambridge: Polity, 2012), 121, 136. For a critique of the reporting of the "Chinese gold farmers," see Lisa Nakamura, "Race and Identity in Digital Media," *Media and Society*, 5th edition, ed. James Curran (New York: Bloomsbury, 2010), 336–47.
32. Edward Castronova, "On Virtual Economies," *Game Studies* 3, no. 2 (December 2003), accessed July 17, 2015, http://www.gamestudies.org/0302/castronova/.
33. Trebor Scholz, ed., *Digital Labor: The Internet as Playground and Factory* (New York: Routledge, 2013), 1.
34. Brett Neilson and Ted Rossiter, "Introduction: Multitudes, Creative Organisation and the Precarious Condition of New Media Labour," *Fibreculture Journal* 5 (2005), accessed August 24, 2014, http://five.fibreculturejournal.org/.
35. See Lauren Berlant et al., "Precarity Talk: A Virtual Roundtable," *TDR: The Drama Review* 56, no. 4 (2012): 163–77, accessed July 11, 2016, https://muse.jhu.edu/article/491900.
36. Galloway, *The Interface Effect*, 120.
37. Neilson and Rossiter, "Introduction."
38. Novgorodoff, *Refresh Refresh*, 96–100.
39. Ibid., 44–45.
40. Sarah Kember and Joanna Zylinska, *Life After New Media: Mediation as a Vital Process* (Cambridge, MA: MIT Press), 77 (original was italicized).
41. Novgorodoff, *Refresh Refresh*, 47–50.
42. Lethem, *Chronic City*, 328.
43. For more on the hologram as digital signifier, see Zara Dinnen, "Case Study no. 1: Holoback," *Exaptation and the Digital Now* panel, *Media N*, CAA conference edition (2014), accessed February 3, 2017, http://median.newmediacaucus.org/caa-edition/.
44. Kollin, "Not Yet Another World," 256.
45. Ibid., 263.

46. Lethem, *Chronic City*, 97. Recent reports estimate that data centers produce as much greenhouse gas emission as the aviation industry but receive nowhere near the same amount of government or media attention. See Adam Vaughn, "How Viral Cat Videos Are Warming the Planet," *Guardian*, September 25, 2015, accessed July 4, 2016, https://www.theguardian.com/environment/2015/sep/25/server-data-centre-emissions-air-travel-web-google-facebook-greenhouse-gas.
47. Lethem, *Chronic City*, 109.
48. For literary and cultural histories of the American decade, the long 1990s, see Samuel Cohen, *After the End of History: American Fiction in the 1990s* (Iowa City: University of Iowa Press, 2009); Philip E. Wegner, *Life between Two Deaths, 1989–2001: US Culture in the Long Nineties* (Durham, NC: Duke University Press, 2009); Jay Prosser, ed. *American Fiction of the 1990s* (New York: Routledge, 2008).
49. Bill Clinton, quoted in Martin Halliwell, "Contemporary American Culture," in *American Thought and Culture in the 21st Century*, ed., Martin Halliwell and Catherine Morley (Edinburgh: Edinburgh University Press, 2008), 211.
50. The most emphatic and pervasive iterations of the post-9/11, post-Y2K cultural conditions have been new media modes of surveillance and profiling. In various ways, the banality of everyday self-surveillance manifest on social media platforms is intimately connected to the overt and violent forms of surveillance carried out under the guise of the US "war on terror." See Shoshana Magnet and Kelly Gates, *The New Media of Surveillance* (New York: Routledge, 2009); see especially Lisa Nakamura's afterword, "The Socioalgorithms of Race: Sorting it Out in Jihad Worlds," in ibid., 149–62.
51. Martin Halliwell and Catherine Morley, "Introduction," in *American Thought and Culture in the 21st Century*, ed., Martin Halliwell and Catherine Morley (Edinburgh: Edinburgh University Press, 2008), 3.
52. Novgorodoff, *Refresh Refresh*, 112–38.

6. SPECULATING ON THE REAL ESTATE OF THE DIGITAL BANAL

1. Stephen Graham, "Beyond the 'Dazzling Light': From Dreams of Transcendence to the 'Remediation' of Urban Life," *New Media & Society* 6, no. 1 (2004): 18, doi:10.1177/1461444804039905.
2. According to a 2013 report by the National Telecommunications and Information Administration, in the United States, "the closer a community lies to a central city, the more likely it is to have access to broadband at higher speeds." See David Beede and Anne Neville, "Breaking Down the Urban-Rural Broadband Divide," *National Telecommunications and Information Administration*, June 5, 2013, accessed September 9, 2014, https://www.ntia.doc.gov/blog/2013/breaking-down-urban-rural-broadband-divide.
3. Lisa Parks and Nicole Starosielski, "Introduction," in *Signal Traffic: Critical Studies of Media Infrastructures*, ed. Lisa Parks and Nicole Starosielski (Urbana: University of Illinois Press, 2015), 2–3.

4. Ibid., 4.
5. Shannon Mattern, "Deep Time of Media Infrastructure," in *Signal Traffic: Critical Studies of Media Infrastructures*, ed. Lisa Parks and Nicole Starosielski (Urbana: University of Illinois Press, 2015), 96.
6. Parks and Starosielski, "Introduction," 3.
7. Nigel Thrift and Shaun French, "The Automatic Production of Space," *Transactions of the Institute of British Geographers* 27, no. 3 (2002): 309, doi:10.1111/1475-5661.00057.
8. For more on the everyday production of space as a code practice, see Anne Galloway, "Intimations of Everyday Life: Ubiquitous Computing and the City," *Cultural Studies* 18, no. 2 (2004): 384–408, doi:10.1080/0950238042000201572; Rob Kitchin and Martin Dodge, *Code/Space: Software and Everyday Life* (Cambridge, MA: MIT Press, 2011); Nigel Thrift, "Electric Animals: New Models of Everyday Life?," *Cultural Studies* 18, no. 2 (2004): 461–82, doi:10.1080/0950238042000201617.
9. This quote is taken from the website for Ingrid Burrington's project, "Seeing Networks in New York City," *Seeing Networks* (blog), accessed July 14, 2016, http://seeingnetworks.in/nyc/. See also Burrington's book, *Networks of New York: An Internet Infrastructure Guide* (self-published, 2015), https://app.moonclerk.com/pay/ljgls7hoch.
10. Jennifer Egan, *A Visit from the Goon Squad* (London: Constable & Robinson / Corsair, 2011), 327.
11. Gary Shteyngart, *Super Sad True Love Story* (London: Granta, 2010), 88, 41.
12. Ibid., 35.
13. Ibid., 25.
14. Ibid., 78.
15. Ibid., 67.
16. Gary Shteyngart and Natalie Jacoby, "The Daily: Gary Shteyngart," *Paris Review*, July 27, 2010, accessed July 28, 2011, http://www.theparisreview.org/blog/2010/07/27/gary-shteyngart/.
17. Shteyngart, *Super Sad True Love Story*, 86.
18. Ibid., 88.
19. Ibid.
20. Ibid., 268.
21. Ibid.
22. Ibid., 268–69.
23. Ibid., 268.
24. Thrift and French, "The Automatic Production of Space," 311.
25. James Franco, "Summer Reading Part 5: *A Visit From the Goon Squad*," *Huffington Post*, June 16, 2012, accessed July 14, 2016, http://www.huffingtonpost.com/entry/summer-reading-part-5_b_1602801.
26. Reading Egan's novel *Look at Me* (2001), Adam Kelly suggests that Egan's work resonates with an uncanniness of historical literary tropes and also the uncanniness of its contemporary moment. Published before 9/11, *Look at Me* appears to predict that event, or at least to premediate it. Certainly Egan's awareness of the political and media texture that might build toward such an event registers as uncanny. In my invoca-

tion of the uncanny, I extend Kelly's reference to suggest that Egan's work is explicitly haunted by digital media. See Adam Kelly, "Beginning with Postmodernism," *Twentieth-Century Literature* 57, nos. 3–4 (Fall/Winter 2011): 391–422, doi:10.1215/0041462X-2011-4009.

27. Egan's interest in media is discussed at length in an interview with the author. For Egan, "The story of media saturation in our lives, beginning with the television of the Vietnam War, feels like the big thing I have to write about, here, the cultural cataclysm that has occurred within my lifetime. I haven't arrived at that conclusion intellectually. It just feels alive and rich and I can't quite seem to stay away from it." Jennifer Egan and Zara Dinnen, "'This Is All Artificial': An Interview with Jennifer Egan," *Post45*, May 20, 2016, accessed July 3, 2016, http://post45.research.yale.edu/2016/05/this-is-all-artificial-an-interview-with-jennifer-egan/.
28. Ben Highmore, *Cityscapes: Cultural Readings in the Material and Symbolic City* (Basingstoke, UK: Palgrave Macmillan, 2005), 121.
29. Egan, *A Visit from the Goon Squad*, 61–62.
30. Jennifer Egan, "Black Box," *New Yorker*, June 4, 11, 2012, accessed July 14, 2016 http://www.newyorker.com/magazine/2012/06/04/black-box-2.
31. Egan, *A Visit from the Goon Squad*, 239.
32. A small selection from UK and US broadsheets includes Christian House, Review of *A Visit from the Goon Squad*, by Jennifer Egan, *Independent*, March 13, 2011, accessed July 14, 2016, http://www.independent.co.uk/arts-entertainment/books/reviews/a-visit-from-the-goon-squad-by-jennifer-egan-2240306.html; Ron Charles, Review of *A Visit from the Goon Squad*, by Jennifer Egan, *Washington Post*, June 16, 2010, accessed July 14, 2016, http://www.washingtonpost.com/wp-dyn/content/article/2010/06/15/AR2010061504751.html; Celia McGee, Review of *A Visit from the Goon Squad*, by Jennifer Egan, *Chicago Tribune*, accessed July 14, 2016, http://www.chicagotribune.com/lifestyles/books/chi-books-review-goon-squad-egan-story.html; Sarah Churchwell, Review of *A Visit from the Goon Squad*, by Jennifer Egan, *Guardian*, March 12, 2011, accessed July 14, 2016, https://www.theguardian.com/books/2011/mar/13/jennifer-egan-visit-goon-squad. For more discussion, see also the Goodreads reviews of *A Visit from the Goon Squad*, accessed July 14, 2016, http://www.goodreads.com/book/show/7331435-a-visit-from-the-goon-squad.
33. Egan and Dinnen, "'This Is All Artificial.'"
34. Egan, *A Visit from the Goon Squad*, 288.
35. Ibid., 248.
36. Allison Carruth, "The Digital Cloud and the Micropolitics of Energy," *Public Culture* 26, no. 2 (Spring 2014): 356, doi:10.1215/08992363-2392093.
37. Egan, *A Visit from the Goon Squad*, 267.
38. Carruth, "The Digital Cloud," 356.
39. Egan, *A Visit from the Goon Squad*, 319.
40. Ibid., 309.
41. Ibid., 311.
42. Ibid., 23 (emphasis in original).

43. Ibid., 318 (italics in original).
44. "Feels" is shorthand for feelings or for being overwhelmed by feeling. According to Urban Dictionary, "feels" is a "wave of emotions that sometimes cannot be adequately explained." KissTheDragon, "Feels," Urban Dictionary, June 28, 2012, accessed July 14, 2016, http://www.urbandictionary.com/define.php?term=Feels.
45. Egan, *A Visit from the Goon Squad*, 323–24.
46. Ibid., 320.
47. Sherry Turkle, *Life on the Screen: Identity in the Age of the Internet* (New York: Touchstone, 1997), 183.
48. Caroline Bassett, *The Arc and the Machine: Narrative and New Media* (Manchester: Manchester University Press, 2007), 129.
49. Egan, *A Visit from the Goon Squad*, 331–32.
50. Ibid., 331.
51. Ibid., 332–33.
52. Ibid., 332.
53. Sarah Kember and Joanna Zylinska, *Life After New Media: Mediation as a Vital Process* (Cambridge, MA: MIT Press, 2012), xv.
54. Colson Whitehead, *Zone One* (London: Vintage, 2012), 26.
55. Glen Duncan, "A Plague of Urban Undead in Lower Manhattan," *New York Times*, October 28, 2011, accessed August 24, 2014, http://www.nytimes.com/2011/10/30/books/review/zone-one-by-colson-whitehead-book-review.html.
56. Whitehead, *Zone One*, 80.
57. Ibid., 210.
58. Ibid., 43.
59. Mark Bresnan, "Resisting Technocracy in Colson Whitehead's *Zone One*," paper presented at What Happens Now conference, University of Lincoln, UK, June 27–30, 2016.
60. Whitehead, *Zone One*, 24, 28.
61. Ibid., 149.
62. Bresnan, "Resisting Technocracy."
63. Soren Forsberg, "'Don't Believe Your Eyes': A Review of Colson Whitehead's *Zone One*," *Transition* 109 (2012): 141, accessed July 14, 2016, https://muse.jhu.edu/article/490143 (italics in original).
64. Whitehead, *Zone One*, 11.
65. Ibid., 231.
66. Leif Sorensen, "Against the Post-Apocalyptic: Narrative Closure in Colson Whitehead's *Zone One*," *Contemporary Literature* 55, no. 3 (2014): 573, doi:10.1353/cli.2014.0029.
67. Ibid.
68. See Christian Fuchs, *Digital Labour and Karl Marx* (New York: Routledge, 2014). See also Lisa Nakamura, "The Unwanted Labour of Social Media: Women of Colour Call Out Culture as Venture Community Management," *New Formations* 86 (2015): 106–12. As Nakamura's work makes clear, it is the work of women of color that explicitly makes social media; this gendered aspect of the culture is elided in *Zone One*.

69. Martin Kevorkian, *Color Monitors: The Black Face of Technology in America* (Ithaca, NY: Cornell University Press, 2006), 2.
70. Whitehead, *Zone One*, 151.
71. Sorensen. "Against the Post-Apocalyptic," 564.
72. Bresnan, "Resisting Technocracy."
73. Whitehead, *Zone One*, 3.
74. Ibid., 4.
75. Ibid.
76. Ibid., 255.
77. Ibid., 7.
78. Ibid., 126.
79. Ibid.
80. Ibid., 202–3.
81. Ibid., 203.
82. Ibid., 16, 20.
83. Whitehead, *Zone One*, 24.
84. Brendan Byrne, "S. D. Chrostowska, Marie Calloway, and the New Media Novel," *Rhizome*, January 6, 2014, accessed August 24, 2014, https://rhizome.org/editorial/2014/jan/06/sd-chrostowska-marie-calloway-and-new-media-novel/.

CONCLUSION: AFTER THE DIGITAL BANAL

1. Hito Steyerl, "Too Much World: Is the Internet Dead?" *e-flux* 49 (November 2013), accessed August 15, 2014, http://www.e-flux.com/journal/too-much-world-is-the-internet-dead/.
2. David M. Berry, "The Computational Turn: Thinking about the Digital Humanities," *Culture Machine* 12 (2011): 2, accessed May 26, 2014, http://www.culturemachine.net/index.php/cm/article/viewarticle/440.
3. Ibid., 2.
4. David E. Gates and Jonathan Lethem, "A Kind of Vast Fiction," *PEN America* 12 (2010): 25–26.
5. Ibid.
6. Laura Miller, "How Novels Came to Terms with the Internet," *Guardian*, January 15, 2011, accessed April 15, 2012, https://www.theguardian.com/books/2011/jan/15/novels-internet-laura-miller.
7. Allison K. Gibson, "He Hit Send: On the Awkward but Necessary Role of Technology in Fiction," *Millions*, August 8, 2012, accessed May 26, 2014, http://www.themillions.com/2012/08/he-hit-send-on-the-awkward-but-necessary-role-of-technology-in-fiction.html.
8. Jacob Silverman, "Screen Play: Fiction about the Internet Fumbles toward Eloquence," *New Republic*, June 20, 2013, accessed May 26, 2014, http://www.newrepublic.com/article/113418/note-self-and-more-you-ignore-me-reviewed-jacob-silverman.

BIBLIOGRAPHY

Abbate, Janet. *Inventing the Internet*. Cambridge, MA: MIT Press, 2000.
Alexander, Susannah. "*Catfish* Host Max Joseph Takes Hiatus, Replaced by Five Guests." *Digital Spy*. January 11, 2015. Accessed July 7, 2015. http://www.digitalspy.com/tv/ustv/news/a620697/catfish-host-max-joseph-takes-hiatus-replaced-by-five-guests/.
Amerika, Mark. *META/DATA: A Digital Poetics*. Cambridge, MA: MIT Press, 2007.
———. *Remixthebook*. Minneapolis: University of Minnesota Press, 2011.
———. "The Renewable Tradition (Extended Play Remix)." *Fibreculture* 15 (2009). Accessed December 10, 2010. http://fifteen.fibreculturejournal.org/fcj-099-the-renewable-tradition-extended-play-remix/.
Anastas, Benjamin. "The Soul of a New Machine." *New York Times*. June 15, 2003. Accessed June 13, 2016. http://www.nytimes.com/2003/06/15/books/review/15ANASTAT.html.
Anderson, Judy. *Plagiarism, Copyright Violation, and Other Thefts of Intellectual Property: An Annotated Bibliography with a Lengthy Introduction*. Jefferson, NC: McFarland, 1998.
Andrejevic, Mark. *Reality TV: The Work of Being Watched*. Lanham, MD: Rowman & Littlefield, 2004.
Atwood, Margaret. "When Privacy Is Theft." *New York Review of Books*. November 21, 2013. Accessed June 22, 2016. http://www.nybooks.com/articles/2013/11/21/eggers-circle-when-privacy-is-theft/.
"BAFTA Introduces New 'Constructed Reality' Award." *BBC News*. November 9, 2011. Accessed June 10, 2016. http://www.bbc.com/news/entertainment-arts-15652404.
Bakardjieva, Maria. *Internet Society: The Internet in Everyday Life*. London: Sage, 2005.
Barbrook, Richard. *The Internet Revolution: From Dot-com Capitalism to Cybernetic Communism*. With Andy Cameron. Network Notebooks 10. Amsterdam: Institute of Network Cultures, 2015.

Barbrook, Richard, and Andy Cameron. "The Californian Ideology." *Science as Culture* 26, no. 6 (1996): 44–72. Published online at *Hypermedia Research Centre*. Accessed June 13, 2016. http://www.hrc.wmin.ac.uk/theory-californianideology-main.html.

Barnet, Belinda. "The Erasure of Technology in Cultural Critique." *Fibreculture* 1 (2003). Accessed April 5, 2012. http://one.fibreculturejournal.org/fcj-005-the-erasure-of-technology-in-cultural-critique.

Barthes, Roland. "The Death of the Author." In *Image Music Text*, 142–48. Trans. Stephen Heath. London: Fontana Press, 1977.

———. "The Reality Effect." In *The Rustle of Language*, 140–49. Trans. Richard Howard. Berkeley: University of California Press, 1989.

———. *S/Z*. Trans. Richard Miller. Oxford: Blackwell, 1992.

Bassett, Caroline. *The Arc and the Machine: Narrative and New Media*. Manchester: Manchester University Press, 2007.

———. "Canonicalism and the Computational Turn." In *Understanding Digital Humanities*, ed. David M. Berry, 105–26. London: Palgrave Macmillan, 2012.

———. "New Maps for Old? The Cultural Stakes of '2.0.'" *Fibreculture* 13 (2008). Accessed April 5, 2012. http://thirteen.fibreculturejournal.org/fcj-088-new-maps-for-old-the-cultural-stakes-of-2-0/.

Bassett, Caroline, and Chris Wilbert. "Where You Want to Go Today (Like It or Not): Leisure Practices in Cyberspace." In *Leisure/Tourism Geographies: Practices and Geographical Knowledge*, ed. David Crouch, 181–95. New York: Routledge, 1999.

Baym, Nancy K. *Personal Connections in the Digital Age*. Cambridge: Polity Press, 2011.

Beede, Dave, and Anne Neville. "Breaking Down the Urban-Rural Broadband Divide." *National Telecommunications and Information Administration*. June 5, 2013. Accessed September 9, 2014. https://www.ntia.doc.gov/blog/2013/breaking-down-urban-rural-broadband-divide.

Bell, David, and Barbara M. Kennedy, eds. *The Cybercultures Reader*. New York: Routledge, 2000.

Benedikt, Michael. *Cyberspace: First Steps*. Cambridge, MA: MIT Press, 1992.

Benson-Allott, Caetlin. "The Algorithmic Spectator" *Film Quarterly* 64, no. 3 (Spring 2011): 55–58. doi:10.1525/fq.2011.64.3.55.

Berlant, Lauren. *Cruel Optimism*. Durham, NC: Duke University Press, 2011.

———. "Faceless Book." *Supervalent Thought* (blog). December 25, 2007. Accessed April 23, 2016. https://supervalentthought.com/2007/12/25/faceless-book/.

———. "Intuitionists: History and the Affective Event." *American Literary History* (August 2008). doi:10.1093/alh/ajn039.

———. "Structures of Unfeeling: *Mysterious Skin*." *International Journal of Politics, Culture, and Society* 28, no. 3 (September 2015): 191–213. doi:10.1007/s10767-014-9190-y.

———. "Thinking about Feeling Historical." *Emotion, Space and Society* 1 (2008): 4–9. doi:10.1016/j.emospa.2008.08.006.

Berlant, Lauren, Judith Butler, Bojana Cvejić, Isabell Lorey, Jasbir Puar, and Ana Vujanović. "Precarity Talk: A Virtual Roundtable." *TDR: The Drama Review* 56, no. 4 (2012): 163–77. Accessed July 11, 2016. https://muse.jhu.edu/article/491900.

Berlant, Lauren, Michael Hardt, Heather Davis, and Paige Sarlin. "'On the Risk of a New Relationality': An Interview with Lauren Berlant and Michael Hardt." *Reviews in Cultural Theory* 2, no. 3 (2011–12). Accessed June 22, 2016. http://reviewsinculture.com/2012/10/15/on-the-risk-of-a-new-relationality-an-interview-with-lauren-berlant-and-michael-hardt/.
Berry, David M. "The Computational Turn: Thinking about the Digital Humanities." *Culture Machine* 12 (2011): 1–22. Accessed May 26, 2014. http://www.culturemachine.net/index.php/cm/article/viewarticle/440.
———. *Copy, Rip, Burn: The Politics of Copyleft and Open Source*. London: Pluto Press, 2008.
Birchall, Clare. "'Data.gov-in-a-Box': Delimiting Transparency." *European Journal of Social Theory* 18, no. 2 (2015): 185–202. Accessed December 15, 2016. http://journals.sagepub.com/doi/abs/10.1177/1368431014555259.
Birchall, Clare, Francien Broekhuizen, Simon Dawes, Danai Mikelli, and Poppy Wilde. "Openness and Opacity: An Interview with Clare Birchall." *Networking Knowledge: Journal of the MeCCSA Postgraduate Network* 9, no. 1 (2016). Accessed December 15, 2016. http://ojs.meccsa.org.uk/index.php/netknow/article/view/419.
Bogard, William. "Distraction and Digital Culture." *CTheory* a088 (October 2000). Accessed July 4, 2016. www.ctheory.net/articles.aspx?id=131.
Bolter, Jay David, and Richard Grusin. *Remediation: Understanding New Media*. Cambridge, MA: MIT Press, 1999.
Boyle, Bill. "Court Orders Interxion to Close Paris Data Center." *DatacenterDynamics*. October 21, 2015. Accessed April 23, 2016. http://www.datacenterdynamics.com/power-cooling/court-orders-interxion-to-close-paris-data-center/95059.fullarticle.
Bradshaw, Peter. Review of *The Social Network*. *Guardian*. October 14, 2010. Accessed May 1, 2016. http://www.theguardian.com/film/2010/oct/14/the-social-network-review.
Braidotti, Rosi. *The Posthuman*. Cambridge: Polity Press, 2013.
Bresnan, "Resisting Technocracy in Colson Whitehead's *Zone One*." Paper presented at What Happens Now conference, University of Lincoln, UK, June 27–30, 2016.
Brickman, S. F. "Face Off." *Harvard Crimson*. November 6, 2003. Accessed January 27, 2017. http://www.thecrimson.com/article/2003/11/6/face-off-computer-guru-mark-e/.
Briz, Nick. "How to / Why Leave Facebook (On My Own Terms, without "Deleting" My Account)." Facebook. July 1, 2014. Accessed July 25, 2016. http://nickbriz.com/facebook/.
Brown, William. *Supercinema: Film-Philosophy for the Digital Age*. New York: Berghahn, 2013.
Buckland, Warren. "Wes Anderson: A 'Smart' Director of the New Sincerity?" *New Review of Film and Television Studies* 10, no. 1 (2012): 1–5. doi:10.1080/17400309.2011.640888.
Burn, Stephen J. *Jonathan Franzen at the End of Postmodernism*. London: Bloomsbury, 2008.
Burrington, Ingrid. *Networks of New York: An Internet Infrastructure Guide*. Self-published, 2015. https://app.moonclerk.com/pay/ljgls7hoch.
———. "Seeing Networks in New York City." *Seeing Networks* (blog). Accessed July 14, 2016. http://seeingnetworks.in/nyc/.
Byrne, Brendan. "S. D. Chrostowska, Marie Calloway, and the New Media Novel." *Rhizome*. January 6, 2014. Accessed August 24, 2014. https://rhizome.org/editorial/2014/jan/06/sd-chrostowska-marie-calloway-and-new-media-novel/.

Carlyon, David. "The Trickster as Academic Comfort Food." *Journal of American & Comparative Cultures* 25, nos. 1–2 (March 2002): 14–18. doi:10.1111/1542-734X.00003.

Carr, Nicholas. *The Shallows: How the Internet is Changing the Way We Think, Read and Remember*. London: Atlantic Books, 2010.

Carruth, Allison. "The Digital Cloud and the Micropolitics of Energy." *Public Culture* 26, no. 2 (Spring 2014): 339–64. doi:10.1215/08992363-2392093.

Castronova, Edward. "On Virtual Economies." *Game Studies* 3, no. 2 (December 2003). Accessed July 17, 2015. http://www.gamestudies.org/0302/castronova/.

Catfish. Directed by Henry Joost and Ariel Schulman. 2007. Rogue Pictures, 2011. DVD.

Catfish: The TV Show. Created by Max Joseph, Ariel Schulman, and Yaniv Schulman. MTV, 2012–.

Chan, Jennifer. "Notes on Post-Internet." In *You Are Here: Art After the Internet*, ed. Omar Kholeif, 106–23. Manchester: Cornerhouse Publications, 2014.

Charles, Ron. Review of *A Visit from the Goon Squad*, by Jennifer Egan. *Washington Post*. June 16, 2010. Accessed July 14, 2016. http://www.washingtonpost.com/wp-dyn/content/article/2010/06/15/AR2010061504751.html.

Chew, Jonathan. "Apple's Huge Irish Data Center Has Hit a Snag." *Fortune*. February 3, 2016. Accessed April 23, 2016. http://fortune.com/2016/02/03/apple-ireland-data-center/.

Chun, Wendy Hui Kyong. *Control and Freedom: Power and Paranoia in the Age of Fiber Optics*. Cambridge, MA: MIT Press, 2008.

———. "Crisis, Crisis, Crisis, or Sovereignty and Networks." *Theory Culture Society* 28, no. 6 (2011): 91–112. doi:10.1177/0263276411418490.

———. "The Enduring Ephemeral, or The Future Is a Memory." *Critical Inquiry* 35 (Autumn 2008): 148–71. doi:10.1086/595632.

———. "On Software, or the Persistence of Visual Knowledge." *Grey Room* 18 (2004): 26–51. doi:10.1162/1526381043320741.

———. "On 'Sourcery,' or Code as Fetish." *Configurations* 16, no. 3 (Fall 2008): 299–324. doi:10.1353/con.0.0064.

———. *Programmed Visions: Software and Memory*. Cambridge, MA: MIT Press, 2011.

———. *Updating to Remain the Same: Habitual New Media*. Cambridge, MA: MIT Press, 2016.

Churchwell, Sarah. Review of *A Visit from the Goon Squad*, by Jennifer Egan. *Guardian*. Accessed July 14, 2016. https://www.theguardian.com/books/2011/mar/13/jennifer-egan-visit-goon-squad.

Clements, James. "Trust Your Makers of Things! The Metafictional Pact in Dave Eggers's *You Shall Know Our Velocity*." *Critique: Studies in Contemporary Fiction* 56, no. 2 (March 2015): 121–37. doi:10.1080/00111619.2013.866541.

Cohen, Julie E. *Configuring the Networked Self: Law, Code and the Play of Everyday Practice*. New Haven, CT: Yale University Press, 2012.

———. "Cyberspace as/and Space." *Columbia Law Review* 107, no. 1 (January 2007): 210–56. http://scholarship.law.georgetown.edu/cgi/viewcontent.cgi?article=1822&context=facpub.

Cohen, Samuel. *After the End of History: American Fiction in the 1990s*. Iowa City: University of Iowa Press, 2009.

Coleman, Beth. *Hello Avatar: Rise of the Networked Generation*. Cambridge, MA: MIT Press, 2011.

Coleman, Gabriella. *Hacker, Hoaxer, Whistleblower, Spy: The Many Faces of Anonymous*. New York: Verso Books, 2014.

Conty, Arianne. "Techno-Phenomenology: Martin Heidegger and Bruno Latour on How Phenomena Come to Presence." *South African Journal of Philosophy* 32, no. 4 (2013): 311–26. doi:10.1080/02580136.2013.865099.

Coole, D., and Samantha Frost, eds. *New Materialisms: Ontology, Agency, and Politics*. Durham, NC: Duke University Press, 2010.

Cramer, Florian. "What is Post-Digital?" *APRJA* 3, no. 1 (2014). Accessed August 15, 2014. http://www.aprja.net/what-is-post-digital/.

Crary, Jonathan. *24/7: Late Capitalism and the End of Sleep*. New York: Verso, 2013.

Cubitt, Sean. *The Cinema Effect*. Cambridge, MA: MIT Press, 2004.

Currie, Mark. *About Time: Narrative Fiction and the Philosophy of Time*. Edinburgh: Edinburgh University Press, 2007.

———. "The Expansion of Tense." *Narrative* 17, no. 3 (October 2009): 353–67. doi:10.1353/nar.0.0027.

Darling, Jesse. "Arcades, Mall Rats, and Tumblr Thugs." *New Inquiry*. February 12, 2012. Accessed January 6, 2015. http://thenewinquiry.com/essays/arcades-mallrats-tumblr-thugs/.

Dean, Jodi. *Blog Theory: Feedback and Capture in the Circuits of Drive*. Cambridge: Polity, 2010.

———. "Communicative Capitalism: Circulation and the Foreclosure of Politics." *Cultural Politics* 1, no. 1 (2005): 51–74. doi:10.2752/174321905778054845.

Derrida, Jacques. *Negotiations: Interventions and Interviews, 1971–2001*. Ed. and trans. Elizabeth Rottenberg. Stanford, CA: Stanford University Press, 2002.

———. *Paper Machine*. Trans. Rachel Bowlby. Stanford, CA: Stanford University Press, 2005.

Dibbell, Julian. "The Life of the Chinese Gold Farmer." *New York Times Magazine*. June 17, 2007. Accessed July 12, 2016. http://www.nytimes.com/2007/06/17/magazine/17lootfarmers-t.html?_r=0.

Dinnen, Zara. "Breaking Out That Perl Script: The Imaging and Imagining of Code in *The Social Network* and *Catfish*." *European Journal of American Culture* 32, no. 2 (Summer 2013). doi:10.1386/ejac.32.2.173_1.

———. "Case Study No. 1: Holoback." *Exaptation and the Digital Now* panel, *Media N*, CAA conference edition (2014). Accessed February 3, 2017. http://median.newmediacaucus.org/caa-edition/.

———. "In the Mix: The Potential Convergence of Literature and New Media in Jonathan Lethem's 'Ecstasy of Influence.'" *Journal of Narrative Theory* 42, no. 2 (Summer 2012). doi:10.1353/jnt.2012.0009.

———. "Things that Matter: Representing Everyday Technological Things in Comics." *Studies in Comics* 3, no. 2 (Winter 2013). doi:10.1386/stic.3.2.313_1.

Doueihi, Milad. *Digital Cultures*. Cambridge, MA: Harvard University Press, 2011.

Douglas, Mary. Foreword to *The Gift: Form and Reason for Exchange in Archaic Societies*, by Marcel Mauss. New York: Routledge, 2002.

Drucker, Johanna. "Digital Ontologies: The Ideality of Form in/and Code Storage; or, Can Graphesis Challenge Mathesis?" *Leonardo* 34, no. 2 (2001): 141–45. Accessed April 15, 2011. http://www.jstor.org/stable/1577017.

———. Review of *Mechanisms: New Media and the Forensic Imagination*, by Matthew Kirschenbaum. *Digital Humanities Quarterly* 3, no. 2 (2009). Accessed April 29, 2016. http://digitalhumanities.org/dhq/vol/3/2/000048/000048.html.

Dubrofsky, Rachel E., and Megan M. Wood. "Posting Racism and Sexism: Authenticity, Agency and Self-Reflexivity in Social Media." *Communication and Critical/Cultural Studies* 11, no. 3 (2014): 282–87. doi:10.1080/14791420.2014.926247.

Duhigg, Charles, and David Barboza. "In China, Human Costs Are Built into an iPad." *New York Times*, January 5, 2012. Accessed April 23, 2016. http://www.nytimes.com/2012/01/26/business/ieconomy-apples-ipad-and-the-human-costs-for-workers-in-china.html?_r=0.

Duncan, Glen. "A Plague of Urban Undead in Lower Manhattan." *New York Times*. October 28, 2011. Accessed August 24, 2014. http://www.nytimes.com/2011/10/30/books/review/zone-one-by-colson-whitehead-book-review.html.

Duncan, Pansy. *The Emotional Life of Postmodern Film: Affect Theory's Other*. New York: Routledge, 2016.

Dyer-Witheford, Nick. "The Circulation of the Common." Paper presented at Immaterial Labour, Multitudes and New Social Subjects: Class Composition in Cognitive Capitalism, King's College, University of Cambridge. April 2006. Accessed May 14, 2016. http://www.fims.uwo.ca/people/faculty/dyerwitheford/commons2006.pdf.

Eco, Umberto. *The Name of the Rose*. Boston: Mariner Books, 2014.

Egan, Jennifer. "Black Box." *New Yorker*. June 4, 11, 2012. Accessed July 14, 2016. http://www.newyorker.com/magazine/2012/06/04/black-box-2.

———. *A Visit from the Goon Squad*. London: Constable & Robinson / Corsair, 2011.

Egan, Jennifer, and Zara Dinnen. "'This Is All Artificial': An Interview with Jennifer Egan." *Post45*. May 20, 2016. Accessed July 3, 2016. http://post45.research.yale.edu/2016/05/this-is-all-artificial-an-interview-with-jennifer-egan/.

Eggers, Dave. *The Circle*. London: Hamish Hamilton, 2013.

Eggers, Dave, and Gaby Wood. "Dave Eggers Interview." *Telegraph*. October 5, 2013. Accessed July 3, 2016. http://www.telegraph.co.uk/culture/books/authorinterviews/10356543/Dave-Eggers-interview.html.

Elias, Amy J. "The Commons . . . and Digital Planetarity." In *The Planetary Turn: Relationality and Geoaesthetics in the Twenty-First Century*, ed. Amy J. Elias and Christian Moraru, 37–69. Evanston, IL: Northwestern University Press, 2015.

Ellison, Nicole B., and danah boyd. "Sociality through Social Network Sites." In *The Oxford Handbook of Internet Studies*, ed. William H. Dutton, 151–71. Oxford: Oxford University Press, 2013.

Emerson, Lori. *Reading Writing Interfaces: From the Digital to the Bookbound*. Minneapolis: Minnesota University Press, 2014.

Ensmenger, Nathan. *The Computer Boys Take Over: Computers, Programmers, and the Politics of Technical Expertise*. Cambridge, MA: MIT Press, 2010.

Enwezor, Okwui. "The Black Box." In *Documenta 11, platform 5*, exhibition catalogue. Ostfildern-Ruit, Ger.: Hatje Cantz, 2002.
Fallows, James. "Inside Foxconn." *Atlantic*. October 18, 2012. Accessed April 23, 2016. http://www.theatlantic.com/international/archive/2012/10/inside-foxconn/263791/.
Faragher, Claire, Brian Hill, Molly Dineen, and Richard McKerrow. "Is Structured Reality Corrupting Documentary?" *BAFTA*. Soundcloud podcast. Accessed June 11, 2016. https://soundcloud.com/bafta/structured-reality-documentary-debate.
Fincher, David. "Commercials / Music Videos." In *The Director's Cut: Picturing Hollywood in the 21st Century*, ed. Stephan Littger, 165–80. New York: Continuum, 2006.
Fitzpatrick, Kathleen. *Planned Obsolescence: Publishing, Technology, and the Future of the Academy*. New York: New York University Press, 2011.
Forsberg, Soren. "'Don't Believe Your Eyes': A Review of Colson Whitehead's *Zone One*." *Transition* 109 (2012): 130–43. Accessed July 14, 2016. https://muse.jhu.edu/article/490143.
Foster, Hal. *The Return of the Real: The Avant-Garde at the End of the Century*. Cambridge, MA: MIT Press, 1996.
Franco, James. "Summer Reading Part 5: *A Visit from the Goon Squad*." *Huffington Post*. June 16, 2012. Accessed July 14, 2016. http://www.huffingtonpost.com/entry/summer-reading-part-5_b_1602801.
Fuchs, Christian. *Digital Labour and Karl Marx*. New York: Routledge, 2014.
Fuller, Matthew, ed. *Behind the Blip: Essays on the Culture of Software*. New York: Autonomedia, 2003.
———. *Software Studies: A Lexicon*. Cambridge, MA: MIT Press, 2008.
Galloway, Alexander R. *The Interface Effect*. Cambridge: Polity, 2012.
———. "Language Wants to Be Overlooked: On Software and Ideology." *Journal of Visual Culture* 5 (2006): 315–31. doi:10.1177/1470412906070519.
———. *Protocol: How Control Exists after Decentralization*. Cambridge, MA: MIT Press, 2004.
Galloway, Anne. "Intimations of Everyday Life: Ubiquitous Computing and the City." *Cultural Studies* 18, no. 2 (2004): 384–408. doi:10.1080/0950238042000201572.
Gates, David E., and Jonathan Lethem. "A Kind of Vast Fiction." *PEN America* 12 (2010): 20–28. https://pen.org/a-kind-of-vast-fiction/.
Gibson, Allison K. "He Hit Send: On the Awkward but Necessary Role of Technology in Fiction." *Millions*. August 8, 2012. Accessed May 26, 2014. http://www.themillions.com/2012/08/he-hit-send-on-the-awkward-but-necessary-role-of-technology-in-fiction.html.
Gibson, William. "My Obsession." In *Everyday eBay: Culture, Collecting, and Desire*, ed. Ken Hillis, Michael Petit, and Nathan Scott Epley, 19–30. New York: Routledge, 2006.
———. *Neuromancer*. 1984. London: Harper-Voyager, 1995.
———. *Pattern Recognition*. London: Penguin, 2003.
Gira Grant, Melissa. "Girl Geeks and Boy Kings." *Dissent* (Winter 2013). Accessed July 22, 2015. https://www.dissentmagazine.org/article/girl-geeks-and-boy-kings.
The Girl with the Dragon Tattoo. Directed by David Fincher. 2011. Sony Pictures Home Entertainment, 2012. DVD.
Gladstone, Jason. "Our Aesthetic Condition." *Contemporary Literature* 55, no. 1 (2014): 192–201. Accessed April 23, 2016. https://muse.jhu.edu/article/545860.

Goldman, Michael. "Going Tapeless." *Millimeter* 34, no. 6 (2006): 8–16. Accessed February 17, 2015. http://www.creativeplanetnetwork.com/news/news-articles/going-tapeless/386899.

Gone Girl. Directed by David Fincher. 20th Century Fox, 2014.

Graham, Stephen. "Beyond the 'Dazzling Light': From Dreams of Transcendence to the 'Remediation' of Urban Life." *New Media & Society* 6, no. 1 (2004): 16–25. doi:10.1177/1461444804039905.

Grier, David Allen. "The ENIAC, the Verb "To Program" and the Emergence of Digital Computers." *IEEE Annals of the History of Computing* 18, no. 1 (1996): 51–55. doi:10.1109/85.476561.

———. *When Computers Were Human*. Princeton, NJ: Princeton University Press, 2005.

Grusin, Richard, ed. *The Nonhuman Turn*. Minneapolis: University of Minnesota Press, 2015.

———. *Premediation: Affect and Mediality in America after 9/11*. London: Palgrave Macmillan, 2010.

Hackett, Pat. Introduction to *The Andy Warhol Diaries*, ed. Pat Hackett. New York: Warner Books, 1989.

Haimson, Oliver L., and Anna Lauren Hoffmann. "Constructing and Enforcing 'Authentic' Identity Online: Facebook, Real Names, and Non-Normative Identities." *First Monday* 21, no. 6 (June 2016). doi:10.5210/fm.v21i6.6791.

Hall, Gary. "Introduction: Pirate Philosophy." *Culture Machine* 10 (2009): 1–5. Accessed February 14, 2015. http://www.culturemachine.net/index.php/cm/article/view/367/374.

———. "Pirate Radical Philosophy." *Radical Philosophy* 173 (May/June 2012). Accessed February, 19 2015. https://www.radicalphilosophy.com/commentary/pirate-radical-philosophy-2.

Halliwell, Martin. "Contemporary American Culture." In *American Thought and Culture in the 21st Century*, ed. Martin Halliwell and Catherine Morley, 211–26. Edinburgh: Edinburgh University Press, 2008.

Halliwell, Martin, and Catherine Morley. "Introduction." In *American Thought and Culture in the 21st Century*, ed., Martin Halliwell and Catherine Morley, 1–20. Edinburgh: Edinburgh University Press, 2008.

Hamilton, Caroline D. *One Man Zeitgeist: Dave Eggers, Publishing and Publicity*. New York: Continuum, 2010.

Hands, Joss. *@ is for Activism: Dissent, Resistance and Rebellion in a Digital Culture*. London: Pluto Press, 2011.

———. "Introduction: Politics, Power and 'Platformativity.'" *Culture Machine* 14 (2013): 1–24. Accessed February 14, 2015. https://www.culturemachine.net/index.php/cm/article/viewArticle/504.

———. "Platform Communism." *Culture Machine* 14 (2013): 1–24. Accessed February 14, 2015. http://www.culturemachine.net/index.php/cm/article/view/510/525.

Hansen, Mark B. N. *New Philosophies for New Media*. Cambridge, MA: MIT Press, 2004.

Haraway, Donna. "A Cyborg Manifesto." In *The Cybercultures Reader*, ed. Daniel Bell and Barbara M. Kennedy, 291–324. New York: Routledge, 2000.

———. *Modest_Witness@Second_Millenium.FemaleMan@Meets_OncoMouse™: Feminism and Technoscience*. New York: Routledge, 1997.

Haraway, Donna, Constance Penley, and Andrew Ross. "Cyborgs at Large: Interview with Donna Haraway." *Social Text* 5, no. 26 (1990): 8–23. doi:10.2307/466237.
Hardt, Michael. "The Common in Communism." In *The Idea of Communism*, ed. Costas Douzinas and Slavoj Žižek, 131–44. New York: Verso, 2010.
———. "Reclaim the Common in Communism." *Guardian*. February 3, 2012. Accessed February 19, 2015. http://www.theguardian.com/commentisfree/2011/feb/03/communism-capitalism-socialism-property.
Harvey, Stefano, and Fred Moten. *The Undercommons: Fugitive Planning and Black Study*. Wivenhoe, UK: Minor Compositions, 2013.
Hayles, N. Katherine. *How We Became Posthuman: Virtual Bodies in Cybernetics, Literature and Informatics*. Chicago: University of Chicago Press, 1999.
———. "Hyper and Deep Attention: The Generational Divide in Cognitive Modes." *Profession* (2007): 187–99. doi:10.1632/prof.2007.2007.1.187.
———. "Intermediation: The Pursuit of a Vision." *New Literary History* 38, no. 1 (2007): 99–125. doi:10.1353/nlh.2007.0021.
———. "Print Is Flat, Code Is Deep: The Importance of Media-Specific Analysis." *Poetics Today* 25, no. 1 (2004): 67–90. doi:10.1215/03335372-25-1-67.
———. "The Seductions of Cyberspace." In *Reading Digital Culture*, ed. David Trend, 305–21. Oxford: Blackwell Publishers, 2001.
———. "Traumas of Code." *Critical Inquiry* 33, no. 1 (2006): 136–57. doi:10.1086/509749.
———. "Virtual Bodies and Flickering Signifiers." In *The Visual Culture Reader*, 2nd edition, ed. Nicholas Mirzoeff, 152–57. New York: Routledge, 2002.
———. *Writing Machines*. Cambridge, MA: MIT Press, 2002.
Haythornwaite, Caroline, and Barry Wellman, eds. *The Internet in Everyday Life*. Oxford: Blackwell, 2002.
Heti, Sheila. *How Should a Person Be?* London: Harvill Secker, 2013.
Heti, Sheila, and Claire Cameron. "How Should a Writer Be? An Interview with Sheila Heti." *Millions*. June 12, 2012. Accessed June 12, 2016. http://www.themillions.com/2012/06/how-should-a-writer-be-an-interview-with-sheila-heti.html.
Highmore, Ben. *Cityscapes: Cultural Readings in the Material and Symbolic City*. Basingstoke, UK: Palgrave Macmillan, 2005.
Hillis, Ken. *Online a Lot of the Time: Ritual, Fetish, Sign*. Durham, NC: Duke University Press, 2009.
Hillis, Ken, Susanna Paasonen, and Michael Petit, eds. *Networked Affect*. Cambridge, MA: MIT Press, 2015.
Hillis, Ken, Michael Petit, and Nathan Scott Epley, eds. *Everyday eBay: Culture, Collecting, and Desire*. New York: Routledge, 2006.
Holland, Mary. "A Lamb in Wolf's Clothing: Postmodern Realism in A. M. Homes's *Music for Torching* and *This Book Will Save Your Life*." *Critique: Studies in Contemporary Fiction* 53, no. 3 (2012): 214–37. doi:10.1080/00111611003767621.
Homes, A. M. *May We Be Forgiven*. London: Granta, 2013.
Horning, Rob. "Know Your Product." *New Inquiry*. July 29, 2015. Accessed July 25, 2016. https://thenewinquiry.com/blog/know-your-product/.

House, Christian. Review of *A Visit from the Goon Squad*, by Jennifer Egan. *Independent*. March 13, 2011. Accessed July 14, 2016. http://www.independent.co.uk/arts-entertainment/books/reviews/a-visit-from-the-goon-squad-by-jennifer-egan-2240306.html.

Huhtamo, Erkki. "Web Stalker Seek Aaron: Reflections on Digital Arts, Codes, and Coders." In *Code: The Language of Our Time, Ars Electronica 2003*, ed. Gerfried Stocker and Christiane Schöpf, 110–28. Ostfildern-Ruit, Ger.: Hatje-Cantz, 2003.

Hyde, Lewis. *The Gift: Imagination and the Erotic Life of Property*. 1983. Edinburgh: Canongate, 2007.

Introna, Lucas D. "The Enframing of Code: Agency, Originality and the Plagiarist." *Theory Culture Society* 28, no. 6 (2011): 113–41. doi:10.1177/0263276411418131.

Jacobs, Alan. *The Pleasures of Reading in an Age of Distraction*. Oxford: Oxford University Press, 2011.

James, Ian. "Bernard Stiegler and the Time of Technics." *Cultural Politics* 6, no. 2 (2010): 207–28. doi:10.2752/175174310X12672016548360.

Jameson, Fredric. *Postmodernism, or, The Cultural Logic of Late Capitalism*. Durham, NC: Duke University Press, 1991.

Kelly, Adam. "Beginning with Postmodernism." *Twentieth Century Literature* 57, nos. 3–4 (Fall/Winter 2011): 391–422. doi:10.1215/0041462X-2011-4009.

Kelty, Chris. "Geeks, Social Imaginaries, and Recursive Publics." *Cultural Anthropology* 20, no. 2 (May 2005): 185–214. Accessed June 22, 2016. http://www.jstor.org/stable/3651533.

———. *Two Bits: The Cultural Significance of Free Software*. Durham, NC: Duke University Press, 2008.

Kember, Sarah, and Joanna Zylinska. *Life After New Media: Mediation as a Vital Process*. Cambridge, MA: MIT Press, 2012.

Kennedy, Helen. "Beyond Anonymity, or Future Directions for Internet Identity Research." *New Media & Society* 8, no. 6 (December 2006): 859–76. doi:10.1177/1461444806069641.

Kevorkian, Martin. *Color Monitors: The Black Face of Technology in America*. Ithaca, NY: Cornell University Press, 2006.

Kirschenbaum, Matthew G. *Mechanisms: New Media and the Forensic Imagination*. Cambridge, MA: MIT Press, 2008.

Kitchin, Rob, and Martin Dodge. *Code/Space: Software and Everyday Life*. Cambridge, MA: MIT Press, 2011.

Kittler, Friedrich. "Code (or, How You Can Write Something Differently)." In *Software Studies / A Lexicon*, ed. Matthew Fuller, 40–47. Cambridge, MA: MIT Press, 2008.

———. "Gramophone, Film, Typewriter." Trans. Dorothea Von Mücke and Philippe L. Similon. *October* 41 (Summer 1987): 101–18. doi:10.2307/778332.

Kollin, Susan. "Not Yet Another World: Ecopolitics and Urban Natures in Jonathan Lethem's *Chronic City*." *LIT: Literature Interpretation Theory* 26, no. 4 (2015): 255–75. doi:10.1080/10436928.2015.1092346.

Konstantinou, Lee. "The Brand as Cognitive Map in William Gibson's *Pattern Recognition*." *boundary 2* 36, no. 2 (2009): 67–97. doi:10.1215/01903659-2009-005.

———. "Periodizing the Present." *Contemporary Literature* 54, no. 2 (Summer 2013): 411–23. doi:10.1353/cli.2013.0013.

———. "We Had to Get Beyond Irony: How David Foster Wallace, Dave Eggers, and a New Generation of Believers Changed Fiction." *Salon*. March 27, 2016. Accessed June 10, 2016. http://www.salon.com/2016/03/27/we_had_to_get_beyond_irony_how_david_foster_wallace_dave_eggers_and_a_new_generation_of_believers_changed_fiction/.

Kramer, Adam D. I., Jamie E. Guillory, and Jeffrey T. Hancock. "Experimental Evidence of Massive-Scale Emotional Contagion through Social Networks." *PNAS* 111, no. 24 (June 2014): 8788–90. doi:10.1073/pnas.1320040111.

Kunzru, Hari. "Smoke and Mirrors." *Bookforum* (September 2009): 24. Accessed April 23, 2016. http://www.bookforum.com/inprint/016_03/4331.

Kushigemachi, Todd. "Nostalgia Goes Digital: Turning Back Time in the Films of David Fincher." *PopMatters*. October 10, 2011). Accessed December 3, 2013. http://www.popmatters.com/feature/144591-nostalgia-goes-digital-turning-back-time-in-the-films-of-david-finch/.

Lessig, Lawrence. *Remix: Making Art and Commerce Thrive in the Hybrid Economy*. London: Bloomsbury, 2008.

Lethem, Jonathan. "Always Crashing in the Same Car (A Mash-Up)." *Conjunctions* 48 (Spring 2007): 222–30.

———. *Chronic City*. London: Faber and Faber, 2010.

———, ed. *Da Capo Best Music Writing 2002*. Boston, MA: Da Capo Press, 2002.

———. *The Disappointment Artist and Other Essays*. London: Faber and Faber, 2005.

———. "The Ecstasy of Influence: A Plagiarism." *Harper's* (February 2007): 59–71. Accessed March 21, 2010. http://harpers.org/archive/2007/02/the-ecstasy-of-influence/.

———. "The Ecstasy of Influence: A Plagiarism Mosaic." In *Cutting Across Media: Appropriation Art, Interventionist Collage, and Copyright Law*, 298–326. Durham, NC: Duke University Press, 2011.

———. "The Ecstasy of Influence: A Plagiarism Mosaic." In *The Ecstasy of Influence*, 93–120. London: Jonathan Cape, 2012.

———. "The Ecstasy of Influence: A Plagiarism Mosaic." In *Sound Unbound: Sampling Digital Music and Culture*, ed. Paul D. Miller aka DJ Spooky That Subliminal Kid, 25–52. Cambridge, MA: MIT Press, 2008.

———. *The Fortress of Solitude*. New York: Doubleday, 2003.

———. "Q & A with Jonathan Lethem." Occasional Music: A Symposium on the Work of Jonathan Lethem. Birkbeck College, London. July 10, 2010.

———. *They Live*. Berkeley, CA: Soft Skull Press, 2010.

Lethem, Jonathan, interview with Zara Dinnen. *Dandelion Journal*. 2, no. 1 (2011). Accessed December 3, 2013. http://dandelionjournal.org/index.php/dandelion/article/view/48/57.

Lethem, Jonathan, interview with David E. Gates. "A Kind of Vast Fiction." *PEN America* 12 (2010): 20–28.

Lethem, Jonathan, and Carter Scholz. *Kafka Americana*. New York: Norton, 2001.

Light, Jennifer S. "When Computers Were Women." *Technology and Culture* 40, no. 3 (1999): 455–83. Accessed December 3, 2013. https://muse.jhu.edu/article/33396.

Losse, Katherine. *The Boy Kings: A Journey into the Heart of the Social Network*. New York: Free Press, 2012.

Lovink, Geert. *Networks without a Cause: A Critique of Social Media*. Cambridge: Polity Press, 2011.

Mackenzie, Adrian. *Cutting Code: Software and Sociality*. New York: Peter Lang, 2006.

Mackenzie, Adrian, and Theo Vurdubakis. "Codes and Codings in Crisis: Signification, Performativity and Excess." *Theory Culture Society* 28, no. 6 (2011): 3–23. doi:10.1177 /0263276411424761.

MacLellan, Matthew, and Margrit Talpalaru. "Editors' Introduction: Remaking the Commons." *Reviews in Cultural Theory* 2, no. 3 (2011–12): 1–5. Accessed August 22, 2012. http:// mediamargins.net/wp-content/uploads/2012/09/RCT-SP-On-the-Commons.pdf.

Magnet, Shoshana, and Kelly Gates, eds. *The New Media of Surveillance*. New York: Routledge, 2009.

Manovich, Lev. *The Language of New Media*. Cambridge, MA: MIT Press, 2001.

Mattern, Shannon. "Deep Time of Media Infrastructure." In *Signal Traffic: Critical Studies of Media Infrastructures*, ed., Lisa Parks and Nicole Starosielski, 94–112. Urbana: University of Illinois Press, 2015.

Mauss, Marcel. *The Gift: Form and Reason for Exchange in Archaic Societies*. New York: Routledge, 2002.

McGee, Celia. Review of *A Visit from the Goon Squad*, by Jennifer Egan. *Chicago Tribune*. Accessed July 14, 2016. http://www.chicagotribune.com/lifestyles/books/chi-books-review -goon-squad-egan-story.html.

McLuhan, Marshall. *Understanding Media: The Extensions of Man*. 1964. New York: Routledge, 1997.

McNeill, Laurie. "Social Networking Sites and Posthuman Auto/Biography." *Biography* 35, no. 1 (Winter 2012): 65–82.

McPherson, Tara, Patrick Jagoda, and Wendy H. K. Chun. "Preface: New Media and American Literature." *American Literature* 85, no. 4 (2013): 615–28. doi:10.1215/00029831-2367265.

Meyer, Robinson. "Everything We Know about Facebook's Secret Mood Manipulation Experiment." *Atlantic*. June 28, 2014. Accessed December 16, 2016. http://www.theatlantic .com/technology/archive/2014/06/everything-we-know-about-facebooks-secret-mood -manipulation-experiment/373648/.

Miller, Daniel. *Tales from Facebook*. Cambridge: Polity Press, 2011.

Miller, Laura. "How Novels Came to Terms with the Internet." *Guardian*. January 15, 2011. Accessed April 15, 2012. https://www.theguardian.com/books/2011/jan/15/novels-internet-laura -miller.

Mishra, Pankaj. "Modernity's Undoing." *London Review of Books* 33, no. 7 (2011): 27–30.

Mitchell, W. J. T. "The Work of Art in the Age of Biocybernetic Reproduction." *Modernism/ modernity* 10, no. 3 (September 2003): 481–500. doi:10.1353/mod.2003.0067.

Mosco, Vincent. *The Digital Sublime*. Cambridge, MA: MIT Press, 2004.

Mulvey, Laura. "Passing Time: Reflections on Cinema from a New Technological Age." *Screen* 45, no. 2 (Summer 2004): 142–55. doi:10.1093/screen/45.2.142.

Murphy, Graham J., and Sherryl Vint. *Beyond Cyberpunk: New Critical Perspectives*. New York: Taylor and Francis, 2010.

Nakamura, Lisa. "The Comfort Women of the Digital Industries: Asian Women in David Fincher's *The Social Network.*" *In Media Res.* January 17, 2011. Accessed July 14, 2016. http://mediacommons.futureofthebook.org/imr/2011/01/17/comfort-women-digital-industries-asian-women-david-finchers-social-network.

———. "Cyberrace." *PMLA* 123, no. 5 (2008): 1673–82. Accessed 14 July, 2016. http://www.jstor.org/stable/25501969.

———. *Cybertypes: Race, Ethnicity, and Identity on the Internet.* New York: Routledge, 2002.

———. "Race and Identity in Digital Media." In *Media and Society*, 5th edition, ed. James Curran, 336–47. New York: Bloomsbury, 2010.

———. "The Socioalgorithms of Race: Sorting it Out in Jihad Worlds," In *The New Media of Surveillance*, ed. Shoshana Magnet and Kelly Gates, 149–62. New York: Routledge, 2009.

———. "The Unwanted Labour of Social Media: Women of Colour Call Out Culture as Venture Community Management." *New Formations* 86 (2015): 106–12.

Navas, Eduardo, Owen Gallagher, and xtine Burrough, eds. *The Routledge Companion to Remix Studies.* New York: Routledge, 2014.

Neilson, Brett, and Ted Rossiter. "Introduction: Multitudes, Creative Organisation and the Precarious Condition of New Media Labour." *Fibreculture* 5 (2005). Accessed August 24, 2014. http://five.fibreculturejournal.org/.

Ngai, Sianne. "Merely Interesting." *Critical Inquiry* 34, no. 4 (Summer 2008): 777–817. doi:10.1086/592544.

———. "On Cruel Optimism." *Social Text Online.* January 15, 2013. Accessed April 23, 2016. http://socialtextjournal.org/periscope_article/on-cruel-optimism/.

———. *Our Aesthetic Categories: Zany, Cute, Interesting.* Cambridge, MA: Harvard University Press, 2012.

———. "Stuplimity: Shock and Boredom in Twentieth-Century Aesthetics." *Postmodern Culture* 10, no. 2 (2000). Accessed July 4, 2016. https://muse.jhu.edu/article/27722.

———. *Ugly Feelings.* Cambridge, MA: Harvard University Press, 2005.

Nixon, Rob. *Slow Violence and the Environmentalism of the Poor.* Cambridge, MA: Harvard University Press, 2011.

Novgorodoff, Danica. *Refresh Refresh.* With Benjamin Percy, and James Ponsoldt. New York: First Second, 2009.

Office Space. Directed by Mike Judge. 1999. Twentieth Century Fox, 2003. DVD.

Olson, Parmy. "Facebook Was the One Network People Used Less in 2014." *Forbes.* January 27, 2015. Accessed July 25, 2016. http://www.forbes.com/sites/parmyolson/2015/01/27/facebook-active-users-decline/#6fad4b3a411b.

Paasonen, Susanna. "Bit on Networked Affect." *Susanna Paasonen* (blog). March 3, 2016. Accessed April 23, 2016. https://susannapaasonen.org/2016/03/03/bit-on-networked-affect/.

———. "'Virgin Mary in Grilled Cheese Not a Hoax! Look & See!': Sublime Kitsch on eBay." In *Everyday eBay: Culture, Collecting, and Desire*, ed. Ken Hillis, Michael Petit, and Nathan Scott Epley, 201–16. New York: Routledge, 2006.

Parks, Lisa, and Nicole Starosielski, eds. *Signal Traffic: Critical Studies of Media Infrastructures.* Urbana: University of Illinois Press, 2015.

Pasquale, Frank. *The Black Box Society: The Secret Algorithms that Control Money and Information.* Cambridge, MA: Harvard University Press, 2015.

Pellegrini, Ann, and Jasbir Puar. "Affect." *Social Text* 27, no. 3, 100 (2009): 35–38. doi:10.1215/01642472-2009-004.

Percy, Benjamin. *Refresh, Refresh.* London: Jonathan Cape, 2008.

Pols, Mary. "Fish Tale." *Time.* September 27, 2010. Accessed April 15, 2011. http://content.time.com/time/magazine/article/0,9171,2019606,00.html.

Poster, Mark. "The Digital Subject and Cultural Theory." In *The Book History Reader*, 2nd edition, ed. David Finkelstein and Alistair McCleery, 486–93. New York: Routledge, 2006.

Prosser, Jay, ed. *American Fiction of the 1990s.* New York: Routledge, 2008.

Punday, Daniel. *Five Strands of Fictionality: The Institutional Construction of American Fiction.* Columbus: Ohio State University Press, 2010.

Ricker Schulte, Stephanie. *Cached: Decoding the Internet in Global Popular Culture.* New York: New York University Press, 2013.

Robson, Duncan. "Let's Enhance." YouTube video. December 13, 2009. Accessed July 25, 2016. https://www.youtube.com/watch?v=Vxq9yj2pVWk.

Rosen, Jonathan. *The Talmud and the Internet: A Journey between Worlds.* London: Continuum, 2000.

Scholz, Trebor, ed. *Digital Labor: The Internet as Playground and Factory.* New York: Routledge, 2013.

Schwarz, Bari M. "Hot or Not? Website Briefly Judges Looks." *Harvard Crimson.* November 4, 2003. Accessed January 27, 2017. http://www.thecrimson.com/article/2003/11/4/hot-or-not-website-briefly-judges/.

Schwartz, Hillel. *The Culture of the Copy: Striking Likeness, Unreasonable Facsimiles.* New York: Zone Books, 1998.

Schwartz, Niles. "'Fuck You You Fucking Fuck': David Fincher's Cyber Fairy Tale of (Mis)Communication, *The Girl With the Dragon Tattoo.*" *Niles Files* (blog). December 27, 2011. Accessed February 17, 2014. http://nilesfilmfiles.blogspot.co.uk/2011/12/fuck-you-you-fucking-fuck-david.html.

Seetharaman, Deepa. "Survey Finds Teens Prefer Instagram, Twitter, Snapchat for Social Networks." *Wall Street Journal.* October 16, 2015. Accessed July 25, 2016. http://blogs.wsj.com/digits/2015/10/16/survey-finds-teens-prefer-instagram-snapchat-among-social-networks/.

Shaviro, Steven. *Post-Cinematic Affect.* Winchester: Zero Books, 2010.

Shaw, Debra Benita. *Technoculture: The Key Concepts.* Oxford: Berg, 2008.

Shteyngart, Gary. *Super Sad True Love Story.* London: Granta, 2010.

Shteyngart, Gary, and Natalie Jacoby. "The Daily: Gary Shteyngart." *Paris Review.* July 27, 2010. Accessed July 28, 2011, http://www.theparisreview.org/blog/2010/07/27/gary-shteyngart.

Silicon Valley. Created by Mike Judge, John Altschuler, and Dave Krinsky. HBO, 2014–.

Silver, David. "Introducing Cyberculture." *Resource Centre for Cyberculture Studies.* Accessed June 13, 2016. http://mysite.du.edu/~lavita/edpx_3770_13s/_docs/Intro%20Cyberculture%20copy.pdf.

———. "Looking Backward, Looking Forward: Cyberculture Studies 1990–2000." In *Web.studies: Rewiring Media Studies for the Digital Age*, ed. David Gauntlett, 19–31. Oxford: Oxford University Press, 2000.

Silverman, Jacob. "Screen Play: Fiction about the Internet Fumbles toward Eloquence." *New Republic*. June 20, 2013. Accessed May 26, 2014. http://www.newrepublic.com/article/113418/note-self-and-more-you-ignore-me-reviewed-jacob-silverman.

Smith, Zadie. "Generation Why?" *New York Review of Books*. November 25, 2010. Accessed April 15, 2011. http://www.nybooks.com/articles/2010/11/25/generation-why/.

The Social Network. Directed by David Fincher. 2010. Sony Pictures Home Entertainment, 2011. DVD.

Solnit, Rebecca. "Resisting Monoculture." *Guernica*. January 7, 2014. Accessed August 17, 2015. https://www.guernicamag.com/daily/rebecca-solnit-resisting-monoculture/.

Sorensen, Leif. "Against the Post-Apocalyptic: Narrative Closure in Colson Whitehead's *Zone One*." *Contemporary Literature* 55, no. 3 (2014): 559-592. doi:10.1353/cli.2014.0029.

Sorkin, Aaron, and David Fincher, with Charlie Rose. "The Social Network." Video. *Charlie Rose*. September 28, 2010. Accessed January 27, 2017. https://charlierose.com/videos/14347.

Stadler, Gustavus. "'My Wife': The Tape Recorder and Warhol's Queer Ways of Listening." *Criticism* 56, no. 3 (Summer 2014): 425–56. doi:10.1353/crt.2014.0025.

Stewart, Garrett. *Framed Time: Toward a Postfilmic Cinema*. Chicago: University of Chicago Press, 2007.

Stewart, Heather. "Facebook Paid £4,327 Corporation Tax despite £35m Staff Bonuses." *Guardian*. October 11, 2015. Accessed July 25, 2016. https://www.theguardian.com/global/2015/oct/11/facebook-paid-4327-corporation-tax-despite-35-million-staff-bonuses.

Stewart, Kathleen. *Ordinary Affects*. Durham, NC: Duke University Press, 2007.

Steyerl, Hito. "In Defense of the Poor Image." *e-flux* 10 (November 2009). Accessed May 22, 2012. http://www.e-flux.com/journal/in-defense-of-the-poor-image/.

———. "Too Much World: Is the Internet Dead?" *e-flux* 49 (November 2013). Accessed August 15, 2014. http://www.e-flux.com/journal/too-much-world-is-the-internet-dead/.

Stiegler, Bernard. "The Carnival of the New Screen: From Hegemony to Isonomy." In *The YouTube Reader*, ed. Pelle Snickards and Patrick Vonderau, 40–59. Stockholm: National Library of Sweden, 2009.

———. "The Most Precious Good in the Era of Social Technologies." In *Unlike Us Reader: Social Media Monopolies and Their Alternatives*, ed. Geert Lovink and Miriam Rasch, 16–30. Amsterdam: Institute of Network Cultures, 2013. Accessed April 28, 2016. http://www.networkcultures.org/_uploads/%238UnlikeUs.pdf.

———. *Technics and Time, 1: The Fault of Epimetheus*. Trans. Richard Beardsworth and George Collins. Stanford, CA: Stanford University Press, 1998.

Stiegler, Bernard, interview with Irit Rogoff. "Transindividuation." *e-flux* 14 (March 2010). Accessed February 26, 2015. http://www.e-flux.com/journal/transindividuation/.

Streeter, Thomas. *The Net Effect: Romanticism, Capitalism, and the Internet*. New York: New York University Press, 2010.

Tabbi, Joseph. "Locating the Literary in New Media." *ebr: The Electronic Book Review.* September 23, 2008. Accessed July 29, 2010. http://electronicbookreview.com/thread/criticalecologies/interpretive.

———. "A Review of Books in the Age of Their Technological Obsolescence." *ebr: The Electronic Book Review* 1 (Winter 1995–96). Accessed June 7, 2010. http://www.altx.com/ebr/tabbi.htm.

Taubin, Amy. "Nerds on a Wire." *Sight and Sound* 17, no. 5 (May 2007): 24–26.

"Technical Workflows." *CEITON Technologies.* Accessed May 22, 2017. http://www.ceiton.de/CMS/EN/workflow/system-centric-bpms.html.

Terranova, Tiziana. "Free Labor." In *Digital Labor: The Internet as Playground and Factory*, ed. Trebor Scholz, 33–77. New York: Routledge, 2013.

"3% of Americans use dial-up at home." *Pew Research Internet Project.* Accessed May 24, 2017, 2014, http://www.pewresearch.org/fact-tank/2013/08/21/3-of-americans-use-dial-up-at-home/.

Thrift, Nigel. "Electric Animals: New Models of Everyday Life?" *Cultural Studies* 18, no. 2 (2004): 461–82. doi:10.1080/0950238042000201617.

Thrift, Nigel, and Shaun French. "The Automatic Production of Space." *Transactions of the Institute of British Geographers* 27, no. 3 (2002): 309–35. doi:10.1111/1475-5661.00057.

Tiku, Nitasha. "*Circle* Jerks: Why Do Editors Love Dave Eggers?" *Gawker.* October 2, 2013. Accessed July 22, 2015. http://gawker.com/circle-jerks-why-do-editors-love-dave-eggers-1440226375.

Timmer, Nicoline. *Do You Feel It Too? The Post-Postmodern Syndrome in American Fiction at the Turn of the Millennium.* Amsterdam: Rodopi, 2010.

Tofts, Darren, and Christian McCrea. "What Now? The Imprecise and Disagreeable Aesthetics of Remix." *Fibreculture* 15 (2009). Accessed April 5, 2011. http://fifteen.fibreculturejournal.org/.

Trottier, Daniel, and Christian Fuchs, eds. "Theorising Social Media, Politics and the State: An Introduction." In *Social Media, Politics and the State: Protests, Revolutions, Riots, Crime and Policing in the Age of Facebook, Twitter and YouTube.* New York: Routledge, 2015.

Turkle, Sherry. *Life on the Screen: Identity in the Age of the Internet.* New York: Touchstone, 1997.

Turner, Fred. *From Counterculture to Cyberculture: Stewart Brand, the Whole Earth Network, and the Rise of Digital Utopianism.* Chicago: University of Chicago Press, 2006.

Twitchell, Elizabeth. "Dave Eggers's *What is the What*: Fictionalizing Trauma in the Era of Misery Lit." *American Literature* 83, no. 3 (2011): 621–48. doi:10.1215/00029831-1339890.

Ullman, Ellen. *The Bug.* New York: Telese/Doubleday, 2003.

———. *Close to the Machine.* San Francisco: City Lights Books, 1997.

Vaughn, Adam. "How Viral Cat Videos Are Warming the Planet." *Guardian.* September 25, 2015. Accessed July 4, 2016. https://www.theguardian.com/environment/2015/sep/25/server-data-centre-emissions-air-travel-web-google-facebook-greenhouse-gas.

Wegner, Philip E. *Life between Two Deaths, 1989–2001: US Culture in the Long Nineties.* Durham, NC: Duke University Press, 2009.

Westerståhl Stenport, Anna, and Cecilia Ovesdotter Alm. "Corporations, Crime, and Gender Construction in Stieg Larsson's *The Girl with the Dragon Tattoo*." *Scandinavian Studies* 81, no. 2 (Summer 2009): 157–78. Accessed January 27, 2017. http://www.jstor.org/stable/40920850.

Westerståhl Stenport, Anna, and Garrett Traylor. "The Eradication of Memory: Film Adaptations and Algorithms of the Digital." *Cinema Journal* 55, no. 1 (Fall 2015): 74–94. doi:10.1353/cj.2015.0058.

Wexler, Aaron. "Notes from the Artist." James Hotels. Accessed June 9, 2016. http://www.jameshotels.com/new-york/soho/explore-hotel/artatthejames/aaron-wexler.

Whitehead, Colson. *Zone One*. London: Vintage, 2012.

Williams, David E. "Cold Case File." *American Cinematographer* 88, no. 4 (April 2007): 32–51. Accessed February 14, 2015. https://www.theasc.com/ac_magazine/April2007/Zodiac/page1.php .

Williams, Mary E. "Horror's First Viral Hit: How *The Blair Witch Project* Revolutionized Movies." *Salon*. June 13, 2014. Accessed July 7, 2015. http://www.salon.com/2014/06/13/horrors_first_viral_hit_how_the_blair_witch_project_revolutionized_movies/.

Wittkower, D. E. "Facebook and Dramauthentic Identity: A Post-Goffmanian Theory of Identity Performance on SNS." *First Monday* 4, no. 19 (April 2014). doi:10.5210/fm.v19i4.4858.

Wolf, Christine T. "DIY Videos on YouTube: Identity and Possibility in the Age of Algorithms." *First Monday* 21, no. 6 (June 2016). doi:10.5210/fm.v21i6.6787.

Wood, James. "True Lives: Sheila Heti's *How Should a Person Be?*" *New Yorker*. June 25, 2012. Accessed June 10, 2016. http://www.newyorker.com/magazine/2012/06/25/true-lives-2.

Wutz, Michael. *Enduring Words: Literary Narrative in a Changing Media Ecology*. Tuscaloosa: University of Alabama Press, 2009.

Zodiac. Directed by David Fincher. 2007. Warner Home Video, 2007. DVD.

INDEX

aesthetics, 9, 94. *See also* Ngai, Sianne
affect. *See* affective novelty; flat affects; minor affects; new media affects; ordinary affects
affective blocking, 1, 6, 10–11, 31, 38, 48, 55, 60, 90, 119, 136, 159. *See also* blocking attention
affective labor, 17, 47, 49–50, 68, 74, 111, 159. *See also* labor
affective novelty, 6–9, 38, 46, 62, 90, 105, 109, 112–14, 129, 137, 142–43, 150–53, 155, 160
algorithms, 6, 8, 24, 64–65, 94, 96, 108, 163
ambivalence, 28, 75, 87, 99, 103, 106–8, 114, 116–17
American decade, 137
Amerika, Mark, 13, 15, 47–56, 67, 98. See also *remixthebook* (Amerika); remix writing
anonymity, 113
Anthropocene, the, 151
anthropomorphization, 12
anxiety, 25, 55–56, 71, 74, 81–82, 85–86, 92, 101, 145
Apple, 26, 125
appropriation, 88
assemblage, 119–21
authenticity: authenticity of representation, 8, 38, 40, 177n37, 177n41; "authentic subject," 73–74, 76, 78–80, 84, 93–96, 128. *See also* code: representation of; subjectivity
automation, 145
avant-garde, 57, 67, 183n33

banal: aesthetic, 8–11, 48, 62, 82, 86–89, 93, 116, 123, 158–61; theory of the, 8–13. *See also* affective novelty; Berlant, Lauren; boredom; digital banal; Ngai, Sianne
banal affects, 7, 9–12, 26, 82, 120, 170n22. *See also* flat affects; minor affects; ordinary affects
Barbrook, Richard, 16, 99, 106–9. *See also* "Californian Ideology," the
Barthes, Roland, 3, 60, 66
Bassett, Caroline, 13, 106
becoming-with media, 6, 16, 31, 134, 170n15. *See also* Kember, Sarah; mediation; Zylinska, Joanna
Berlant, Lauren: on cruel optimism, 136, 171n27; and Facebook, 7; on flat affect, 9–10, 86; on the historical present, 10, 12, 31, 102; on nonsovereign love, 173n45. *See also* flat affects; intimacy

Berry, David M., 50, 60, 163
Black Box (Egan), 149, 153
black box technologies, 32, 38, 43, 103, 107–8, 113, 115
blocking attention, 31, 119, 136
Bolter, Jay David, 4. *See also* remediation
boredom, 10–11, 92, 120–21, 125
Boy Kings, The (Losse), 115–16
Bresnan, Mark, 157–58
Bug, The (Ullman), 97–104, 107–8, 116–17, 119
bugs, computer, 98, 100–103
Burrington, Ingrid, 142
Butler, Judith, 131

"Californian Ideology," the, 16, 103–8. *See also* Barbrook, Richard; Cameron, Andy
Cameron, Andy, 16, 29, 99, 106–9
campuses, in Silicon Valley, 14, 103–6, 112, 165
capital and capitalism, 8–10, 16, 46, 49–51, 59–60, 67–68, 71, 74, 81, 87, 92, 94–95, 106, 109, 122, 130–31, 159
Carruth, Alison, 150–51. *See also* computers: computer servers and storage
Catfish (film and TV show), 5, 13, 15–16, 73–82, 85, 95–96
Chan, Jennifer, 74, 92, 107
Chronic City (Lethem), 10, 17, 119–23, 126–32, 134–38, 140, 143
Chun, Wendy Hui Kyong: on "enduring ephemeral," 28–29, 31; on networks, 173n45; on programming, 98–99; on source code, 11–12, 26, 28–29, 37–39, 42; on sourcery, 15, 57, 172n37; on sovereignty, 30, 40, 172n37; on women in computing history, 39–40. *See also* code; software
Circle, The (Eggers), 16–17, 97–117
climate change, 132, 138, 147, 151
cloud, the, 1, 111
code: executability of, 4, 11–12, 26, 28, 35, 42, 51–52, 99, 102–3, 108; and programming languages, 11, 24, 26, 28, 99–100; representation of, 7, 11, 12–14, 21–26, 32–33, 40–43, 99–100, 102; source code, 11–12, 26, 28–29, 30, 37–39, 42, 102; and time, 27–29; and the Zodiac Killer, 32–38. *See also* mediation; software
Coleman, Gabriella, 185n22. *See also* jesters; tricksters
collage, 68–70, 123
commodification, 9, 44, 51, 67, 74, 93, 95, 131
commonality, 57, 64
commons, the, 15, 48–52, 55–60, 63–64, 67–68, 71, 173n43, 178n1; digital commons, 47, 50, 53, 67–68, 71; literary commons, 49, 55–56, 164. *See also* Berry, David M.; Creative Commons; Hands, Joss; Hardt, Michael; sharing; undercommons
communicative capitalism, 67, 92, 94, 181, 184
complexity, 4, 21, 33, 48, 55, 103, 108, 114–15, 147
computers, 2, 10, 35, 39–40, 54; computer memory, 29–30, 103, 155; computer monitors, 21–22, 40–41, 81, 104, 121, 124–25, 127–29, 134, 139–40; computer servers and storage, 113, 150–51, 188n59. *See also* laptops; women: in computing history
connectivity, 1, 4, 6–7, 8, 49, 52–54, 74, 76, 121–24, 136, 141–42, 147, 150–51
control: logic, 16, 109; society of, 75, 89, 116; technology as means of, 19, 51, 68–69, 172n37
copyleft, 60
Creative Commons, 50, 57, 59–60
cruel optimism, 136, 171n27, 172n28, 173n45
Currie, Mark, 15, 20, 28–30, 38
cyberpunk, 191n19. *See also* Gibson, William
cyberspace, 31, 120–21, 135
cyberterrorism, 139
cyber-utopianism, 1, 106. *See also* "Californian Ideology," the
cyborg manifesto, the, 45–46. *See also* Haraway, Donna

Darling, Jesse, 49–51, 57, 68, 70, 74
data: database, 101–2, 174n5; storage, 6, 21, 29, 32, 52, 62, 113; subject, 7, 10, 67, 145–46,

157–58, 170n22; visualization, 21; workflow, 20. *See also* digitization; social media: profiles

data centers, 21, 193n46. *See also* computers: computer servers and storage

Dean, Jodi, 67, 92. *See also* communicative capitalism

depresentification, 15, 29

Derrida, Jacques, 36, 174n1

dial-up Internet access, 121, 128–31, 135

digital banal, 1–5, 12, 18, 21, 27–28, 32, 38–39, 46, 51, 60, 64, 66–67, 75–76, 89–92, 94, 106–8, 111, 121–23, 128, 136, 138, 147, 151

digital cinema, 27–28, 30, 37–38, 175n6. *See also* workflow

digital devices, 14, 145, 157. *See also* computer; digital recorders; laptops

digital media. *See* becoming-with media; computers; digital cinema; digital recorders; digitization; mediation; networks; new media

digital recorders, 13, 89–90, 157

digital time, 20, 27, 32, 37, 61, 98, 101, 119, 159

digitization, 46–48, 51–52, 54, 57, 60, 152

distraction, 17, 26, 119–21, 125, 136, 151

eBay, 10, 13, 17, 127–28, 131, 135, 138

Ecstasy of Influence, The (Lethem), 48–49, 56–72

Egan, Jennifer, 13, 17, 117, 142–43, 148–50, 152–54. *See also Black Box* (Egan); *Visit from the Goon Squad, A* (Egan)

Eggers, Dave, 13, 16, 94, 99, 108, 110–11, 115–16. *See also Circle, The* (Eggers)

e-mail, 31, 40, 90, 123

embodiment, 59, 107, 109, 154

ENIAC girls, 39. *See also* women: in computing history

environmental damage, 14, 138. *See also* climate change

ephemerality, 32, 42, 98, 154. *See also* Chun, Wendy Hui Kyong: on "enduring ephemeral"

everyday life, 2–3, 6–7, 18, 20–24, 34, 52, 64, 98–99, 120, 124–26, 139, 142, 150, 189n7. *See also* ordinary affects

Facebook, 1, 5–8, 14, 16, 22–24, 26–27, 29–31, 38, 49, 69, 73, 78, 82, 109, 115–16, 144; history of, 5–7, 22–24; platform, 5–7; and sexism, 22–24, 44–46; timeline, 30, 69. *See also Social Network, The* (2010 film); Zuckerberg, Mark

feminism, 44–45

Fincher, David, 7, 9, 11, 13–15, 19–46, 75, 95. *See also Girl with the Dragon Tattoo, The* (2011 film); *Social Network, The* (2010 film); *Zodiac* (2007 film)

flat affects, 8–9, 12, 86, 110, 159

Foster, Hal, 88, 94

French, Sean. *See* Thrift, Nigel

friendship, 3–6, 13, 78–79, 81–83, 85–86, 90–92, 94–95

Galloway, Alexander R.: on affective identity, 110, 192n31; on "Chinese gold farmers," 130, 192n31; on "interface effect," 16, 75–76, 78–79, 82, 91; on software as language, 102, 172n37. *See also* intraface; mediation; postfordist society

geeks, 22, 187n44

gender, 22–24, 39–40, 45, 110, 112–14, 170n22. *See also* masculinity; misogyny; patriarchy; sexism

Gibson, William, 189n7, 191n19, 191n26. See *Neuromancer* (Gibson)

gift economies, 48, 57–60, 68, 70–71, 109, 135. *See also* reciprocity; sharing

Girl with the Dragon Tattoo, The (2011 film), 14, 20–21, 38–42, 44–46. *See also* Salander, Lisbeth

glitch, 8, 13, 98, 100, 117, 131, 143
Google, 57, 62; Google Maps, 79–80
Graphical User Interface (GUI), 100

hackers, 22, 67, 98. *See also* geeks; programmers; Salander, Lisbeth; Zuckerberg, Mark
hacking, 21–23, 25–26, 28, 39, 45, 52, 67, 145
Hands, Joss, 1, 51, 67–68. *See also* commons, the; platform politics
handwriting. *See* writing
Haraway, Donna, 45, 127
Hardt, Michael, 48
hardware, 32, 39–40, 43, 67. *See also* computer
Harvey, Stefano. *See* undercommons
Hayles, N. Katherine, 12, 120
Heti, Sheila, 5, 13, 15, 74, 82–87, 89–95. *See also How Should a Person Be?* (Heti)
hologram, 93, 135, 184n56
Homes, A. M., 2–5. *See also May We Be Forgiven* (Homes)
How Should a Person Be? (Heti), 5, 16, 73–75, 82–86, 88, 92–96

individuation, 63, 65. *See also* Stiegler, Bernard; transindividuation
infrastructure. *See* media infrastructure
instant messaging, 3, 41, 77, 144, 147, 152–54. *See also* e-mail
interface effect. *See* Galloway, Alexander R.
Internet: infrastructure and protocols of the, 49–50, 68, 70, 129, 132, 141; "Internet-as-Frontier," 105–8, 137–38; Internet of Things, 4, 167; post-Internet, 92–93, 163; studies on the, 189n7. *See also* connectivity; cyberspace; dial-up Internet access; media infrastructure; networks
interpersonal relations, 92–94, 109–11
intimacy, 7, 42, 46, 79, 91, 114, 138, 149, 158

intraface, 16, 75–76, 78, 89–93, 151
iPhone, 1, 26, 145

Jameson, Fredric: on affect, 8; on postmodern nonrepresentation, 184n56. *See also* postmodernism; post-postmodernism
jesters, 103, 185n22

Kelty, Chris, 187n44
Kember, Sarah: on Facebook, 6, 78; on life *after* new media, 87, 104, 157; on mediation, 4, 16, 31, 64, 78, 134, 157, 170n15. *See also* becoming-with media
Kirschenbaum, Matthew G., 21, 188n59
Kittler, Friedrich, 37, 52, 54, 179n18, 180n20

labor: authorial and artistic, 74, 92; exploitation, 24, 116, 130–31, 159, 192n31; immaterial, 92, 99, 117, 130–31, 158; machine, 20, 43, 111, 158; programming, 24–26, 40–41, 99, 108. *See also* affective labor
laptops, 2, 22, 40–42, 114, 121, 124–26, 132–34
Lethem, Jonathan, 10, 13, 15, 17, 48–49, 56–72, 98, 117, 120–21, 127, 129–31, 135. *See also Chronic City* (Lethem); *Ecstasy of Influence, The* (Lethem)
literary criticism, 71, 94, 167
literary genre, 94
Losse, Katherine, 7, 115–16. *See also Boy Kings, The* (Losse)

masculinity, 81–82, 116, 123, 138. *See also* gender; misogyny; patriarchy; sexism
mastery, 36–37, 39–40, 43, 46. *See also* hackers; programmers; sovereignty
May We Be Forgiven (Homes), 2–5
McLuhan, Marshall, 169n13
media ecology, 55
media infrastructure, 14, 21, 105, 107, 117, 130, 141–43, 145–47, 150, 153, 155, 160–62
mediation: digital, 11, 20–21, 31, 51, 54, 78, 87–90, 101, 150, 163; entanglement, 14,

43–45, 76, 82–83, 101, 112, 136; ethics of mediation, 78, 94, 112, 147; everyday, 3–5, 94, 114, 120, 126, 141–42; as vital process, 4, 7, 20, 30–31, 43, 62, 64, 74–75, 78, 80, 82, 85–90, 109, 116, 128, 134, 150, 155–56, 170n15. *See also* Kember, Sarah; premediation; remediation; Stiegler, Bernard; unmediation; Zylinska, Joanna
"merely interesting," 9, 12, 87–88, 172n28. *See also* Ngai, Sianne
messaging. *See* e-mail; instant messaging
minor affects, 8–9, 171n27. *See also* flat affects; Ngai, Sianne; ordinary affects
misogyny, 19, 26, 42–43, 45–46, 112–14, 115–16, 134, 178n50. *See also* masculinity; patriarchy; sexism
Mondo 2000 (magazine), 105
Moten, Fred. *See* undercommons

Nakamura, Lisa, 24, 170n22, 175n14
narrative theory, 28–30
neoliberalism, 43–44, 74, 177n45. *See also* Chun, Wendy Hui Kyong: on sovereignty
networks, 4, 27, 33–35, 62, 131–32, 134–36, 142, 173n45; digital, 43, 47, 49, 50, 52, 62, 76–77, 107, 121, 129–30, 141–42, 146–48, 151, 159–60. *See also* social networks
networked affect, 172n35
Neuromancer (Gibson), 189n7, 191n26
new media, 4, 10, 21, 27–29, 31, 46, 49, 75, 78, 91–95, 105–7, 110, 143, 150, 157–58, 172n35, 193n50. *See also* digital media; Kember, Sarah; writing: after new media; Zylinska, Joanna
new media affects, 10, 31–32, 104–5, 110, 150, 172n35
newness, 1, 4, 8, 12, 44, 46, 55, 105–6, 137. *See also* commodification; novelty; reification
new sincerity, 73–74, 93
New York City, NY, 14, 79, 96, 121–22, 128, 141–43, 150–51, 153, 162
Ngai, Sianne: on Andy Warhol, 87–88; on minor aesthetics, 8–10, 87–88, 171n27,

183n33; on postwar aesthetics, 9, 87. *See also* minor affects
9/11 terror attacks, 101, 122, 136–39, 142
nonhuman, 6, 15, 20, 28, 31, 39, 44, 48, 75, 78, 94–95, 100, 114
nonhuman agency, 95
nonsovereignty, 173n45
novelty, 1–2, 5, 8–9, 18, 21–22, 48, 51, 60, 75, 82, 86–88, 111, 114, 116–17, 146, 150, 167–68. *See also* affective novelty; reification
Novgorodoff, Danica, 10, 17, 117, 120, 124–26, 132–33. See *Refresh Refresh* (Novgorodoff)

obfuscation, 12, 18, 22, 39–40, 52, 94, 97, 99, 108–10, 161
online identity, 44, 74–76, 80, 96, 110, 170n22, 192n31
ordinary affects, 4–6, 172n28. *See also* anxiety; flat affects; minor affects

Paasonen, Susanna, 10
patriarchy, 22–24, 40, 134, 178n5. *See also* feminism; masculinity; misogyny; sexism
Percy, Benjamin, 123, 189n6
personalized media culture, 7, 61, 84, 90, 103–6, 109–11, 143, 145, 153. *See also* interpersonal relations
plagiarism, 48, 51, 55–56, 62, 64–65, 71, 115–16
platform politics, 1, 49–51, 65, 67–69, 73–74, 95, 126, 130, 169n2. *See also* eBay; Facebook: platform; social media
postdigital, 15, 73–96, 107, 147, 152, 157, 163
postfordist society, 110–11, 131
posthuman, 2, 44–46, 94. *See also* cyborg manifesto; nonhuman
postmodernism, 2, 8, 16, 73–75, 93–94, 153
post-postmodernism, 75, 93–94. *See also* postmodernism
PowerPoint, 150. See *Visit from the Goon Squad, A* (Egan)
precarity, 78–79, 107, 109, 122, 130–32, 136–37, 147, 159
premediation, 33, 153

presentification, 15, 28, 30, 32, 39, 42, 98, 101, 119–21, 146, 159. *See also* Currie, Mark; narrative theory
privacy, 110–13, 115, 145. *See also* data: subject; platform politics
privilege, 49, 57, 67, 101, 122, 145, 151, 170n22. *See also* connectivity; precarity
programmers, 14, 16, 22–24, 28, 39, 98–99, 104, 107–8, 116, 172n37
programming, 11–12, 21–30, 39–40, 42, 44–46, 97–102, 108, 116, 172n37
protocols, 49, 65, 71, 105, 156
public sphere, 49–50, 64, 68, 131, 173n43. *See also* commons; platform politics

race and racism, 24, 144, 159, 170n22, 192n31, 196n68
reading, 51, 53, 57, 63, 65, 117; code, 7–8, 11, 21, 24–26, 28, 39, 48–49
realism, 2–5, 74, 84, 150
reality TV, 5, 15, 18, 21, 76, 80, 84, 93
real-time, 20–21, 33, 44, 56, 111, 153
reappropriation, 53, 55–57, 62–63, 65, 69, 71
reciprocity, 60, 69, 109, 120
Refresh Refresh (Novgorodoff), 10–11, 121–26, 132–34, 139–40; and Benjamin Percy, 123
reification, 4, 12, 32, 51, 60, 64, 83, 89–90, 99, 106, 109, 110, 146, 150, 162. *See also* banal affects; digital banal
remediation, 4, 47, 52, 57, 60, 62, 65
remix, 15, 49, 51–56, 59, 62, 65–66, 68, 71, 73
remixthebook (Amerika), 53–55
remix writing, 15, 48, 51–53, 55, 59, 62, 65–66. See also *Ecstasy of Influence, The* (Lethem); *remixthebook* (Amerika)
romance, 8, 38, 76, 80–82
rote. *See* banal; everyday life; ordinary affects

Salander, Lisbeth, 19–20, 38–46, 98, 114, 122
Schulman, Nev, 76–82
screens, 14–15, 17, 21–22, 24, 27, 31–32, 38, 40, 44, 77–78, 104–5, 120–21, 127–29, 132, 139.

See also computers: computer monitors; digital cinema; laptops; smartphones
seamful experience, 61, 146
seamless experience, 20, 37, 53, 65, 90, 103, 109, 121, 146
Second Life, 123
September 11, 2001, terror attacks. *See* 9/11 terror attacks
servers. *See* computers: computer servers and storage
sex and sexuality, 42–43, 81–82, 110, 112–13, 134
sexism, 39–40, 110, 112–14, 115–16, 178n49, 196n68. *See also* misogyny
sharing, 10, 15, 49, 59, 74, 94, 99, 109, 115. *See also* reciprocity
Shteyngart, Gary, 5, 13, 17, 117, 143–48. See also *Super Sad True Love Story* (Shteyngart)
Silicon Valley, 105–7, 165
sincerity, 74, 91, 93–96, 153. *See* authenticity; new sincerity
slowness, 121, 124, 129, 138, 154, 161
Slow Violence (Nixon), 190n9
smartphones, 1, 104–5, 124, 145, 152, 154
social media, 4, 22, 24, 27, 49–51, 67–68, 70, 75, 78–81, 84–85, 92, 95, 116, 130, 136, 144–45, 155; profiles, 7, 22–23, 26, 31, 80, 82, 170n22. *See also* Facebook; *Social Network, The* (2010 film)
Social Network, The (2010 film), 7–8, 14, 21–30, 32, 37–40, 42, 45–46, 75
social networks, 6–8, 22–24, 27, 62, 76–77, 95, 131, 152
society, 9, 57, 62–63, 75, 89, 94–95, 108, 116, 159. *See also* control: society of
software, 11–12, 20, 28–32, 39–40, 52, 64–65, 67, 73–74, 97–100, 102–4, 108, 110–11, 115, 117, 148. *See also* Chun, Wendy Hui Kyong; Galloway, Alexander R.; Thrift, Nigel
source code. *See* Chun, Wendy Hui Kyong; code: source code

sourcery. *See* Chun, Wendy Hui Kyong
sovereignty, 12, 16, 26, 40, 108, 130, 135. *See also* Chun, Wendy Hui Kyong: on sovereignty; mastery; neoliberalism; nonsovereignty
Stewart, Kathleen. *See* ordinary affects
Steyerl, Hito, 163
Stiegler, Bernard, 62–64. *See also* technics; transindividuation
subjectivity, 6–7, 10, 30–31, 42–44, 48–50, 60, 63–64, 73–74, 87–89, 93–94, 112–14, 131–32, 147, 149–50. *See also* authenticity; becoming-with media; data: subject; programmers; users
Super Sad True Love Story (Shteyngart), 5, 17, 142–43, 145, 153, 162
surveillance, 42, 45, 84, 130, 139, 154, 193n50

technics, 51, 62–63
television. See *Catfish* (film and TV show); reality TV
Terranova, Tiziana, 92
Thrift, Nigel, 148
time and temporality, 20–21, 23, 27–31, 37–38, 40–44, 46, 62–63, 78, 81, 87, 98, 100–102, 111, 122–23, 129, 132–33, 142–43, 149, 161. *See also* digital time; real-time
transindividuation, 62–63, 180n35. *See also* individuation; Stiegler, Bernard
transparency, 35, 95, 99, 110–11
tricksters, 103, 185n22
Turner, Fred, 107
2003 Invasion of Iraq, 121, 134, 139
typewriters, 34, 86. *See also* writing: and typing

ubiquitous computing, 137
Ullman, Ellen, 9, 13, 16, 97, 99, 101–2, 104, 106–8, 113. See also *Bug, The* (Ullman)
undercommons, 178n5

unmediation, 157–61
users, 5–6, 10–11, 21, 25–26, 42–43, 49–50, 68, 99, 103, 105, 107, 114, 120, 131, 170n22. *See also* mastery; programmers

virtual class (Barbrook and Cameron), 109
virtual economies, 130, 136
virtual environments, 17, 50, 106–7, 121, 128, 130, 132, 134–37
Visit from the Goon Squad, A (Egan), 17, 142–43, 148, 154, 162

Warhol, Andy, 86–89, 93
Web 2.0, 5, 14. *See also* platform politics
Wexler, Aaron, 68–70
Whitehead, Colson, 5, 13, 17, 117, 142–43, 156, 158–59, 161. See also *Zone One* (Whitehead)
Wired (magazine), 105–6
women: in computing history, 39–40, 43, 46; in technology industry, 23–24, 46, 115–16
workflow, 20, 32, 42, 44
writing: 15, 45, 48, 51–53, 55, 57, 59, 62, 65, 67, 90–93; after new media, 62, 65, 67, 90–93, 154; and handwriting, 37; and typing, 3, 53, 66; and writing code, 7–8, 11–12, 21–26, 28, 32, 36, 52, 55, 99–102

Y2K bug, 139

Zodiac (2007 film), 14, 21, 32–38, 39, 45–46
Zone One (Whitehead), 5, 17, 142–43, 156–62
Zuckerberg, Mark: character in *The Social Network*, 22–24, 26–27, 30, 40, 45–46, 57; founder of Facebook, 5, 24, 27, 38, 94, 98
Zylinska, Joanna: and Facebook, 6, 78; on life *after* new media, 87, 104, 157; on mediation, 4, 16, 31, 64, 78, 134, 157, 170n15. *See also* becoming-with media

GPSR Authorized Representative: Easy Access System Europe, Mustamäe tee
50, 10621 Tallinn, Estonia, gpsr.requests@easproject.com

www.ingramcontent.com/pod-product-compliance
Lightning Source LLC
Chambersburg PA
CBHW021944290426
44108CB00012B/955